Web
Dragons

Web Dragons

Ian H. Witten
Marco Gori
Teresa Numerico

Inside the Myths
of Search Engine Technology

AMSTERDAM • BOSTON • HEIDELBERG • LONDON
NEW YORK • OXFORD • PARIS • SAN DIEGO
SAN FRANCISCO • SINGAPORE • SYDNEY • TOKYO

ELSEVIER

Morgan Kaufmann Publishers is an imprint of Elsevier

MK

MORGAN KAUFMANN PUBLISHERS

Publisher	Diane D. Cerra
Publishing Services Manager	George Morrison
Project Manager	Marilyn E. Rash
Assistant Editor	Asma Palmeiro
Cover Design	Yvo Riezebos Design
Text Design	Mark Bernard, Design on Time
Composition	CEPHA Imaging Pvt. Ltd.
Copyeditor	Carol Leyba
Proofreader	Daniel Stone
Indexer	Steve Rath
Interior Printer	Sheridan Books
Cover Printer	Phoenix Color Corp.

Morgan Kaufmann Publishers is an imprint of Elsevier.
500 Sansome Street, Suite 400, San Francisco, CA 94111

This book is printed on acid-free paper.

Library of Congress Cataloging-in-Publication Data
Witten, I. H. (Ian H.)
 Web dragons: inside the myths of search engine technology / Ian H.
Witten, Marco Gori, Teresa Numerico.
    p. cm. — (Morgan Kaufmann a series in multimedia and information systems)
 Includes bibliographical references and index.
 ISBN-13: 978-0-12-370609-6 (alk. paper)
 ISBN-10: 0-12-370609-2 (alk. paper)
1. Search engines. 2. World Wide Web. 3. Electronic information resources literacy. I. Gori, Marco.
II. Numerico, Teresa. III. Title. IV. Title: Inside the myths of search engine technology.
TK5105.884.W55 2006
025.04--dc22   2006023512

For information on all Morgan Kaufmann Publishers visit our Web site
at www.books.elsevier.com

Printed in the United States of America
06 07 08 09 10   10 9 8 7 6 5 4 3 2 1

CONTENTS

LIST OF FIGURES

LIST OF TABLES

PREFACE

In the eye-blink that has elapsed since the turn of the millennium, the lives of those of us who work with information have been utterly transformed. Much—most—perhaps even all—of what we need to know is on the World Wide Web; if not today, then tomorrow. The web is where society keeps the sum total of human knowledge. It's where we learn and play, shop and do business, keep up with old friends and meet new ones. And what has made all this possible is not just the fantastic amount of information out there, it's a fantastic new technology: search engines. Efficient and effective ways of searching through immense tracts of text is one of the most striking technical advances of the last decade. And today search engines do it for us. They weigh and measure every web page to determine whether it matches our query. And they do it all for free. We call on them whenever we want to find something that we need to know. To learn how they work, read on!

We refer to search engines as "web dragons" because they are the gatekeepers of our society's treasure trove of information. Dragons are all-powerful figures that stand guard over great hoards of treasure. The metaphor fits. Dragons are mysterious: no one *really* knows what drives them. They're mythical: the subject of speculation, hype, legend, old wives' tales, and fairy stories. In this case, the immense treasure they guard is society's repository of knowledge. What could be more valuable than that? In oriental folklore, dragons not only enjoy awesome grace and beauty, they are endowed with immense wisdom. But in the West, they are often portrayed as evil—St. George vanquishes a fearsome dragon, as does Beowulf—though sometimes they are friendly (Puff). In both traditions, they are certainly magic, powerful, independent, and unpredictable. The ambiguity suits our purpose well because, in addition to celebrating the joy of being able to find stuff on the web, we want to make you feel uneasy about how everyone has come to rely on search engines so utterly and completely.

The web is where we record our knowledge, and the dragons are how we access it. This book examines their interplay from many points of view: the philosophy of knowledge; the history of technology; the role of libraries, our traditional knowledge repositories; how the web is organized; how it grows and evolves; how search engines work; how people and companies try to take advantage of them to promote their wares; how the dragons fight back; who controls information on the web and how; and what we might see in the future.

We have laid out our story from beginning to end, starting with early philosophers and finishing with visions of tomorrow. But you don't have to read this book that way: you can start in the middle. To find out how search engines work, turn to Chapter 4. To learn about web spam, go to Chapter 5. For social issues about web democracy and the control of information, head straight for Chapter 6. To see how the web is organized and how its massively linked structure grows, start at Chapter 3. To learn about libraries and how they are finding their way onto the web, go to Chapter 2. For philosophical and historical underpinnings, read Chapter 1. Unlike most books, which you start at the beginning, and give up when you run out of time or have had enough, we recommend that you consider reading this book starting in the middle and, if you can, continuing right to the end. You don't really need the early chapters to understand the later parts, though they certainly provide context and add depth. To help you chart a passage, here's a brief account of what each chapter has in store.

The information revolution is creating turmoil in our lives. For years it has been opening up a wondrous panoply of exciting new opportunities and simultaneously threatening to drown us in them, dragging us down, gasping, into murky undercurrents of information overload. Feeling confused? We all are. Chapter 1 sets the scene by placing things in a philosophical and historical context. The web is central to our thinking, and the way it works resembles the very way we think—by linking pieces of information together. Its growth reflects the growth in the sum total of human knowledge. It's not just a storehouse into which we drop nuggets of information or pearls of wisdom. It's the stuff out of which society's knowledge is made, and how we use it determines how humankind's knowledge will grow. That's why this is all so important. How we access the web is central to the development of humanity.

The World Wide Web is becoming ever larger, qualitatively as well as quantitatively. It is slowly but surely beginning to subsume "the literature," which up to now has been locked away in libraries. Chapter 2 gives a bird's-eye view of the long history of libraries and then describes how today's custodians are busy putting their books on the web, and in their public-spirited way giving as much free access to them as they can. Initiatives such as the Gutenberg Project, the United States, China, and India Million Book Project, and the Open Content Alliance, are striving to create open collections of public domain material. Web bookstores such as Amazon present pages from published works and let you sample them. Google is digitizing the collections of major libraries and making them searchable worldwide. We are witnessing a radical convergence of online and print information, and of commercial and noncommercial information sources.

Chapter 3 paints a picture of the overall size, scale, construction, and organization of the web, a big picture that transcends the details of all those millions of websites and billions of web pages. How can you measure the size of this beast? How fast is it growing? What about its connectivity: is it one network, or does it drop into disconnected parts? What's the likelihood of being able to navigate through the links from one randomly chosen page to another? You've probably heard that complete strangers are joined by astonishingly short chains of acquaintanceship: one person knows someone who knows someone who…through about six degrees of separation…knows the other. How far apart are web pages? Does this affect the web's robustness to random failure—and to deliberate attack? And what about the deep web—those pages that are generated dynamically in response to database queries—and sites that require registration or otherwise limit access to their contents?

Having surveyed the information landscape, Chapter 4 tackles the key ideas behind full-text searching and web search engines, the Internet's new "killer app." Despite the fact that search engines are intricate pieces of software, the underlying ideas are simple, and we describe them in plain English. Full-text search is an embodiment of the classical concordance, with the advantage that, being computerized, it works for all documents, no matter how banal—not just sacred texts and outstanding works of literature. Multiword queries are answered by combining concordance entries and ranking the results, weighing rare words more heavily than commonplace ones. Web search services augment full-text search with the notion of the *prestige* of a source, which they estimate by counting the web pages that cite the source, and *their* prestige—in effect weighting popular works highly. This book focuses exclusively on techniques for searching text, for even when we seek pictures and movies, today's search engines usually find them for us by analyzing associated textual descriptions.

Chapter 5 turns to the dark side. Once the precise recipe for attribution of prestige is known, it can be circumvented, or "spammed," by commercial interests intent on artificially raising their profile. On the web, visibility is money. It's excellent publicity—better than advertising—and it's free. We describe some of the techniques of spamming, techniques that are no secret to the spammers, but will come as a surprise to web users. Like e-mail spam, this is a scourge that will pollute our lives. Search engine operators strive to root it out and neutralize it in an escalating war against misuse of the web. And that's not all. Unscrupulous firms attack the advertising budget of rival companies by mindlessly clicking on their advertisements, for every referral costs money. Some see click fraud as the dominant threat to the search engine business.

There's another problem: access to information is controlled by a few commercial enterprises that operate in secret. This raises ethical concerns that have been concealed by the benign philosophy of today's dominant players and the exceptionally high utility of their product. Chapter 6 discusses the question of democracy (or lack of it) in cyberspace. We also review the age-old system of copyright—society's way of controlling the flow of information to protect the rights of authors. The fact that today's web concentrates enormous power over people's information-seeking activities into a handful of major players has led some to propose that the search business should be nationalized—or perhaps "internationalized"—into public information utilities. But we disagree, for two reasons. First, the apolitical nature of the web—it is often described as anarchic—is one of its most alluring features. Second, today's exceptionally effective large-scale search engines could only have been forged through intense commercial competition—particularly in a mere decade of development.

We believe that we stand on the threshold of a new era, and Chapter 7 provides a glimpse of what's in store. Today's search engines are just the first, most obvious, step. While centralized indexes will continue to thrive, they will be augmented—and for many purposes usurped—by local control and customization. Search engine companies are already experimenting with personalization features, on the assumption that users will be prepared to sacrifice some privacy and identify themselves if they thereby receive better service. Localized rather than centralized control will make this more palatable and less susceptible to corruption. Information gleaned from end users—searchers and readers—will play a more prominent role in directing searches. The web dragons are diversifying from search alone toward providing general information processing services, which could generate a radically new computer ecosystem based on central hosting services rather than personal workstations. Future dragons will offer remote application software and file systems that will augment or even replace your desktop computer. Does this presage a new generation of operating systems?

We want you to get involved with this book. These are big issues. The natural reaction is to concede that they may be important in theory but to question what difference they really make in practice—and anyway, what can you do about them? To counter any feeling of helplessness, we've put a few activities at the end of each chapter in gray boxes: things you *can* do to improve life for yourself—perhaps for others too. If you like, peek ahead before reading each chapter to get a feeling for what practical actions it might suggest.

ACKNOWLEDGMENTS

The seeds for this project were sown during a brief visit by Ian Witten to Italy, sponsored by the Italian Artificial Intelligence Society, and the book was conceived and begun during a more extended visit generously supported by the University of Siena. We would all like to thank our home institutions for their support for our work over the years: the University of Waikato in New Zealand, and the Universities of Siena and Salerno in Italy. Most of Ian's work on the book was done during a sabbatical period while visiting the École Nationale Supérieure des Télécommunications in Paris, Google in New York (he had to promise not to learn anything there), and the University of Cape Town in South Africa (where the book benefited from numerous discussions with Gary Marsden); the generous support of these institutions is gratefully acknowledged. Marco benefited from insightful discussions during a brief visit to the Université de Montréal, and from collaboration with the Automated Reasoning System division of IRST, Trento, Italy. Teresa would like to thank the Leverhulme Foundation for its generous support and the Logic group at the University of Rome, and in particular Jonathan Bowen, Roberto Cordeschi, Marcello Frixione, and Sandro Nannini for their interesting, wise, and stimulating comments.

In developing these ideas, we have all been strongly influenced by our students and colleagues; they are far too numerous to mention individually but gratefully acknowledged all the same. We particularly want to thank members of our departments and research groups: the Computer Science Department at Waikato, the Artificial Intelligence Research Group at Siena, and the Department of Communication Sciences at Salerno. Parts of Chapter 2 are adapted from *How to Build a Digital Library* by Witten and Bainbridge; parts of Chapter 4 come from *Managing Gigabytes* by Witten, Moffat, and Bell.

We must thank the web dragons themselves, not just for providing such an interesting topic for us to write about, but for all their help in ferreting out facts and other information while writing this book. We may be critical, but we are also grateful! In addition, we would like to thank all the authors in the Wikipedia community for their fabulous contributions to the spread of knowledge, from which we have benefited enormously.

The delightful cover illustration and chapter openers were drawn for us by Lorenzo Menconi. He did it for fun, with no thought of compensation, the only reward being to see his work in print. We thank him very deeply and sincerely hope that this will boost his sideline in imaginative illustration. We are extremely grateful to the reviewers of this book, who have helped us focus our thoughts and correct and enrich the text: Rob Akscyn, Ed Fox, Jonathan Grudin, Antonio Gulli, Gary Marchionini, Edie Rasmussen, and Sarah Shieff.

We received sterling support from Diane Cerra and Asma Palmeiro at Morgan Kaufmann while writing this book. Diane's enthusiasm infected us from the very beginning, when she managed to process our book proposal and give us the go-ahead in record time. Marilyn Rash, our project manager, has made the production process go very smoothly for us.

Finally, without the support of our families, none of our work would have been possible. Thank you Agnese, Anna, Cecilia, Fabrizio, Irene, Nikki, and Pam; this is your book too!

About the Authors

Ian H. Witten is professor of computer science at the University of Waikato in New Zealand. He directs the New Zealand Digital Library research project. His research interests include information retrieval, machine learning, text compression, and programming by demonstration. He received an MA in mathematics from Cambridge University in England, an MSc in computer science from the University of Calgary in Canada, and a PhD in electrical engineering from Essex University in England. Witten is a fellow of the ACM and of the Royal Society of New Zealand. He has published widely on digital libraries, machine learning, text compression, hypertext, speech synthesis and signal processing, and computer typography. He has written several books, the latest being *How to Build a Digital Library* (2002) and *Data Mining, Second Edition* (2005), both published by Morgan Kaufmann.

Marco Gori is professor of computer science at the University of Siena, where he is the leader of the artificial intelligence research group. His research interests are machine learning with applications to pattern recognition, web mining, and game playing. He received a Laurea from the University of Florence and a PhD from the University of Bologna. He is the chairman of the Italian Chapter of the IEEE Computational Intelligence Society, a fellow of the IEEE and of the ECCAI, and a former president of the Italian Association for Artificial Intelligence.

Teresa Numerico teaches network theory and communication studies at the University of Rome. She is also a researcher in the philosophy of science at the University of Salerno (Italy). She earned her PhD in the history of science and was a visiting researcher at London South Bank University in the United Kingdom in 2004, having been awarded a Leverhulme Trust Research Fellowship. She was formerly employed as a business development and marketing manager for several media companies, including the Italian branch of Turner Broadcasting System (CNN and Cartoon Network).

Web
Dragons

SETTING THE SCENE

The universe (which others call the Library) is composed of an indefinite and perhaps infinite number of hexagonal galleries, with vast air shafts between, surrounded by very low railings…

Thus begins Jorge Luis Borges's fable *The Library of Babel*, which conjures up an image not unlike the World Wide Web. He gives a surreal description of the Library, which includes spiral staircases that "sink abysmally and soar upwards to remote distances" and mirrors that lead the inhabitants to conjecture whether or not the Library is infinite (". . . I prefer to dream that their polished surfaces represent and promise the infinite," declares Borges's anonymous narrator). Next he tells of the life of its inhabitants, who live and die in this bleak space, traveling from gallery to gallery in their youth and in later years specializing in the contents of a small locality of this unbounded labyrinth. Then he describes the contents: every conceivable book is here, "the archangels' autobiographies, the faithful catalogue of the Library, thousands and thousands of false catalogues, the demonstration of the fallacy of those catalogues, the demonstration of the fallacy of the true catalogue . . . ."

Although the celebrated Argentine writer wrote this enigmatic little tale in 1941, it resonates with echoes of today's World Wide Web. "The impious maintain that nonsense is normal in the Library and the reasonable is an almost

---

Inside the Library of Babel.

miraculous exception." But there are differences: travelers confirm that no two books in Borges's Library are identical—in sharp contrast with the web, replete with redundancy.

The universe (which others call the Web) is exactly what this book is about. And the universe is not always a happy place. Despite the apparent glut of information in Borges's Library of Babel, its books are completely useless to the reader, leading the librarians to a state of suicidal despair. Today we stand at the epicenter of a revolution in how our society creates, organizes, locates, presents, and preserves information—and misinformation. We are battered by lies, from junk e-mail, to other people's misconceptions, to advertisements dressed up as hard news, to infotainment in which the borders of fact and fiction are deliberately smeared. It's hard to make sense of the maelstrom: we feel confused, disoriented, unconfident, wary of the future, unsure even of the present.

Take heart: there have been revolutions before. To gain a sense of perspective, let's glance briefly at another upheaval, one that caused far more chaos by overturning not just information but science and society as well. The Enlightenment in the eighteenth century advocated rationality as a means of establishing an authoritative system of knowledge and governance, ethics, and aesthetics. In the context of the times, this was far more radical than today's little information revolution. Up until then, society's intellectual traditions, legal structure, and customs were dictated partly by an often tyrannical state and partly by the Church—leavened with a goodly dose of irrationality and superstition. The French Revolution was a violent manifestation of Enlightenment philosophy. The desire for rationality in government led to an attempt to end the Catholic Church and indeed Christianity in France, as well as bringing a new order to the calendar, clock, yardstick, monetary system, and legal structure. Heads rolled.

Immanuel Kant, a great German philosopher of the time, urged thinkers to have the courage to rely on their own reason and understanding rather than seeking guidance from other, ostensibly more authoritative, intellects as they had been trained to do. As our kids say today, "Grow up!" He went on to ask new philosophical questions about the present—what is happening "right now." How can we interpret the present when we are part of it ourselves, when our own thinking influences the very object of study, when new ideas cause heads to roll? In his quest to understand the revolutionary spirit of the times, he concluded that the significance of revolutions is not in the events themselves so much as in how they are perceived and understood by people who are not actually front-line combatants. It is not the perpetrators—the actors on the world stage—who come to understand the true meaning of a revolution, but the rest of society, the audience who are swept along by the plot.

In the information revolution sparked by the World Wide Web, we are all members of the audience. We did not ask for it. We did not direct its development.

We did not participate in its conception and launch, in the design of the protocols and the construction of the search engines. But it has nevertheless become a valued part of our lives: we use it, we learn from it, we put information on it for others to find. To understand it we need to learn a little of how it arose and where it came from, who were the pioneers who created it, and what were they trying to do.

The best place to begin understanding the web's fundamental role, which is to provide access to the world's information, is with the philosophers, for, as you probably recall from early university courses in the liberal arts, early savants like Socrates and Plato knew a thing or two about knowledge and wisdom, and how to acquire and transmit them.

ACCORDING TO THE PHILOSOPHERS...

Seeking new information presents a very old philosophical conundrum. Around 400 B.C., the Greek sage Plato spoke of how his teacher Socrates examined moral concepts such as "good" and "justice", important everyday ideas that are used loosely without any real definition. Socrates probed students with leading questions to help them determine their underlying beliefs and map out the extent of their knowledge—and ignorance. The Socratic method does not supply answers but generates better hypotheses by steadily identifying and eliminating those that lead to contradictions. In a discussion about Virtue, Socrates' student Meno stumbles upon a paradox.

> **Meno**: And how will you enquire, Socrates, into that which you do not know? What will you put forth as the subject of enquiry? And if you find what you want, how will you ever know that this is the thing which you did not know?
>
> **Socrates**: I know, Meno, what you mean; but just see what a tiresome dispute you are introducing. You argue that man cannot enquire either about that which he knows, or about that which he does not know; for if he knows, he has no need to enquire; and if not, he cannot; for he does not know the very subject about which he is to enquire.
>
> – *Plato Meno, XIV 80d–e/81a (Jowett, 1949)*

In other words, what is this thing called "search"? How can you tell when you have arrived at the truth when you don't know what the truth is? Web users, this is a question for our times!

KNOWLEDGE AS RELATIONS

Socrates, typically, did not answer the question. His method was to use inquiry to compel his students into a sometimes uncomfortable examination of their own beliefs and prejudices, to unveil the extent of their ignorance. His disciple Plato was more accommodating and did at least try to provide an answer. In philosophical terms, Plato was an idealist: he thought that ideas are not created by human reason but reside in a perfect world somewhere out there. He held that knowledge is in some sense innate, buried deep within the soul, but can be dimly perceived and brought out into the light when dealing with new experiences and discoveries—particularly with the guidance of a Socratic interrogator.

Reinterpreting for the web user, we might say that we do not begin the process of discovery from scratch, but instead have access to some preexisting model that enables us to evaluate and interpret what we read. We gain knowledge by relating new information and experience to our existing model in order to make sense of our perceptions. At a personal level, knowledge creation—that is, learning—is a process without beginning or end.

The American philosopher Charles S. Peirce (1839–1914) founded a movement called "pragmatism" that strives to clarify ideas by applying the methods of science to philosophical issues. His work is highly respected by other philosophers. Bertrand Russell thought he was "certainly the greatest American thinker ever," and Karl Popper called him one of the greatest philosophers of all time. When Peirce discussed the question of how we acquire new knowledge, or as he put it, "whether there is any cognition not determined by a previous cognition," he concluded that knowledge consists of relations.

> All the cognitive faculties we know of are relative, and consequently their products are relations. But the cognition of a relation is determined by previous cognitions. No cognition not determined by a previous cognition, then, can be known. It does not exist, then, first, because it is absolutely incognizable, and second, because a cognition only exists so far as it is known.
>
> – *Peirce (1868a, p. 111)*

What thinking, learning, or acquiring knowledge does is create relations between existing "cognitions"—today we would call them cognitive structures, patterns of mental activity. But where does it all begin? For Peirce, there is no such thing as the first cognition. Everything we learn is intertwined—nothing comes first, there is no beginning.

Peirce's pragmatism sits at the very opposite end of the philosophical spectrum to Plato's idealism. But the two reached strikingly similar conclusions: we acquire knowledge by creating relationships among elements that were formerly unconnected. For Plato, the relationships are established between the perfect world of ideas and the world of actual experience, whereas Peirce's relations are established among different cognitions, different thoughts. Knowing is relating. When philosophers arrive at the same conclusion from diametrically opposing starting points, it's worth listening.

The World Wide Web is a metaphor for the general knowledge creation process that both Peirce and Plato envisaged. We humans learn by connecting and linking information, the very activity that defines the web. As we will argue in the next chapters, virtually all recorded knowledge is out there on the web— or soon will be. If linking information together is the key activity that under- lies learning, the links that intertwine the web will have a profound influence on the entire process of knowledge creation within our society. New knowledge will not only be born digital; it will be born fully contextualized and linked to the existing knowledge base at birth—or, more literally, at conception.

KNOWLEDGE COMMUNITIES

We often think of the acquisition of new knowledge as a passive and solitary activity, like reading a book. Nothing could be further from the truth. Plato described how Socrates managed to elicit Pythagoras's theorem, a mathemati- cal result commonly attributed to the eponymous Greek philosopher and mathematician who lived 200 years earlier, from an uneducated slave—an extraordinary feat. Socrates led the slave into "discovering" this result through a long series of simple questions. He first demonstrated that the slave (incor- rectly) thought that if you doubled the side of a square, you doubled its area. Then he talked him through a series of simple and obvious questions that made him realize that to double the area, you must make the *diagonal* twice the length of the side, which is not the same thing as doubling the side.

We can draw two lessons from this parable. First, discovery is a dialogue. The slave could never have found the truth alone, but only when guided by a master who gave advice and corrected his mistakes. Learning is not a solitary activity. Second, the slave reaches his understanding through a dynamic and active process, gradually producing closer approximations to the truth by cor- recting his interpretation of the information available. Learning, even learning a one-off "fact," is not a blinding flash of inspiration but a process of discov- ery that involves examining ideas and beliefs using reason and logic.

Turn now from Plato, the classical idealist, to Peirce, the modern pragma- tist. He asked, what is "reality"? The complex relation between external reality, truth, and cognition has bedeviled philosophers since time immemorial, and we'll tiptoe carefully around it. But in his discussion, Peirce described the acquisition and organization of knowledge with reference to a community:

The very origin of the conception of reality shows that this conception essentially involves the notion of a Community, without definite limits, and capable of a definite increase of knowledge.

– Peirce (1868b, p. 153)

Knowledge communities are central to the World Wide Web—that is, *the universe (which others call the Web)*. In fact, community and knowledge are so intertwined that one cannot be understood without the other. As Peirce notes, communities do not have crisp boundaries in terms of membership. Rather, they can be recognized by their members' shared beliefs, interests, and concerns. Though their constituency changes and evolves over time, communities are characterized by a common intellectual heritage. Peirce's "reality" implies the shared knowledge that a community, itself in constant flux, continues to sustain and develop into the future. This social interpretation of knowledge and reality is reflected in the staggering number of overlapping communities that create the web. Indeed, as we will learn in Chapter 4, today's search engines analyze this huge network in an attempt to determine and quantify the degree of authority accorded to each page by different social communities.

KNOWLEDGE AS LANGUAGE

We learned from Plato that people gain knowledge through interaction and dialogue, and from Peirce that knowledge is community-based and that it develops dynamically over time. Another philosopher, Ludwig Wittgenstein (1889–1951), one of last century's most influential and original thinkers, gave a third perspective on how information is transformed into knowledge. He was obsessed with the nature of language and its relationship with logic. Language is clearly a social construct—a language that others cannot understand is no use at all. Linguistic communication involves applying rules that allow people to understand one another even when they do not share the same world vision. Meaning is attributed to words through a convention that becomes established over time within a given community. Understanding, the process of transforming information into knowledge, is inextricably bound up with the linguistic habits of a social group. Thinking is inseparable from language, which is inseparable from community.

Though Wittgenstein was talking generally, his argument fits the World Wide Web perfectly. The web externalizes knowledge in the form of language, generated and disseminated by interacting communities.

We have discussed three very different thinkers from distant times and cultures: Plato, Peirce, and Wittgenstein, and discovered what they had to say about the World Wide Web—though, of course, they didn't know it. Knowing is relating. Knowledge is dynamic and community-based; its creation is both discovery and dialogue. Thinking is inseparable from language, which is inseparable from community. Thus prepared, we are ready to proceed with Kant's challenge of interpreting the revolution.

ENTER THE TECHNOLOGISTS

Norbert Wiener (1894–1964) was among the leaders of the technological revolution that took place around the time of the Second World War. He was the first American-born mathematician to win the respect of top intellects in the traditional European bastions of learning. He coined the term *cybernetics* and introduced it to a mass audience in a popular book entitled *The Human Use of Human Beings*. Though he did not foresee in detail today's amazing diffusion of information and communication technologies, and its pivotal role in shaping our society, he had much to say about it.

THE BIRTH OF CYBERNETICS

Wiener thought that the way to understand society is by studying messages and the media used to communicate them. He wanted to analyze how machines can communicate with each other, and how people might interact with them. Kids today discuss on street corners whether their portable music player can "talk to" their family computer, or how ineptly their parents interact with TiVo, but in the 1950s it was rather unusual to use machines and interaction in the same sentence. After the war, Wiener assembled to work with him at MIT some of the brightest young researchers in electrical engineering, neuropsychology, and what would now be called artificial intelligence.

Wiener began the study of communication protocols and human-computer interaction, and these underpin the operation of the World Wide Web. Although systems like search engines are obviously the product of human intellectual activity, we interact with them as entities in their own right. Though patently not humanoid robots from some futuristic world or science fiction tale, we nevertheless take their advice seriously. We rely on them to sift information for us and do not think, not for a moment, about how they work inside. Even all the software gurus who developed the system would be hard pressed to explain the precise reason why a particular list of results came up for a particular query at a particular time. The process is too intricate and the information it uses too dynamic and distributed to be able to retrace all the steps involved. No single person is in control: the machine is virtually autonomous.

When retrieving information from the web, we have no option but to trust tools whose characteristics we cannot comprehend, just as in life we are often forced to trust people we don't really know. Of course, no sources of information in real life are completely objective. When we read newspapers, we do not expect the reporter's account to be unbiased. But we do have some idea where he or she is coming from. Prominent journalists' biases are public knowledge; the article's political, social, and economic orientation is manifest in its first few lines; the newspaper's masthead sets up appropriate expectations. Web search agents give no hint of their political inclinations—to be fair, they probably have none. But the most dangerous biases are neither political nor commercial, but are implicit in the structure of the technology. They are virtually undetectable even by the developers, caught up as they are in leading the revolutionary vanguard.

All those years ago, Wiener raised ethical concerns that have, over time, become increasingly ignored. He urged us to consider what are legitimate and useful developments of technology. He worried about leaving delicate decisions to machines; yet we now uncritically rely on them to find relevant information for us. He felt that even if a computer could learn to make good choices, it should never be allowed to be the final arbiter—particularly when we are only dimly aware of the methods it uses and the principles by which it operates. People need to have a basis on which to judge whether they agree with the computer's decision. Responsibility should never be delegated to computers, but must remain with human beings.

Wiener's concern is particularly acute in web information retrieval. One aim of this book is to raise the issue and discuss it honestly and openly. We do not presume to have a final response, a definitive solution. But we do aspire to increase people's awareness of the ethical issues at stake. As Kant observed, the true significance of a revolution comes not from its commanders or foot soldiers, but from its assimilation by the rest of us.

INFORMATION AS PROCESS

In 1905, not long after the Wright Brothers made the first successful powered flight by a heavier-than-air machine, Rudyard Kipling wrote a story that envisaged how technology—in this case, aeronautics—might eventually come to control humanity. He anticipated how communication shapes society and international power relationships today. *With the Night Mail* is set in A.D 2000, when the world becomes fully globalized under the Aerial Board of Control (ABC), a small organization of "semi-elected" people who coordinate global transportation and communication. The ABC was founded in 1949 as an international authority with responsibility for airborne traffic and "all that that implies." Air travel had so united the world that war had long since become obsolete. But private property was jeopardized: any building could be legitimately damaged by a plane engaged in a tricky landing procedure. Privacy was completely abandoned in the interests of technological communication and scientific progress. The machines were effectively in control.

This negative vision exasperated Wiener. He believed passionately that machines cannot *in principle* be in control, since they do their work at the behest of man. Only human beings can govern.

He [Kipling] has emphasized the extended physical transportation of man, rather than the transportation of language and ideas. He does not seem to realize that where a man's word goes, and where his power of perception goes, to that point his control and in a sense his physical existence is extended. To see and to give commands to the whole world is almost the same as being everywhere.

– Wiener (1950, p. 97)

Kipling's dystopia was based on transportation technology, but Wiener took pains to point out that transporting information (i.e., bits) has quite different consequences from the transport of matter. (This was not so clear in 1950 as it is to us today.) Weiner deployed two arguments. The first was based on analyzing the kind of systems that were used to transport information. He argued that communicating machines, like communicating individuals, transcend their physical structure. Two interconnected systems comprise a new device that is greater than the sum of its parts. The whole acquires characteristics that cannot be predicted from its components. Today we see the web as having a holistic identity that transcends the sum of all the individual websites.

The second argument, even more germane to our topic, concerns the nature of information itself. In the late 1940s, Claude Shannon, a pioneer of information theory, likened information to thermodynamic entropy, for it obeys some of the same mathematical laws. Wiener inferred that information, like entropy, is not conserved in the way that physical matter is. The world is constantly changing, and you can't store information and expect it to retain its value indefinitely. This led to some radical conclusions. For example, Wiener decried the secrecy that shrouded the scientific and technological discoveries of the Second World War; he felt that stealth was useless—even counterproductive—in maintaining the superiority of American research over the enemy's. He believed that knowledge could best be advanced by ensuring that information remained open.

Information is not something that you can simply possess. It's a process over time that involves producer, consumer, and intermediaries who assimilate and transmit it. It can be refined, increased, and improved by anyone in the chain. Technological tools play a relatively minor role: the actors are the beings who transform information into knowledge in order to pass it on. The activities of users affect the information itself. We filter, retrieve, catalogue, distribute, and evaluate information: we do not preserve it objectively. Even the acts of reading, selecting, transmitting, and linking transmute it into something different. Information is as delicate as it is valuable. Like an exquisite gourmet dish that is destroyed by transport in space or time, it should be enjoyed now, here at the table. Tomorrow may be too late. The world will have moved on, rendering today's information stale.

THE PERSONAL LIBRARY

Vannevar Bush (1890–1974) is best remembered for his vision of the Memex, the forerunner of the personal digital assistant and the precursor of hypertext. One of America's most successful scientists leading up to the Second World War, he was known not just for prolific scientific and technological achievements, but also for his prowess as a politician and scientific administrator. He became vice president and dean of engineering at MIT, his alma mater, in 1931. In 1940, he proposed an organization that would allow scientists to develop critical technologies as well as cutting-edge weapons, later named the Office for Scientific Research and Development. This placed him at the center of a network of leading scientists cooperating with military partners. With peacetime, the organization evolved under his direction into the National Science Foundation, which still funds research in the United States.

Bush's experience as both scientist and technocrat provided the background for his 1945 vision:

A Memex is a device in which an individual stores all his books, records, and communications, and which is mechanized so that it may be consulted with exceeding speed and flexibility.

– Bush (1945)

He put his finger on two new problems that scientists of the time were beginning to face: specialization and the sheer volume of the scientific literature. It was becoming impossible to keep abreast of current thought, even in restricted fields. Bush wrote that scientific records, in order to be useful, must be stored, consulted, and continually extended—echoing Wiener's "information as process."

The dream that technology would solve the problem of information overload turned out to be a mirage. But Bush proposed a solution that even today is thought-provoking and inspirational. He rejected the indexing schemes used by librarians as artificial and stultifying and suggested an alternative.

The human mind... operates by association. With one item in its grasp, it snaps instantly to the next that is suggested by the association of thoughts, in accordance with some intricate web of trails carried by the cells of the brain.

– Bush (1945)

People make associative leaps when following ideas, leaps that are remarkably effective in retrieving information and making sense of raw data. Although Bush did not believe that machines could really emulate human memory, he was convinced that the Memex could augment the brain by suggesting and recording useful associations.

What Bush was suggesting had little in common with the giant calculating machines that were constructed during the 1940s. He was thinking of a desk-size workstation for information workers—lawyers, physicians, chemists, historians. Though he failed to recognize the potential of the new digital medium, his vision transcended technology and gave a glimpse of tools that might help deal with information overload. He foresaw the *universe (which others call the Web)* and inspired the pioneers who shaped it: Doug Engelbart, Ted Nelson, and Tim Berners-Lee.

THE HUMAN USE OF TECHNOLOGY

Although Bush did not participate directly in the artificial intelligence debate, he knew about it through his assistant Claude Shannon, who later created the theory of information that is still in use today (and also pioneered computer chess). The artificial *intelligentsia* of the day were striving to automate logical reasoning. But Bush thought that the highest form of human intelligence— the greatest accomplishment of the human mind, as he put it—was not logic but judgment. Judgment is the ability to select from a multitude of arguments and premises those that are most useful for achieving a particular objective. Owing more to experience than reasoning, it conjures up free association and loose connections of concepts and ideas, rather than the rigid classification structures that underlie library methods of information retrieval. He wanted machines to be able to exercise judgment:

> Memex needs to graduate from its slavish following of discrete trails, even as modified by experience, and to incorporate a better way in which to examine and compare information it holds.
>
> – *Bush (1959, p. 180)*

Judgment is what stops people from making mistakes that affect human relationships—despite faulty data, despite violation of logic. It supplants logical deduction in the face of incomplete information. In real life, of course, data is never complete; rationality is always subject to particular circumstances and bounded by various kinds of limit. The next step for the Memex, therefore, was to exercise judgment in selecting the most useful links and trails according to the preferences of what Bush called its "master." Today we call this "user modeling." By the mid-1960s, his still-hypothetical machine embodied advanced features of present-day search engines.

How did Bush dream up a vision that so clearly anticipated future developments? He realized that if the information revolution was to bring us closer to what he called "social wisdom," it must be based not just on new technical gadgets, but on a greater understanding of how to use them. "Know the user" is today a popular slogan in human-computer interface design, but in Bush's day the technologists—not the users—were in firm control. New technology can only be revolutionary insofar as it affects people and their needs. While

Wiener's ethical concerns emphasized the human use of human beings, Bush wanted technologies that were well adapted to the needs of their human users.

THE INFORMATION REVOLUTION

The World Wide Web arose out of three major technical developments. First, with the advent of interactive systems, beginning with time-sharing and later morphing into today's ubiquitous personal computer, people started to take the issue of human-computer interaction seriously. Second, advances in communication technology made it feasible to build large-scale computer networks. Third, changes in the way we represent knowledge led to the idea of explicitly linking individual pieces of information.

COMPUTERS AS COMMUNICATION TOOLS

J. C. R. Licklider (1915–1990) was one of the first to envision the kind of close interaction between user and computer that we now take for granted in our daily work and play. George Miller, doyen of modern psychologists, who worked with him at Harvard Laboratory during the Second World War, described him as the "all-American boy—tall, blond, and good-looking, good at everything he tried." Unusually for a ground-breaking technologist, Lick (as he was called) was educated as an experimental psychologist and became expert in psychoacoustics, part of what we call neuroscience today. In the 1930s, psychoacoustics researchers began to use state-of-the-art electronics to measure and simulate neural stimuli. Though his background in psychology may seem tangential to his later work, it inspired his revolutionary vision of computers as tools for people to interact with.

Computers did not arrive on the scene until Lick was in mid-career, but he rapidly came to believe that they would become essential for progress in psychoacoustic research. His links with military projects gave him an opportunity to interact (helped by an expert operator) with a PDP-1, an advanced computer of the late 1950s. He described his meeting with the machine as akin to a religious conversion. As an early minicomputer, the PDP-1 was smaller and less expensive than the mainframes of the day, but nevertheless very powerful—particularly considering that it was only the size of a couple of refrigerators. An ancestor of the personal computer, it was far more suited to interactive use than other contemporary machines. Though inadequate for his needs, the PDP-1 stimulated a visionary new project: a machine that could become a scientific researcher's assistant.

In 1957, Lick performed a little experiment: he noted down the activities of his working day. Fully 85 percent of his time was spent on clerical and mechanical tasks such as gathering data and taking notes—activities that he thought could be accomplished more efficiently by a machine. While others regarded computers as giant calculating engines that performed all the number-crunching that lies behind scientific work, as a psychologist Licklider saw them as interactive assistants that could interpret raw data in accordance with the aphorism that "the purpose of computing is insight, not numbers."

Believing that computers could help scientists formulate models, Licklider outlined two objectives:

> 1) to let the computers facilitate formulative thinking as they now facilitate the solution of formulated problems, and 2) to enable men and computers to cooperate in making decisions and controlling complex situations without inflexible dependence on predetermined programs.
>
> *– Licklider (1960)*

He was more concerned with the immediate benefits of interactive machines than with the fanciful long-term speculations of artificial intelligence aficionados. He began a revolution based on the simple idea that, in order for computers to *really* help researchers, effective communication must be established between the two parties.

TIME-SHARING AND THE INTERNET

Licklider synthesized Bush's concept of a personal library with the communication and control revolution sparked by Wiener's cybernetics. He talked of "man-computer symbiosis": cooperative and productive interaction between person and computer. His positive, practical attitude and unshakable belief in the fruits of symbiosis gave him credibility. Though others were thinking along the same lines, Lick soon found himself in the rare position of a man who could make his dream come true.

The U.S. Defense Department, alarmed by Russia's lead in the space race—*Sputnik*, the world's first satellite, was launched in 1957—created the Advanced Research Project Agency (ARPA) to fund scientific projects that could significantly advance the state of the art in key technologies. The idea was to bypass bureaucracy and choose projects that promised real breakthroughs. And in 1962, Licklider was appointed director of ARPA's Information Processing Techniques Office, with a mandate to raise awareness of the computer's potential, not just for military command but for commercial enterprises and the advancement of laboratory science. Human-computer symbiosis was elevated from one person's dream to a national priority.

The first advance was time-sharing technology. Interacting one-on-one with minicomputers was still too expensive to be practical on a wide scale, so systems were created that allowed many programmers to share a machine's resources simultaneously. This technical breakthrough caused a cultural change. Suddenly programmers realized that they belonged to the same community as the computer's end users: they shared objectives, strategies, and ways of thinking about their relationship with the machine. The idea that you could type on the keyboard and see an immediate output produced a seismic shift in how people perceived the machine and their relationship with it. This was a first step toward the symbiosis that Licklider had imagined.

The second advance was the world's first wide-area computer network, designed to connect scientists in different institutions and facilitate the exchange of ideas. In a series of memos that foreshadowed almost everything the Internet is today, Licklider had, shortly before he was appointed, formulated the idea of a global (he light-heartedly baptized it "galactic") computer network. Now he had the resources to build it. Time-sharing reformed communication between people and machines; the network spawned a new medium of communication between human beings. Called the ARPAnet, in 1969 it grew into the Internet.

In 1968, Licklider wrote of a time in which "men will be able to communicate more effectively through a machine than face to face." He viewed the computer as something that would allow creative ideas to emerge out of the interaction of minds. Unlike passive communication devices such as the telephone, it would participate actively in the process alongside the human players. His historic paper explicitly anticipated today's online interactive communities:

> [They] will consist of geographically separated members, sometimes grouped in small clusters and sometimes working individually. They will be communities not of common location, but of common interest.
> – *Licklider and Taylor (1968)*

Although the future was bright, a caveat was expressed: access to online content and services would have to be universal for the communication revolution to achieve its full potential. If this were a privilege reserved for a few people, the existing discontinuity in the spectrum of intellectual opportunity would be increased; if it were a birthright for all, it would allow the entire population to enjoy what Licklider called "intelligence amplification."

The same reservation applies today. Intelligence amplification will be a boon if it is available universally; a source of great inequity otherwise. The United Nations has consistently expressed profound concern at the deepening mal-distribution of access, resources, and opportunities in the information and communication field, warning that a new type of poverty, "information poverty," looms. The Internet is failing the developing world. The knowledge gap between nations is widening. For the sake of equity, our society must focus on guaranteeing open, all-inclusive, and cooperative access to the universe of human knowledge—*which others call the Web*.

AUGMENTING HUMAN INTELLECT

Doug Engelbart (1925–) wanted to improve the human condition by inventing tools that help us manage our world's growing complexity. Like Licklider, he believed that machines should assist people by taking over some of their tasks. He was the key figure behind the development of the graphical interface we all use every day. He invented the mouse, the idea of multiple overlapping windows, and an advanced collaborative computing environment of which today's "group-ware" is still but a pale reflection. He strove to augment human intellect though electronic devices that facilitate interaction and collaboration with other people. He came up with the radical new notion of "user-friendliness," though his early users were programmers and their systems were not as friendly as one might hope.

He thought that machines and people would co-evolve, mutually influencing one another in a manner reminiscent of Licklider's "man-computer symbiosis." Engelbart's groundbreaking hypermedia groupware system represented information as a network of relations in which all concepts could be reciprocally intertwined, an approach inspired by Bush's vision of the "intricacy of the web of trails." In fact, Engelbart wrote to Bush acknowledging his article's influence on his own work. Links could be created at any time during the process of organizing information—the genesis of today's hypertextual world.

Engelbart recognized from the outset that knowledge management was a crucial part of the enterprise. He foresaw a revolution that would "augment human intellect," in which knowledge workers would be the principal actors. An essential step was to make the computer a personal device, another radical notion in the mid-1960s. Engelbart recognized that the greatest challenge was the usability of the data representation, which could be achieved only by increasing the collaborative capabilities of both individuals and devices. The key was to allow the "augmented person" to create relations easily, relations that the "augmented computer" kept track of automatically. His sci-fi vision was that human beings could evolve through interaction with their machines—and vice versa.

Engelbart's innovative perspective caught the eye of the establishment. ARPA funded his work under the auspices of the prestigious Stanford Research Institute. When Xerox's Palo Alto Research Center (PARC) was established at the beginning of the 1970s—it would soon become the world's greatest human-computer research incubator—its founders recognized the importance of Engelbart's work and began to entice researchers away from his group. In 1981, PARC produced the Star workstation, the culmination of a long line of development. Though not a commercial success in itself, Star inspired Apple's

Macintosh, which eventually provoked Microsoft into producing their now-ubiquitous Windows operating system. Through these developments, it was Engelbart and his collaborators who made the computer what it is today: a user-friendly hypertextual networked machine.

THE EMERGENCE OF HYPERTEXT

The spirit of hypertext was in the air during the 1960s. Humanities scholars imagined a tangled world of relations in which avid readers followed trails through intertwined webs of concepts. The first to try to actualize these "literary machines" was Ted Nelson (1937–), who coined the term *hypertext*. He discovered computers while at Harvard graduate school, and under Bush's influence imagined that they might be used to keep track of his stream of ideas and of notes. While he thought this would be easy to realize, he later confessed that he mistook a clear view for a short distance, an endemic problem in computer programming.

Nelson saw the computer not just as a communication aid but as a completely new tool: a device to create the very content that would be communicated. He had no doubt that computers could help people in their creative thought processes. What he really wanted was something that kept track of all the author's revisions and changes of mind, so they could revert to previous versions at will. He also imagined adding links that were like special footnotes where reader and author could skip hand in hand from one part of the work to another, transcending the traditional serial presentation of content. He developed these ideas independently of Engelbart, though he too was inspired by Bush.

Around the end of the 1970s, Nelson began Xanadu, a vision and embryo software design for a universal system of electronic information storage and access that provided inspiration to others but was never completed in itself. His contribution was to see computers as creative tools that would revolutionize the way in which literature is read and written. Computers had always been aimed at science; Nelson was among the first to direct their attention toward the humanities. This is as significant a gesture as Galileo's four hundred years earlier when he pointed his telescope at the sky. Before that, it was a terrestrial instrument, used to spot faraway ships. Simply changing the direction of the lens transformed it into a new tool that shed fresh light onto our relationship with the world about us.

Nelson is a colorful and controversial figure who describes himself as a designer, generalist, and contrarian. He often repeats the four maxims by which he claims to lead his life: "most people are fools, most authority is malignant, God does not exist, and everything is wrong." There's something here to offend everyone! He imagined a community built around Xanadu, an anarchic group whose economy would be based on a system of reciprocal royalties for using one another's text. This community was born some years later, but rested on a different economic principle: mutual cooperation in which members share their content, rewarded by little more than positive reputation and social recognition.

AND NOW, THE WEB

Nelson's vision was transformed into reality by a young physicist. In 1980, Tim Berners-Lee (1955–) was a consultant at CERN, the European particle physics laboratory in Geneva. Stimulated by the need to communicate among dozens of institutions, he developed a program to help people track one another's work. He whimsically called it *Enquire*, after a Victorian self-help book, *Enquire Within Upon Everything*, which had fascinated him as a boy. It was a remarkable project, even though—as we have seen—the basic idea of hypertext had already been established.

Following its conception, the web remained *in utero* for nearly a decade. The hypertext environment was intended only for CERN's internal document repository. Berners-Lee continued to tinker with it, and in 1991 he sent to an Internet newsgroup a description of a project that would allow links to be made to any information, anywhere in the world. He announced a prototype hypertext editor for the NeXT, a powerful but little-used computer, and a browser for old-fashioned line-oriented terminals. He wrote: "If you're interested in using the code, mail me. It's very prototype, but available from [an Internet address]. It's copyright CERN but free distribution and use is not normally a problem."

One year later, the World Wide Web was demonstrated and distributed, along with browser software. But it only became popular when Marc Andreessen, a young programmer in the National Center for Supercomputing Applications at the University of Illinois, created a graphical web browser called Mosaic that significantly improved upon Berners-Lee's original design. Then the web exploded and has now populated every corner of our planet.

The World Wide Web allows people to create and organize their own information spaces and share them with others. In Berners-Lee's own words:

> There was no central computer "controlling" the Web, no single network on which these protocols worked, not even an organization anywhere that "ran" the Web. The Web was not a physical "thing" that existed in a certain "place". It was a "space" in which information could exist.
>
> – *Berners-Lee (2000, p. 39)*

The core ideas were a distributed, public information space freely accessible by all; organization of information into hypertext documents; no central authority to control the distribution of content; and a system for access based on the creation of web "trails" (as Bush had anticipated). Each of these characteristics is essential to the nature of the web as we know it.

The WWW is one of the greatest success stories in the history of technology. Although it exploded into the world without warning, like a supernova, the ground had been prepared over several decades: it is the culmination of the conjoint effort of philosophers, engineers, and humanities scholars. Between them, these people conjured up two revolutions, one in information dissemination and the other in human-computer interaction.

THE WORLD WIDE WEB

We opened with Borges' *Library of Babel* as an analogy for the parlous state of the web, the universe with which this book is concerned. After briefly placing the information revolution in context by comparison with other revolutions (the Enlightenment and the French Revolution), we heard what three very different thinkers from distant times and cultures, Plato, Peirce and Wittgenstein, had to say about the World Wide Web. We turned to early technologists and cited some of their concerns: Wiener's preoccupation with communication as the basis for society and with the dynamic nature of information, and Bush's belief in the personal library and the primacy of judgment over logic. The information revolution itself was fertilized by technical developments in computer science and required a reconceptualization of the notion of who the "users" of computers really are. Finally, we recounted how the web was born in a corner of a small country at the center of Europe.

We close by reflecting on how the web is used. It's created by people, and communities, and corporations—let's call them "writers." Its contents constitute a huge world archive of information. Although it certainly supports minority viewpoints, it is not a reflection of our world as it exists, as people often claim, but a reflection of our world as perceived by the writers. Although in principle almost anyone can be a writer, in practice few are—though wikis and blogs are redressing the balance. Ordinary people—let's call them "readers"—consult the web for information every day, and they do so through search engines. For many readers, their favorite search engine is synonymous with the web. What we read is not the repository but a biased view of it, biased by our search engine.

A UNIVERSAL SOURCE OF ANSWERS?

Gottfried Wilhelm Leibniz (1646–1716) was one of the most prominent thinkers of his time. A brilliant scientist and illustrious philosopher, he was also an ambassador and influential political consultant. As a youth, he dreamed of discovering how to settle all philosophical and scientific questions by calculating the results of a specified mathematical procedure. His plan was to design a formal language (*Lingua Characteristica*) and inference technique (*Calculus Ratiocinator*) and then find a way to express questions in the language and apply the rules of the calculus mechanically. He fantasized that savants would sit together and calculate the outcome of their debate without any disagreement or confusion. Leibniz hoped that the project would avoid effort wasted in pointless discussion and argumentation. It would supply definitive, incontrovertible answers to all questions—along with an assurance that the solutions were wise, effective, and trustworthy. It would make reasoning as easy as talking and liberate us from the anxiety and injustice of wrong decisions and judgments.

Leibniz's dream was hopelessly utopian. For a start, it presupposes that every philosophical, ethical, and scientific problem has a definitive answer, which unfortunately is not the case. The history of thought is littered with "dream of reason" projects like this. We all shrink from the insecurity inherent in decision-making, the stress involved in exercising judgment to come up with answers to delicate questions upon which our reputation rests. The myth that a fixed system of reasoning can provide a panacea to all doubts and difficulties is hard to dispel.

The web is the largest collection of information ever known. One might speculate that it contains the answer to every conceivable question—if not today, perhaps tomorrow, or next year—and revive the dream of a universal machine that can answer everything. As Leibniz suggested three centuries ago, the key would reside in the information representation. He wanted to couch everything in an artificial language in such a way that the answer to any question could be either retrieved or calculated. Fifty years ago, the computing world embarked on an analogous but far less ambitious venture: the construction of massive databases of company information. Data was normalized, fields were mandatory, data entry procedures were formalized, and rigid interrogation strategies were used to retrieve results. In the closed world of company databases, logical procedures returned the correct answer to every conceivable question.

When the web appeared, a painful adjustment took place. The logical foundation of document retrieval differs fundamentally from that of data retrieval. It is simply not possible to represent textual documents—web pages—uniformly in a way that supports answering questions about what they mean. The calculations performed by search engines recognize the lexical and statistical properties of text, but not its meaning.

Contrast a database query with a web request. To the database, we pose a clear question that implies a direct and well-defined answer: "how many students are enrolled in Harvard courses this year?" In the worst case, the information is absent; perhaps this year's figures are not yet available. Even then the answer is useful. But when users interrogate the web, they do not expect a unique reply but rather a set of documents that probably includes some useful information on the topic. We could ask about the U.S. government's position on the Middle East. The response will necessarily be indeterminate and nondeterministic—and will require the user's judgment in determining which links to follow. It is meaningless to classify the query's outcome in stark terms of success or failure.

The web user is faced with an indefinitely long list of results, most of them irrelevant. Contrast this with the precise answer obtained by a database user. Unfortunately, this deep shift in perspective is not always perceived clearly. When querying a database, the interrogator knows that there is a clear connection between request and reply. When the same question is posed to a web search engine, there is no guarantee of user satisfaction—indeed, we cannot even measure it. If the web is our sole information source and we interact using a particular tool, we have no way of evaluating the results obtained, comparing them with others, or knowing whether what we have found even scratches the surface of what is available.

Most users blindly trust their search tool, a single information source, when at their feet lies a subtle, collective, multiply-linked structure. Why? Like Leibniz, we are all seduced by the dream of reason. We feel, or hope, that it is possible to obtain a unique, definitive solution—just as we used to do when searching databases. We yearn to avoid ambiguity, the obligation to select results, the need to investigate the fallibility and evaluate the performance of search tools, to judge the quality of resources. There is no shame in this: Leibniz suffered the same misconception.

But be aware: The dream of reason is a dangerous nightmare. Users should not become victims. We must continually invent creative new procedures for searching. We must employ judgment to evaluate search tools. We must spend time and mental energy. We must not behave as though database-style integrity is guaranteed by the search tools we use every day.

WHAT USERS KNOW ABOUT WEB SEARCH

There is a mind-boggling supply of information on the web. Search engines—the "web dragons" of the book's title—mediate between this treasure and its consumers, and purport to guarantee access to all that we require. We all use them in an attempt to find what we need to know. In the words of a recent report on Internet usage, searchers are confident, satisfied, and trusting—but they are also unaware and naïve.

The overwhelming majority of adult Internet users have used a search engine. Well over half the people online consult one on any given day (in 2006). Search engine usage rivals e-mail, which is impressive because e-mail is a private interpersonal communication activity. People employ search engines for important and trivial questions alike. They have become part of everyday life.

Though hundreds of search engines are freely and publicly available, a very few capture the overwhelming majority of the audience. According to the well-known 80/20 rule, 80 percent of users are concentrated on 20 percent of applications. The proportion is even more extreme with search engines because of a strong economic feedback loop: popular ones attract a greater volume of advertising and produce the highest revenues, which funds improved and diversified services. The dragons are out to capture our attention.

Users trust their own ability as web searchers. More than 90 percent of people who use search engines say they are confident in the answers; half are very confident. Users also judge their research activities as successful in most cases. "But how do you know," Plato would retort, recalling Socrates' conversation with Meno. Users should recognize Plato's dilemma of knowledge: you cannot tell when you have arrived at the truth when you don't know what the truth is.

The less Internet experience people have, the more successful they regard their own searches. Neophytes have overwhelming confidence that their search results are satisfactory; they grow more skeptical as their experience with search engines increases. Use is particularly prevalent among the younger generation, who feel daunted by the prospect of seeking information on the web (or anywhere else) without the help of search engines.

A report on the critical thinking of higher education students in the Internet era sums up its message in the title: "Of course it's true; I saw it on the Internet!" Students tend to place supreme confidence in the results of search engines, without having any idea how they work or being aware that they are fundamentally commercial operations. Researchers asked students in a first-year university class on Computers and the Internet to answer several questions, some of which were prone to misinformation. The results were remarkable. Though they were not obliged to use the Internet for their information, fewer than 2 percent of students cited any other source. Students were extraordinarily confident in search engines and remained faithful to their dragon of choice throughout the survey, even when the desired answer eluded them. More interesting than the quantitative results were the students' attitudes toward search capability. When their answers were correct, they rarely verified them against an alternative source, even though this would have been easy for them to do.

Given these findings, it is particularly disturbing that users think their search activity is successful. The students in this survey apparently place blind trust in whatever is presented to them by their favorite search engine. This is a dangerous vicious circle: users believe they are capable searchers precisely because they are uncritical toward the results that their search engine returns.

Surveys have revealed that more than two-thirds of users believe that search engines are a fair and unbiased source of information. In spite of the trust they place in these tools, the most confident users are those who are less knowledgeable and experienced in the world of search. In particular, many are unaware of two issues: commercialism, in the form of sponsored links, and privacy, or the fact that search engines have an opportunity to track each user's search behavior. Only around 60 percent of users can identify commercially sponsored links in the search results, a proportion that has remained unchanged over the past two years. Even more prevalent is ignorance of potential privacy issues: nearly 60 percent of users are unaware that their online searches can be tracked.

SEARCHING AND SERENDIPITY

In a letter of January 28, 1754, to a British envoy in Florence, the English politician and writer Horace Walpole coined a new term: *serendipity*. Succinctly characterized as the art of finding something when searching for something else, the word comes from a tale called *The Three Princes of Serendip* (an old name for Sri Lanka). These princes journeyed widely, and as they traveled they continually made discoveries, by accident and sagacity, of things they were not seeking.

Serendipity shares salient characteristics with online information discovery. First, seeking answers to questions is not a static activity, but involves a quest, a journey. Second, exploration of new territory requires navigation tools: compass and sextant, perhaps a map and previous travelers' diaries. Third, luck and intelligence are needed to make new discoveries: we must sagaciously interpret what we bump into by chance. Fourth, it is not possible to plan all research steps in full detail; we must be flexible enough to integrate our preliminary thoughts with hints collected in the field and adapt our strategy as required. Fifth, we often find what we are not seeking, but it nevertheless behooves us to understand and interpret the discovery. Sixth, while traveling, we will rarely encounter something completely new, for indigenous tribes already inhabit the spaces we are in the process of discovering. Innovation is about creating new connections and new relations with already known territory. Finally, serendipity implies that logical trails of discovery can never guarantee certainty. Every result is provisional and temporary, subject to revision as new vistas unfold.

Just as nature is continuously changing, so is the web. It's a dynamic world: a collective memory that is in constant flux, not a static database that yields the same answer to the same question. Creating and using the web are activities for craftsmen as much as scholars. We strive to increase our knowledge despite the fact that we will never see the whole picture. The process is fascinating—but hardly reassuring, and to some, unnerving. There is no fixed point, no guiding star, and no guarantee. We travel with light hearts and a positive spirit, eager to face the continual challenges that a dynamic archive poses. We must be resourceful and embrace a diverse set of tools. To make sense of *the universe (which others call the Web)*, we must recognize its social character, accept that discovery is never-ending, and exercise our judgment at all times. We must succeed where the librarians of Babel failed.

SO WHAT?

The World Wide Web is exerting a profound influence on the way we think, work, and play. It's an absolutely unprecedented phenomenon. But although it exploded onto the scene in the space of a few years, in a way that was totally unexpected, it didn't arise out of nowhere. The groundwork had been laid over centuries by philosophers and over decades by technological visionaries. Though they knew nothing of the web itself, looking back over their work we can see that they had a lot to say about it.

In the next chapter we will tease out another strand of our intellectual heritage, one that did not sow the seeds of the web but is now rushing headlong toward convergence with it: libraries and the world of books.

WHAT CAN *YOU* DO ABOUT ALL THIS?

- Read Jorge Luis Borges' little story.
- Be creative about the tools you use to find information.
- Split your everyday search tasks into groups that call for different techniques.
- Don't get stuck in a rut: try a different dragon for a change.
- Ask your friends whether they regard search engines as an unbiased source of information.
- Try the same search on the same search engine a week later.
- Enjoy serendipitous adventures when you next surf the web.
- Discuss the paradox of inquiry with your friends.
- Find *MyLifeBits* on the web and trace its origins back to Bush's Memex.
- Express your view on the evolution of science in the Internet era.
- Read *The Onion*'s zany satirical article "Factual error found on Internet."

NOTES AND SOURCES

To avoid breaking up the flow of the main text, all references are collected together at the end of each chapter. This first *Notes and Sources* section describes papers, books, and other resources relevant to the material covered in Chapter 1.

The Library of Babel originally appeared in Spanish in Borges' 1941 collection of stories, *El Jardín de Senderos que se Bifurcan* (*The Garden of Forking Paths*). Borges (2000) is a translation illustrated with beautiful, evocative etchings by Erik Desmazières. We found inspiration in Michel Foucault's writings (1984, 1994), in particular his interpretation of Kant's essay *What is Enlightenment* (1784) and Kant's views on the French Revolution in *The Conflict of the Faculties* (1798). First published in 1953, two years after the author's death, Wittgenstein's *Philosophical Investigations* (2003) was a major contribution to last century's philosophical debate that raised new questions about language and its interpretation.

Turning to the technologists, Wiener sets out his ideas in two books on cybernetics (1948, 1950), while Heims (1980) provides an independent account of Wiener's ideas and achievements. Vannevar Bush's seminal paper (1945) is available in many anthologies on the history of technology; Nyce and Kahn (1991) give a compendium of his contributions, including his papers and archival material, along with editorial comment and discussion of his far-sighted ideas. Lick's early ideas are set out in Licklider (1960), and his vision of how men (*sic*) will be able to communicate more effectively through a machine than face to face is in Licklider and Taylor (1968). Waldrop (2002) gives a detailed description of Lick's influence on the development of man-computer symbiosis through personal computers, while Chapter 7 of Rheingold (2000) recounts his contributions to user-friendliness and the history of computer networks.

Engelbart's Bootstrap Institute website[1] provides electronic copies of all his work, including the invention of the mouse, window, and hypermedia groupware. Bardini (2000) and Lana (2004) (the latter in Italian only) describe the role of people and machines in Engelbart's "Augmentation of human intellect" project. You can read about Ted Nelson and how he pioneered two of the most influential cyberspace artifacts, hypertext and the Docuverse, on his website.[2] The fascinating history of the web, told by its inventor Berners-Lee in his book

---

[1] *www.bootstrap.org*

[2] *xanadu.com.au/ted;* a detailed bibliography appears at *www.mprove.de/diplom/ referencesNelson.html*

Weaving the Web (2000), recounts from the very first step the developments that brought us where we are now.

Pew Internet & American Life Project[3] surveyed search engine users in a January 2005 report. The study of college students in a Computers and the Internet course was undertaken by Graham and Metaxas (2003).

---

[3] *www.pewinternet.org*

LITERATURE AND THE WEB

The subject of this book, the web, is a young teenager. It's hard to believe it was *in utero* in 1990, emerged from the cradle with the introduction of the Netscape browser five years later, and only became widely known to the outside world around the turn of the millennium. *Teenager*, a juvenile between the onset of puberty and maturity, is an apt metaphor: agile, bumptious, cool, disrespectful, energetic, fun, gangly, hilarious, inane, jaunty, keen, loyal, noisy, obstreperous, promiscuous, quirky—the web is all these and more.

Today, this teenager has all but usurped our literature. The web is where people go to find things out. And while it is often denigrated as a damaged and unreliable source of questionable information, its aspiration knows no bounds: it is now threatening to take over our libraries. In future chapters, we will dissect the web, measure its size, probe its flaws and failings, review its past, and assess its future. But first, this chapter takes a look at the kind of literature that is stored in libraries: how much there is, how it has grown, how it is organized … and what is happening to it now. To understand a revolution, we must place it in the context of what has gone before.

Can the alchemists transmute a mess of books into an ethereal new structure?

You probably think of libraries as bastions of conservatism, institutions that have always been there and always will be, musty and dank, unlit by the beacons of progress in our society. But you would be wrong: they have changed greatly over the centuries. They have had their own revolutions, seen turmoil and fire, even rape and plunder. And there has been no time of greater uncertainty than the present. For librarians are without doubt among those whose working lives are most radically affected by the tremendous explosion of networked information sparked by the Internet. For them, advances in information technology generate shockwave after shockwave of opportunities and problems that must seem like a fierce, and sustained, onslaught on their own self-image.

How would you react if a technology juggernaut like Google suddenly declared that its mission was something that you thought society had entrusted to you alone, which you had been doing well for centuries: "to organize the world's information and make it universally accessible and useful"? How do librarians feel when people turn from their doors and instead visit web bookstores to check their references, to ferret out related books, or to see what others recommend—even to check out facts in standard reference works? Like everyone else, they are acutely aware that the world is changing, and they know their job descriptions and institutions must follow suit. Their clients now work online, and part of the contemporary librarian's job is to create websites, provide web interfaces to the catalogue, link to full text where available, and tend the e-mail help desk.

This is not normal evolution, it's violent revolution. The bumptious teenager is really throwing his weight around. Now they're digitizing libraries and chucking out the books!—not (usually) into the garbage; they're going into remote storage depots where they will never again see the light of day nor illuminate the minds of readers who have been used to browsing library shelves. Massive digitization programs are underway that will change forever the way in which people find and use information. The events of the last quarter-century have shaken our confidence in the continued existence of the traditional library. Of course, there is a backlash: defensive tracts with titles like *Future Libraries: Dreams, Madness and Reality* deride "technolust" and the empty promises of early technophiles. But it is a plain fact that the web is placing libraries as we know them in serious jeopardy.

THE CHANGING FACE OF LIBRARIES

Libraries are society's repositories for knowledge—temples, if you like, of culture and wisdom. Born in an era where agriculture was humankind's greatest preoccupation, they experienced a resurgence with the invention of printing in the Renaissance, and really began to flourish when the industrial revolution prompted a series of inventions—such as the steam press—that mechanized the printing process.

Although libraries have been around for more than twenty-five centuries, only one has survived more than five or six centuries, and most are far younger. The exception is a collection of two thousand engraved stone slabs or "steles" situated in Xi'an, an ancient walled city in central China. This collection was established in the Song dynasty (ca. A.D. 1100) and has been gradually expanded with new work ever since. Each stele stands 2 or 3 meters high and is engraved with a poem, story, or historical record (see Figure 2.1). Confucius's works are here, as is much classic poetry, and an account of how a Christian sect spread eastward to China along the Silk Road. Chinese writing is an art form, and this library gathers together the work of outstanding calligraphers over a period of two millennia. It contains the weightiest books in the world!

We think of the library as the epitome of a stable, solid, unchanging institution, and indeed the silent looming presence of two thousand enormous stone slabs—tourist guidebooks call it the "forest of steles"—certainly projects an air of permanence. But this is an exception. Over the years, libraries have evolved beyond recognition. Originally intended for storage and preservation, they have refocused to place users and their information needs at center stage.

Ancient libraries were only useful to the tiny minority of people who could read. Even then access was strictly controlled. Medieval monastic and university libraries held chained copies of books in public reading areas. Other copies

Figure 2.1 Rubbing from a stele in Xi'an.

were available for loan, although substantial security was demanded for each volume borrowed.

The public library movement took hold in the nineteenth century. Libraries of the day had bookstacks that were closed to the public. Patrons perused the catalog, chose their books, and received them over the counter. In continental Europe, most libraries continue to operate this way; so do many research libraries in other countries. However, progressive twentieth-century librarians came to realize the advantage of allowing readers to browse the shelves and make their own selection. The idea of open-shelf libraries gained wide acceptance in English-speaking countries, marking the fulfillment of the principle of free access to libraries by all—the symbolic snapping of the links of the chained book.

Today we stand on the threshold of the digital library. The information revolution not only supplies the technological horsepower that drives digital libraries, it fuels an unprecedented demand for storing, organizing, and accessing information—a demand that is, for better or worse, economically, rather than curiosity, driven as in days gone by. If information is the currency of the knowledge economy, digital libraries are the banks where it is invested. Indeed, Goethe once remarked that visiting a library was like entering the presence of great wealth that was silently paying untold dividends.

BEGINNINGS

The fabled library of Alexandria, which Ptolemy I created in around 300 B.C., is widely recognized as the first great library. There were precedents, though. 350 years earlier the King of Assyria established a comprehensive, well-organized collection of tens of thousands of clay tablets, and long before that Chinese written records began, extending at least as far back as the eighteenth century B.C.

The Alexandrian Library grew at a phenomenal rate and, according to legend, contained 200,000 volumes within ten years. The work of the acquisitions department was rather more dramatic than in today's libraries. During a famine, the king refused to sell grain to the Athenians unless he received in pledge the original manuscripts of leading authors. The manuscripts were diligently copied and the copies returned to the owners, while the originals went into the library. By far the largest single acquisition occurred when Mark Antony stole the rival library of Pergamum and gave it lock, stock, and barrel—200,000 volumes—to Cleopatra as a love token. She passed it over to Alexandria for safe keeping.

By the time Julius Caesar fired the harbor of Alexandria in 47 B.C., the library had grown to 700,000 volumes. More than 2000 years would pass before another library attained this size, notwithstanding technological innovations such as the printing press. Tragically, the Alexandrian Library was destroyed. Much remained after Caesar's fire, but this was willfully laid waste (according to the Moslems) by Christians in A.D. 391 or (according to the Christians) by Moslems in A.D. 641. In the Arab conquest, Amru, the captain of Caliph Omar's army, would have been willing to spare the library, but the fanatical Omar is said to have disposed of the problem of the information explosion with the tragic words, "If these writings of the Greeks agree with the Koran, they are useless and need not be preserved; if they disagree, they are pernicious and ought to be destroyed."

THE INFORMATION EXPLOSION

Moving ahead a thousand years, let us peek into the library of a major university near the center of European civilization a century or two after Gutenberg's introduction of the movable-type printing press around 1450.[4] Trinity College, Dublin, one of the oldest universities in Western Europe, was founded in 1592 by Queen Elizabeth I. In 1600 the library contained a meager collection of 30 printed books and 10 handwritten manuscripts. This grew rapidly, by several thousand, when two of the Fellows mounted a shopping expedition to England, and by a further 10,000 when the library received the personal collection of Archbishop Ussher, a renowned Irish man of letters, on his death in 1661.

There were no journals in Ussher's collection. The first scholarly journals appeared just after his death: the *Journal des Sçavans* began in January 1665 in France, and the *Philosophical Transactions* of the Royal Society began in March 1665 in England. These two have grown, hydra-like, into hundreds of thousands of scientific journals today—although many are being threatened with replacement by electronic archives.

Trinity's library was dwarfed by the private collection of Duke August of Wolfenbüttel, Germany, which reached 135,000 works by his death in 1666. It was the largest contemporary library in Europe, acclaimed as the eighth wonder of the world. The pages, or "imprints," were purchased in quires (i.e., unbound) and shipped to the duke in barrels, who had them bound in 31,000 volumes with pale parchment bindings that you can still see today. Incidentally, Casanova, after visiting the library for a week in 1764, declared that "I have sometimes thought that the life of those in heaven may be somewhat similar to [this visit]"—high praise indeed from the world's most renowned lover!

But Trinity College was to have a windfall that would vault its library far ahead of Wolfenbüttel's. In 1801, the British Parliament passed an act decreeing that a copy of every book printed in the British Isles was to be donated

---

[4] The printing press was invented in China much earlier, around five centuries before Gutenberg.

to the College. The privilege extends to this day, and is shared by five other libraries—the British National Library, the University Libraries of Oxford and Cambridge, and the National Libraries of Scotland and Wales. This "legal deposit" law had a precedent in France, where King François I decreed in 1537 that a copy of every book published was to be placed in the Bibliothèque du Roi (long since incorporated into the French National Library). Likewise, the Library of Congress receives copies of all books published in the United States.

In the eighteenth century, the technology of printing really took hold. For example, more than 30,000 titles were published in France during a sixty-year period in the mid-1700s. Ironically, the printing press that Gutenberg had developed in order to make the Bible more widely available became the vehicle for disseminating the European Enlightenment—the emancipation of human thinking from the weight of authority of the Church that we mentioned in Chapter 1—some 300 years later.

Across the Atlantic, the United States was a late starter. President John Adams created a reference library for Congress when the seat of government was moved to the new capital city of Washington in 1800, the year before the British Parliament belatedly passed their legal deposit law. He began by providing $5000 "for the purchase of such books as may be necessary for the use of Congress—and for putting up a suitable apartment for containing them therein." The first books were ordered from England and shipped across the Atlantic in eleven trunks and a map case.

The library was housed in the new Capitol until August 1814, when—in a miniature replay of Julius Caesar's exploits in Alexandria—British troops invaded Washington and burned the building. The small congressional collection of 3000 volumes was lost in the fire, and began again with the purchase of Jefferson's personal library. Another fire destroyed two-thirds of the collection in 1851. Unlike Alexandria, however, the Library of Congress has regrown—indeed, its rotunda is a copy of the one built in Wolfenbüttel two centuries earlier. Today it's the largest library in the world, with 128 million items on 530 miles of bookshelves. Its collection includes 30 million books and other printed material, 60 million manuscripts, 12 million photographs, 5 million maps, and 3 million sound recordings.

Back in Trinity College, the information explosion began to hit home in the middle of the nineteenth century. Work started in 1835 on the production of a printed library catalog, but by 1851 only the first volume, covering the letters *A* and *B*, had been completed. The catalog was finally finished in 1887, but only by restricting the books that appeared in it to those published up to the end of 1872. Other libraries were wrestling with far larger volumes of information. By the turn of the century, Trinity had a quarter of a million books, while the Library of Congress had nearly three times as many.

Figure 2.2 A page from the original Trinity College Library catalog.

Both were dwarfed by the British Museum (now part of the British National Library), which at the time had nearly 2 million books, and the French National Library in Paris with more than 2.5 million.

THE ALEXANDRIAN PRINCIPLE: ITS RISE, FALL, AND REBIRTH

An Alexandrian librarian was reported as being "anxious to collect, if he could, all the books in the inhabited world, and, if he heard of, or saw, any book worthy of study, he would buy it." Two millennia later, this early statement of library policy was formulated as a self-evident principle of librarianship: *It is a librarian's duty to increase the stock of his library.* When asked how large a library should be, librarians answered "bigger. And with provision for further expansion."

Only recently did the Alexandrian principle come under question. In 1974, commenting on a ten-year building boom unprecedented in library history, the *Encyclopedia Britannica* observed that "even the largest national libraries are doubling in size every 16 to 20 years," and warned that such an increase can hardly be supported indefinitely. In the twentieth century's closing decade, the national libraries of the United Kingdom, France (see Figure 2.3), Germany, and Denmark all opened new buildings. The first two are monumental in scale: their country's largest public buildings of the century. Standing on the bank of the Seine, the Bibliothèque Nationale de France consists of four huge towers that appear like open books, surrounding a sunken garden plaza. The reading rooms occupy two levels around the garden, with bookshelves encircling them on the outer side.

Sustained exponential growth cannot continue, at least not in the physical world. A collection of essays published in 1976 entitled *Farewell to Alexandria: Solutions to Space, Growth, and Performance Problems of Libraries* dwells on the issues that arise when growth must be abandoned and give way to a steady state. Sheer physical space has forced librarians to rethink their principles. Now they talk about weeding and culling, no-growth libraries, the optimum size for collections, and even dare to ask "could smaller be better?" In a striking example of aggressive weeding, in 1996 the library world was rocked when it learned that the San Francisco Public Library had surreptitiously dumped

Figure 2.3 The Bibliothéque Nationale de France; Dominique Perrault, architect.

Copyright © Alain Goustard, photographer.

200,000 books, or 20 percent of its collection, into landfills, because its new building, though lavishly praised by architecture critics, was too small for all the books. Of course, the role of a public library is to serve the needs of the local community, whereas national libraries have a commitment to preserve the nation's heritage.

Over the last fifty years, the notion of focused collections designed to fulfill the needs of the reader has gradually replaced the Alexandrian ideal of a library that is vast and eternally growing. The dream of a repository for all the world's knowledge gave way to the notion of service to library users. Libraries that had outgrown their physical boundaries in the city center or university campus retired their books, or (more commonly) moved them to vast storehouses out of town, where they could be kept far more cheaply and still ordered by readers on request.

But everything changed at the start of the millennium. Our brash teenager, the World Wide Web, was born into a family where sustained exponential growth was the norm and had been for years. Gordon Moore, co-founder of Intel, observed in 1965 that the number of transistors that can be squeezed onto an electronic chip doubled every two years, a phenomenon that continues even today—only better, doubling every eighteen months or so. The term Moore's law is commonly used to refer to the rapidly continuing advance in computing power per unit cost. Similar advances occur in disk storage—in fact, progress over the past decade has outpaced semiconductors: the cost of storage falls by half every twelve months, while capacity doubles. That Alexandrian librarian has come home at last: now he can have his heart's desire. There are no physical limitations any more. Today, all the text in your local library might fit on your teenage child's handheld digital music player.[5]

THE BEAUTY OF BOOKS

What will become of books in the brave new web world? Bibliophiles love books as much for the statements they make as objects as for the statements they contain as text. Early books were works of art. The steles in Xi'an are a monumental example. They are studied as much for their calligraphic beauty as for the philosophy, poetry and history that they record. They are a permanent record of earlier civilizations. The *Book of Kells* in Trinity College Library,

---

[5] Assume the library contains half a million 80,000-word novels. At 6 letters per word (including the inter-word space), each novel comes to half a million bytes, or 150,000 bytes when compressed. The whole library amounts to about 75 gigabytes, about the capacity of a high-end iPod today (2006). This is text only: it does not allow for illustrations.

laboriously lettered by Irish monks at the scriptorium of Iona about 1200 years ago, is one of the masterpieces of Western art; a thirteenth-century scholar fancifully enthused that "you might believe it was the work of an angel rather than a human being." Figure 2.4 shows part of a page from the *Book of Kells* that exhibits an extraordinary array of pictures, interlaced shapes and ornamental details.

Beautiful books have always been prized for their splendid illustrations, for colored impressions, for beautifully decorated illuminated letters, for being printed on uncommon paper (or uncommon materials), for their unusual bindings, or for their rarity and historic significance. In India, you can see ancient books—some 2000 years old—written on palm leaves, bound with string threaded through holes in the leaves. Figure 2.5 shows an example, which includes a picture of a deity (Sri Ranganatha) reclining with his consort on a serpent (Adishesha).

For many readers, handling a book is an enjoyably exquisite part of the information seeking process. Beauty is functional: well-crafted books give their readers an experience that is rich, enlightening, memorable. Physical characteristics—the book's size, heft, the patina of use on its pages, and so on—communicate ambient qualities of the work. Electronically presented books may never achieve the standards set by the beautiful books of a bygone age. Most web pages are appallingly brash and ugly; the better ones are merely

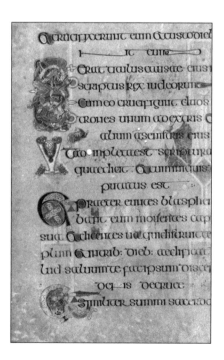

Figure 2.4 Part of a page from the *Book of Kells*.

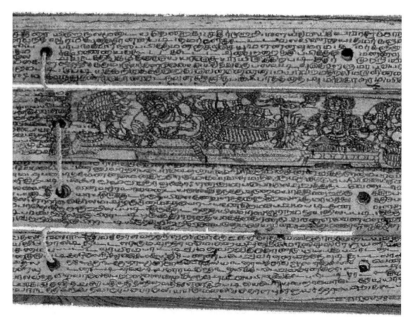

Figure 2.5 Pages from a palm-leaf manuscript in Thanjavur, India.
Thanjavur Maharaja Serfoji's Sarasvat Maha Library, Tamil Nadu (1995).

bland and utilitarian. Designers of electronic books do pay some attention to the look and feel of the pages, with crisp text clearly formatted and attractively laid out. Many digital collections offer page images rather than electronic text, but although sometimes rather beautiful, they are blandly presented as flat, two-dimensional framed objects.

The British National Library has made a rare attempt to provide an electronic reading experience that more closely resembles reading a traditional book. Readers sit at a large screen showing a double-page spread of what appears to be a physical book. They flick their finger across the touch-sensitive screen to metaphorically pick up a page and turn it. Pages look three-dimensional; they flip over, guided by your finger, and the book's binding eases imperceptibly as each one is turned. Page edges to right and left indicate how far through you are. The simulation is compelling, and users rapidly become absorbed in the book itself. Families cluster around the screen, discussing a beautifully illustrated text, turning pages unthinkingly. What a contrast from a web page and scroll bar! But the drawback is cost: these books are painstakingly photographed in advance to give a slow movie animation of every single page-turn.

A simulated three-dimensional book can be obtained from any electronic text by creating a computer model of the page-turn using techniques developed by the entertainment industry for animated movies. This yields a dynamic representation of a physical document that imitates the way it looks in nature, achieved

Figure 2.6 Views of an electronic book.

by interactive graphics—albeit rendered on a two-dimensional screen and manipulated using an ordinary mouse or touch-panel. The simulation nevertheless conveys the impression of handling a physical book.

The electronic book of Figure 2.6 uses a model whose parameters are page size and thickness, number of pages, paper texture, cover image, and so on. The model captures, in excruciating detail, the turning of each page of a completely blank book, depending on where you grab it (with the mouse or touch-panel). Then the textual page images of the actual book are mapped onto the blank pages before the page-turning operation is applied, a job that the computer can do in somewhat less than the twinkling of an eye. Future library patrons can (metaphorically) handle the book, heft it, flip through the pages, sample excerpts, scan for pictures, locate interesting parts, and so on. This gives a sense of numerous salient properties: the book's thickness, layout, typographic style, density of illustrations, color plates, and so on. When it comes to actual reading, page by page, readers switch to a conventional two-dimensional view, optimized for legibility and sequential access.

People have valuable and enjoyable interactions with books without necessarily reading them from cover to cover. And even when they do read right through, they invariably take a good look at the outside—and inside—first. When web bookstores opened, they soon began to provide front and back cover images, and progressed to the table of contents and subject index, then to sample chapters, and finally to full-page images of the books in their stock. These clues help provide readers with a sense of what it is that they are going to acquire.

Real documents give many clues to their age and usage history. Pages change color and texture with age, becoming yellow and brittle. Books fall open to well used parts, which bear the marks of heavier handling. Simulations can emulate these features and use them to enhance the reader's experience. But computers can go further, transcending reality. Other information can be used to augment the physical model. Fingertip recesses are cut into the page edges of old-fashioned dictionaries and reference works to indicate logical sections— letters of the alphabet, in the case of dictionaries. This can be simulated in a three-dimensional book model to show chapters and sections. Simulation offers key advantages over real life: the process can be applied to any book, and it can be switched on and off according to the user's taste and current needs.

Future virtual books will do far more than just mimic their physical counter- parts. Section headings will pop out from the side, forming a complete table of contents that is keyed to physical locations within the book, or—less intrusively— as "rollover text" that pops up when your finger strokes the page edges. The result of textual searches will be indicated by coloring page edges to indicate clusters of terms. Back-of-book indexes, or lists of automatically extracted terms and phrases, will be keyed to pages in the book. It will be easy to flick through just the illustrations, as many people do when encountering a new book. (Did you, when you picked this one up?)

The invention of the "codex," or book form, counts as one of history's greatest innovations. Unlike the papyrus scrolls in the Library of Alexandria, books provide random access. They can be opened flat at any page. They can be read easily—and shelved easily, with title, author, and catalog number on the spine. From a starkly utilitarian point of view, three-dimensional visualiza- tions communicate interesting and useful document features to the reader.

Life, including our interactions with digital technology, involves—or should involve—far more than merely maximizing efficiency and effectiveness. Subjective impact—how much pleasure users gain, how engaged they become—should not be overlooked or downplayed. Readers will be intrigued and enthusiastic as they interact with future three-dimensional books. The familiar, comforting, enjoyable, and useful nature of book visualizations will go some way toward helping to open up digital browsing to a broader audi- ence than technophiles—including those with little enthusiasm for bland information experiences.

METADATA

The contents of the World Wide Web are often called "virtual." To paraphrase the dictionary definition, something is *virtual* if it exists in essence or effect though not in actual fact, form, or name. In truth, a virtual representation of books has been at the core of libraries right from the beginning: the catalog.

Even before Alexandria, libraries were arranged by subject, and catalogs gave the title of each work, the number of lines, the contents, and the opening words. In 240 B.C., an index was produced to provide access to the books in the Alexandrian Library that was a classified subject catalog, a bibliography, and a biographical dictionary all in one.

A library catalog is a complete model that represents, in a predictable manner, the books within. It provides a summary of—sometimes a surrogate for—the library's holdings. Today we call this information "metadata," often dubbed "data about data."[6] And it is highly valuable in its own right. In the generous spirit of self-congratulation, a late nineteenth-century librarian declared:

> Librarians classify and catalog the records of ascertained knowledge, the literature of the whole past. In this busy generation, the librarian makes time for his fellow mortals by saving it. And this function of organizing, of indexing, of time-saving and thought-saving, is associated peculiarly with the librarian of the 19th Century.
>
> *—Bowker (1883)*

Along with the catalog, libraries contain other essential aids to information seeking, such as published bibliographies and indexes. Like catalogs, these are virtual representations—metadata—and they provide the traditional means of gaining access to journal articles, government documents, microfiche and microfilm, and special collections.

Organizing information on a large scale is far more difficult than it seems at first sight. In his 1674 Preface to the Catalogue for the Bodleian Library in Oxford, Thomas Hyde lamented the lack of understanding shown by those who had never been charged with building a catalog:

> "What can be more easy (those lacking understanding say), having looked at the title-pages than to write down the titles?" But these inexperienced people, who think making an index of their own few private books a pleasant task of a week or two, have no conception of the difficulties that arise or realize how carefully each book must be examined when the library numbers myriads of volumes. In the colossal labour, which exhausts both body and soul, of making into an alphabetical catalogue a multitude of books gathered from every corner of the earth there are many intricate and difficult problems that torture the mind.
>
> *— Hyde (1674)*

Two centuries later, the Trinity College librarians, still laboring over their first printed catalog, would surely have agreed.

Librarians have a wealth of experience in classifying and organizing information in ways that make relevant documents easy to find. Although some

---

[6] Because most traditional library catalogers are women whereas men tend to dominate digital libraries, metadata has been defined tongue-in-cheek as "cataloging for men."

aspects are irrelevant for digital collections—such as the physical constraint of arranging the library's contents on a linear shelving system—we can still benefit from their experience. Casual library patrons often locate information by finding one relevant book on the shelves and then looking around for others in the same area, but libraries provide far more systematic and powerful retrieval structures.

THE LIBRARY CATALOG

Few outside the library profession appreciate the amount of effort that goes into cataloging books. Librarians have created a detailed methodology for assigning catalog information, or metadata, to documents in a way that makes them easy to locate. The methodology is designed for use by professionals who learn about cataloging during intensive courses in librarianship graduate programs. The idea is that two librarians, given the same document to catalog, will produce exactly the same record.

A conscientious librarian takes an average of two hours to create a catalog record for a single item, and it has been estimated that a total of more than a billion records have been produced worldwide—a staggering intellectual investment. How can it take two hours to write down title, author, and publisher information for a book? It's not that librarians are slow; it's that the job is far harder than it first sounds. Of course, for web documents, the painstaking intellectual effort that librarians put into cataloging is completely absent. Most web users don't know what they're missing. What are some of the complexities? Let's look at what librarians have to reckon with.

Authors

Authors' names seem the most straightforward of all bibliographic entities. But they often present problems. Some works emanate from organizations or institutions: are they the author? Modern scientific and medical papers can have dozens of authors because of the collaborative nature of the work and institutional conventions about who should be included. Many works are anthologies: is the editor an "author"? If not, what about anthologies that include extensive editorial commentaries: when is this deemed worthy of authorship? And what about ghostwriters?

Digital documents may or may not represent themselves as being written by particular authors. If they do, authorship is generally taken at face value. However, this is problematic—not so much because people misrepresent authorship, but because differences arise in how names are written. For one thing, people sometimes use pseudonyms. But a far greater problem is simply inconsistency in spelling and formatting. Librarians go to great pains to normalize names into a standard form so that you can tell whether two documents are by the same person or not.

Table 2.1

Spelling Variants of the Name *Muammar Qaddafi*

Qaddafi, Muammar	Muammar al-Qadhafi	Qathafi, Muammar
Gadhafi, Mo ammar	Mu ammar al-Qadhdhafi	Gheddafi, Muammar
Kaddafi, Muammar	Qadafi, Mu ammar	Muammar Gaddafy
Qadhafi, Muammar	El Kazzafi, Moamer	Muammar Ghadafi
El Kadhafi, Moammar	Gaddafi, Moamar	Muammar Ghaddafi
Kadhafi, Moammar	Al Qathafi, Mu ammar	Muammar Al-Kaddafi
Moammar Kadhafi	Al Qathafi, Muammar	Muammar Qathafi
Gadafi, Muammar	Qadhdhafi, Mu ammar	Muammar Gheddafi
Mu ammar al-Qadafi	Kaddafi, Muammar	Khadafy, Moammar
Moamer El Kazzafi	Muammar al-Khaddafi	Qudhafi, Moammar
Moamar al-Gaddafi	Mu amar al-Kad'afi	Qathafi, Mu'Ammar el
Mu ammar Al Qathafi	Kad'afi, Mu amar al-	El Qathafi, Mu'Ammar
Muammar Al Qathafi	Gaddafy, Muammar	Kadaffi, Momar
Mo ammar el-Gadhafi	Gadafi, Muammar	Ed Gaddafi, Moamar
Muammar Kaddafi	Gaddafi, Muammar	Moamar el Gaddafi
Moamar El Kadhafi	Kaddafi, Muamar	

Table 2.1, admittedly an extreme example, illustrates just how difficult the problem can become. It shows different ways in which the name of *Muammar Qaddafi* (the Libyan leader) is represented on documents received by the Library of Congress. The catalog chooses one of these forms, ostensibly the most common—*Qaddafi, Muammar* in this case—and groups all variants under this spelling, with cross-references from all the variants. In this case, ascribing authorship by taking documents at face value would yield 47 different authors.

The use of standardized names is called authority control, and the files that record this information are authority files. This is an instance of the general idea of using a controlled vocabulary or set of preferred terms to describe entities. Terms that are not preferred are "deprecated" (which does not necessarily imply disapproval) and are listed explicitly, with a reference to the preferred term. Controlled vocabularies contrast with the gloriously unrestricted usage found in free text. Poets exploit the fact that there are no restrictions at all on how authors may choose to express what they want to say.

Titles

Most documents have titles. In digital collections, they (like authors) are often taken at face value from the documents themselves. In the world of books, they can exhibit wide variation, and vocabulary control is used for titles as well as for authors. Table 2.2 shows what is represented on the title pages of fifteen different editions of Shakespeare's *Hamlet*.

Amleto, Principe di Danimarca	*Montale Traduce Amleto*
Der erste Deutsche Buhnen-Hamlet	*Shakespeare's Hamlet*
The First Edition of the Tragedy of Hamlet	*Shakspeare's Hamlet*
Hamlet, A Tragedy in Five Acts	*The Text of Shakespeare's Hamlet*
Hamlet, Prince of Denmark	*The Tragedy of Hamlet*
Hamletas, Danijos Princas	*The Tragicall Historie of Hamlet*
Hamleto, Regido de Danujo	*La Tragique Histoire d'Hamlet*
The Modern Reader's Hamlet	

Table 2.2

Title Pages of Different Editions of *Hamlet*

Subjects

Librarians assign subject headings to documents from a standard controlled vocabulary—such as the *Library of Congress Subject Headings*. Subjects are far more difficult to assign objectively than titles or authors, and involve a degree of, well, subjectivity. The dictionary tellingly defines subjective as both

> pertaining to the real nature of something; essential

and

> proceeding from or taking place within an individual's mind such as to be unaffected by the external world.

The evident conflict between these meanings speaks volumes about the difficulty of defining subjects objectively!

It is far easier to assign subject descriptors to scientific documents than to literary ones, particularly works of poetry. Many literary compositions and artistic works—including audio, pictorial, and video compositions—have subjects that cannot readily be named. Instead, they are distinguished as having a definite style, form, or content, using artistic categories such as "genre."

Classification Codes

Library shelves are arranged by classification code. Each work is assigned a unique code, and books are placed on the shelves in the corresponding order. Classification codes are not the same as subject headings: any particular item has several subjects but only one classification. Their purpose is to place works into categories so that volumes treating similar topics fall close together. Classification systems that are in wide use in the English-speaking world are the Library of Congress Classification, the Dewey Decimal Classification, and India's Colon Classification System.

Readers who browse library shelves have immediate access to the full content of the books, which is quite different from browsing catalog entries that give only summary metadata. Placing like books together adds a pinch of serendipity to searching that would please the Three Princes of Chapter 1. You catch sight of an interesting book whose title seems unrelated, and a quick glance inside—the table of contents, chapter headings, illustrations, graphs, examples, tables, bibliography—gives you a whole new perspective on the subject.

Physical placement on shelves, a one-dimensional linear arrangement, is a far less expressive way of linking content than the rich hierarchy that subject headings provide. But digital collections have no dimensionality restriction. Their entire contents can be rearranged at the click of a mouse, and rearranged again, and again, and again, in different ways depending on how you are thinking.

THE DUBLIN CORE METADATA STANDARD

As we have seen, creating accurate library catalog records is a demanding job for trained professionals. The advent of the web, with its billions of documents, calls for a simpler way of assigning metadata. Dublin Core is a minimalist standard, intended for ordinary people, designed specifically for web documents.[7] It is used not just for books, but for what it terms "resources." This subsumes pictures, illustrations, movies, animations, simulations, even virtual reality artifacts, as well as textual documents. A resource has been defined as "anything that has identity." That includes you and me.

Table 2.3 shows the metadata standard. These fifteen attributes form a "core" set that may be augmented by additional ones for local purposes. In addition, many of the attributes can be refined through the use of qualifiers. Each one can be repeated where desired.

The *Creator* might be a photographer, illustrator, or author. *Subject* is typically expressed as a keyword or phrase that describes the topic or content of the resource. *Description* might be a summary of a textual document, or a textual account of a picture or animation. *Publisher* is generally a publishing house, university department, or corporation. *Contributor* could be an editor, translator, or illustrator. *Date* is the date of resource creation, not the period

---

[7] Named after a meeting held in Dublin, Ohio, not Molly Malone's fair city, in 1995.

Metadata	Definition
Title	A name given to the resource
Creator	An entity primarily responsible for making the content of the resource
Subject	A topic of the content of the resource
Description	An account of the content of the resource
Publisher	An entity responsible for making the resource available
Contributor	An entity responsible for making contributions to the content of the resource
Date	A date of an event in the lifecycle of the resource
Type	The nature or genre of the content of the resource
Format	The physical or digital manifestation of the resource
Identifier	An unambiguous reference to the resource within a given context
Source	A reference to a resource from which the present resource is derived
Language	A language of the intellectual content of the resource
Relation	A reference to a related resource
Coverage	The extent or scope of the content of the resource
Rights	Information about rights held in and over the resource

Table 2.3

The Dublin Core Metadata Standard

covered by its contents. A history book will have a separate *Coverage* date range that defines the time period to which the book relates. *Coverage* might also include geographical locations that pertain to the content of the resource. *Type* might indicate a home page, research report, working paper, poem, or any of the media types listed before. *Format* can be used to identify software systems needed to run the resource.

This standard does not impose any kind of vocabulary control or authority files. Two people might easily generate quite different descriptions of the same resource. However, work is underway to encourage uniformity by specifying recommended sets of values for certain attributes. For example, the *Library of Congress Subject Headings* are encouraged as one way of specifying the *Subject*. There are standard schemes for encoding dates and languages, which Dublin Core adopts.

The original minimalist Dublin Core standard is being augmented with new ways to increase expressiveness by accommodating complexity. Certain attributes can be refined. For example, *Date* can be qualified as *date created*, *date valid*, *date available*, *date issued*, or *date modified*; multiple specifications are possible. *Description* can be couched as an *abstract* or a *table of contents*. Standard refinements of the *Relation* field include *is version of*, *is part of*, *replaces*, *requires*, and *references*.

DIGITIZING OUR HERITAGE

How big is our literature? And how does it compare with the web? The Library of Congress has 30 million books. The one you are reading contains 103,304 words, or 638,808 characters (including spaces)—say 650,000 bytes of text in uncompressed textual form (compression might reduce it to 25 percent without sacrificing any accuracy). Although it has few illustrations, they add quite a bit, depending on how they are stored. But let's consider the words alone. Suppose the average size of a book in the Library of Congress is a megabyte. That makes a total of 30 terabytes for the Library's total textual content—or maybe 100,000 copies of the *Encyclopedia Britannica*.

How big is the web? In the next chapter, we will learn that it was estimated at 11.5 billion pages in early 2005, totaling perhaps 40 terabytes of textual content. That's a little more than the Library of Congress. Or take the Internet Archive. Today, according to its website,[8] its historical record of the web (which probably includes a great deal of duplication) contains approximately one petabyte (1,024 terabytes) of data and is growing at the rate of 20 terabytes per month—all the text in the Library of Congress every six weeks.

The amounts we have been talking about are for text only. Text is miniscule in size compared with other electronic information. What about all the information produced on computers everywhere, not just the web? It took two centuries to fill the Library of Congress, but today's world takes about 15 minutes to churn out an equivalent amount of new digital information, stored on print, film, magnetic, and optical media. More than 90 percent of this is stored on ordinary hard disks. And the volume doubles every three years.

You might take issue with these figures. They're rough and ready and could be off by a large factor. But in today's exponentially growing world, large factors are overcome very quickly. Remember the local library that we mentioned might fit on a teenager's portable digital music player? It had half a million books. Wait six years until storage has improved by a factor of 60, and the Library of Congress will fit there. Wait another couple to store the world's entire literature. What's a factor of 10, or 100, in a world of exponential growth? Our teenager the web has reached the point where it dwarfs its entire ancestry.

What are the prospects for getting all our literature onto the web? Well, storage is not a problem. And neither is cost, really. If we show page images, backed up by the kind of low-accuracy searchable text that automatic optical character recognition can produce, it might cost $10 per book to digitize all

---

[8] *www.archive.org/about/faqs.php*

the pages. The 30 million books in the Library of Congress would cost $300 million. That's half the Library's annual budget.

The main problem, of course, is copyright.[9] There are three broad classes of material: works that are in the public domain, commercially viable works currently in print and being sold by publishers, and works still under copyright that are no longer being commercially exploited. We briefly discuss current projects that are digitizing material in these three areas. But be warned: things are moving very quickly. Indeed, the doubling every two years that Gordon Moore observed in semiconductor technology seems rather sluggish by the standards of large-scale digitization projects in the early twenty-first century! Many radical new developments will have occurred by the time you read these pages.

PROJECT GUTENBERG

Project Gutenberg was conceived in 1971 by Michael Hart, then a student, with the goal of creating and disseminating public domain electronic text. Its aim was to have 10,000 texts in distribution thirty years later. The amount added to the collection doubles every year, with one book per month in 1991, two in 1992, four in 1993, and so on. The total should have been reached in 2001, but the schedule slipped a little, and in October 2003 the 10,000th electronic text was added to the collection—the Magna Carta. A new goal was promptly announced: to grow the collection to one million by the end of the year 2015. By early 2006, the project claimed 18,000 books, with a growth of 50 per week.

Gutenberg's first achievement was an electronic version of the U.S. Declaration of Independence, followed by the Bill of Rights and the Constitution. The Bible and Shakespeare came later. Unfortunately, however, the latter was never released, due to copyright restrictions. You might wonder why: surely Shakespeare was published long enough ago to be indisputably in the public domain? The reason is that publishers change or edit the text enough to qualify as a new edition, or add new extra material such as an introduction, critical essays, footnotes, or an index, and then put a copyright notice on the whole book. As time goes by, the number of original surviving editions shrinks, and eventually it becomes hard to prove that the work is in the public domain since few ancient copies are available as evidence.

Project Gutenberg is a grass-roots phenomenon. Text is input by volunteers, each of whom can enter however much they want—a book a week, a book a year, or just one book in a lifetime. The project does not direct the

---

[9] Chapter 6 introduces salient aspects of copyright law.

volunteers' choice of material; instead, people are encouraged to choose books they like and enter them in a manner in which they are comfortable. In the beginning, books were typed in. Now they are scanned using optical character recognition but are still carefully proofread and edited before being added to the collection. An innovative automated scheme distributes proofreading among volunteers on the Internet. Each page passes through two proofreading rounds and two formatting rounds. With thousands of volunteers each working on one or more pages, a book can be proofed in hours.

Gutenberg deals only with works that are in the public domain. It has sister projects in other countries, where the laws are sometimes slightly different.[10]

MILLION BOOK PROJECT

The Million Book project was announced in 2001 by Carnegie Mellon University, with the goal of digitizing one million books within a few years. The idea was to create a free-to-read, searchable digital library about as big as Carnegie Mellon University's library, and far larger than any high school library. The task involves scanning the books, recognizing the characters in them, and indexing the full text. Pilot Hundred- and Thousand-book projects were undertaken to test the concept.

Partners were quickly established in India and China to do the work. The United States supplies equipment, expertise, training, and copyright experts, while the partner countries provide labor and perform the actual digitization. To kick start the venture, Carnegie Mellon University pulled books published before 1923 from its shelves and boxed them for shipment to India, sending a total of 45,000 titles, mainly biographies and science books. Further material originates in the partner countries. The Chinese are digitizing rare collections from their own libraries, while the Indians are digitizing government-sponsored textbooks published in many of the country's eighteen official languages. By the end of 2005, more than half a million books had been scanned: 28 percent in India and 69 percent in China, with the remaining 3 percent in Egypt. Roughly 135,000 of the books are in English; the others are in Indian, Chinese, Arabic, French, and other languages. However, not all are yet available online, and they are distributed between sites in three countries. The project

---

[10] For example, the Australian project has more freedom because until recently its copyright laws were more permissive—works entered the public domain only 50 years after the author's death. In early 2005, the copyright term was extended by 20 years as part of the Australia–U.S. Free Trade Agreement, bringing it into line with U.S. practice. However, material for which copyright had previously expired—that is, if the author died in 1954 or before—remains in the public domain in Australia, though not in the United States. We discuss copyright further in Chapter 6.

is on track to complete a million books by 2007. It recently joined the Open Content Alliance (see page 55).

Unlike Project Gutenberg, which places great emphasis on accurate electronic text that can be both displayed and searched, the Million Book Project makes books available in the form of highly compressed image files (using DjVu, which is a commercial technology). Part of the project is developing optical character recognition technology for Chinese and for the Indian languages, an ambitious goal considering the variability and intricacy of the scripts. The project is daunting in scale and many details are unclear, such as how many of the currently scanned books have actually been converted to electronic text form, how much emphasis is being placed on accuracy, and to what extent the output is being manually corrected. It is intended that 10,000 of the million books will be available in more than one language, providing a test bed for machine translation and cross-language information retrieval research.

As well as public domain works, in-copyright but out-of-print material will be digitized. Books will be free to read on the web, but printing and saving may be restricted to a page at a time to deter users from printing or downloading entire books—this is facilitated by the use of DjVu technology for display (although open source viewers exist). Publishers are being asked for permission to digitize all their out-of-print works; others who wish to have book collections digitized are invited to contact the project. Donors receive digital copies of their books.

INTERNET ARCHIVE AND THE BIBLIOTHECA ALEXANDRINA

The Internet Archive was established in 1996 with the aim of maintaining a historical record of the World Wide Web. Its goal is to preserve human knowledge and culture by creating an Internet library for researchers, historians, and scholars. By 2003, its total collection was around 100 terabytes, growing by 12 terabytes per month; today it includes more than 40 billion web pages and occupies a petabyte of storage, growing by 20 terabytes per month.

The Internet Archive is deeply involved in digitization initiatives and now provides storage for the Million Book Project. On April 23, 2002, UNESCO's International Day of the Book, a partnership was announced with Bibliotheca Alexandrina, an Egyptian institution that has established a great library near the site of the original Library of Alexandria. A copy of the entire Internet Archive is now held there—including the Million Book Project.

In December 2004, the Internet Archive announced a new collaboration with several international libraries to put digitized books into open-access archives. At that time, their text archive contained 27,000 books, and a million books had already been committed. This collaboration includes Carnegie Mellon University and subsumes the Million Book Project. It includes some of the original partners in India and China, as well as the Bibliotheca Alexandrina in Egypt and new partners in Canada and the Netherlands.

The Internet Archive does not target commercially successful books—ones that are available in bookstores. But neither does it want to restrict scope to the public domain. It has its eye on what are often called "orphan" works—ones that are still in copyright but not commercially viable—and is taking legal action in an attempt to obtain permission to include such books. In 2004, it filed a suit against the U.S. Attorney General claiming that statutes that extend copyright terms unconditionally—like the 1998 Sonny Bono Copyright Term Extension Act discussed in Chapter 6—are unconstitutional under the free speech clause of the First Amendment. It is requesting a judgment that copyright restrictions on works that are no longer available violate the U.S. Constitution. The U.S. District Court dismissed the case, but the ruling has been appealed.

AMAZON: A BOOKSTORE

What about commercially successful books? In October 2003, Amazon, the world's leading online bookstore, announced a new online access service to the full text of publications called "Search inside the book." This dramatic initiative opened with a huge collection of 120,000 fiction and nonfiction titles supplied by nearly 200 book publishers, with an average of 300 pages per title. The goal was to quickly add most of Amazon's multimillion-title catalog.

The "search inside" feature allows customers to do just that: search the full text of books and read a few pages. Amazon restricts the feature to registered users, or ones who provide a credit card, and limits the number of pages you can see. Each user is restricted to a few thousand pages per month and at most 20 percent of any single book. You cannot download or copy the pages, or read a book from beginning to end. There's no way to link directly to any page of a book. You can't print using the web browser's print function, though even minor hackers can easily circumvent this. Anyone could save a view of their screen and print that, but it's a tedious way of obtaining low-quality hardcopy.

Our teenager is flexing its muscles. Publishers did not welcome this initiative, but they had no real choice—you can't ignore the call of the web.[11]

---

[11] However, many publishers balk at making popular textbooks available through this program, for they fear that a concerted effort by a group of bright students could completely undermine their copyright.

The fact that Amazon's mission is to sell books helped convince publishers to agree to have their content included. When the service was introduced, there was a lively debate over whether it would help sales or damage them. The Authors Guild was skeptical: its staff managed to print out 100 consecutive pages from a best-selling book using a process that was quite simple though a bit inconvenient (Amazon immediately disabled the print function). Amazon reported that early participants experienced sales gains of 9 percent from the outset. Customers reported that the service allowed them to find things they would never have seen otherwise, and gave them a far stronger basis for making a purchase decision. Pundits concluded that while it may not affect a book's central audience, it would extend the edges. Some felt that it would hurt the sales of reference books because few people read them from cover to cover, but now most major publishers have joined the program to avoid the risk of losing significant sales to the competition.

There is evidence that putting full text on the web for free access can actually boost sales. When the National Academy Press did this for all new books, print sales increased (to the surprise of many). The Brookings Institute placed an experimental 100 books online for free and found that their paper sales doubled.

Amazon's service is entirely voluntary: publishers choose whether to make their books available. Before doing so, they must ensure that their contract with the author includes a provision for digital rights that entitles them to exploit the work in this way. Then they supply the electronic text or a physical copy. Amazon sends most books to scanning centers in low-wage countries like India and the Philippines. Some are scanned in the United States using specialist machines to handle oversize volumes and ensure accurate color reproduction.

This initiative heralds a profound change in the bookselling business. Amazon provides an electronic archive in which readers can find books, sample them, and, if they like what they see, purchase them. It is now able to earn a profit by selling a far wider variety of books than any previous retailer. The popularity curve has a long tail—there are many books that are not profitable to stock, though they would sell a few copies every year. Under the traditional publishing model, titles become inefficient at hundreds of sales per year, whereas Amazon's model remains profitable at far lower sales volumes.

GOOGLE: A SEARCH ENGINE

Just a year later, in October 2004, Google announced its own book search service. There is a key difference from Amazon's program: Google does not sell books. When Google Book Search generates a search result, it lists online bookstores: you can click on one to buy the book. Publishers could purchase one of the links and sell the book directly, thereby reducing their reliance on book retailers. This provides an intriguing new business model. Google underwrites the cost of digitizing out-of-print editions for publishers who want to have their books in the Google index; it then splits advertising revenue with the publisher.

Of course, viewing restrictions like Amazon's are imposed. Users can only see a few pages around their search hits, and there is an upper limit to the number of pages you can view (determined, in this case, by the publisher). In order to help protect copyright, certain pages of every in-copyright book are unconditionally unavailable to all users.

A few months later, at the end of 2004, Google announced a collaboration with five major libraries[12] to digitize vast quantities of books. Works are divided into three categories. Those in the public domain will be available on an open-access basis—you can read their full content. For copyrighted material covered by an agreement between the publisher and Google, you can view pages up to a predetermined maximum limit, as with Amazon. For copyrighted books that are scanned without obtaining copyright permission, users will only see small snippets of text—a line or two—that contain their query in context, plus bibliographic information. The snippets are intended to inform readers about the relevance of the book to their subject of inquiry. Google will place links to bookstores and libraries next to search results.

Some of the collaborating libraries intend to offer their entire book collection for Google to scan. Others will offer just a portion; still others are giving rare materials only. A total of 15 million books are involved. What's in it for the libraries? Google gives back the digitized versions for them to use in whatever ways they like. Whereas Google can't offer the full content publicly, libraries can show their patrons electronic copies. For libraries that have already been spending big bucks to digitize parts of their collection, this is an offer from heaven.

The announcement rocked the world of books. There have been many enthusiasts and a few detractors. Some denounce it as an exercise in futility, others as a massive violation of copyright; others fret that it will distort the course of scholarship. The president of France's National Library warned of the risk of "crushing American domination in the definition of how future generations conceive the world" and threatened to build a European version. To which Google characteristically replied, "Cool!"

---

[12] The University of Michigan, Harvard, Oxford, and Stanford; and the New York Public Library.

OPEN CONTENT ALLIANCE

One year further on, toward the end of 2005, the Open Content Alliance was announced. Prompted by the closed nature of Google's initiative, the Internet Archive, Yahoo, and Microsoft, along with technology organizations such as Adobe and HP Labs and many libraries, formed a consortium dedicated to building a free archive of digital text and multimedia. Initially, the Internet Archive will host the collection and Yahoo will index the content. The cost of selecting and digitizing material is borne by participating institutions based on their own fundraising and business models; the Internet Archive undertakes nondestructive digitization at 10¢ per page. Yahoo is funding the digitization of a corpus of American literature selected by the University of California Digital Library.

The aim is to make available high-resolution, downloadable, reusable files of the entire public domain, along with their metadata. Donors have the option to restrict the bulk availability of substantial parts of a collection, although in fact Yahoo and the University of California have decided not to place any restrictions. Use will be made of the Creative Commons license described in Chapter 6 (page 197), which allows authors to explicitly relinquish copyright and place their work in the public domain.

Whether an open consortium can rival Google's project is moot. Google has the advantage of essentially limitless funding. But the Open Content Alliance is distinguishing its efforts from Google's by stressing its "copyright-friendly" policy: it intends to respect the rights of copyright holders before digitizing works that are still under copyright. This may restrict the Alliance's scope, but will leave it less exposed to discontent.

NEW MODELS OF PUBLISHING

Project Gutenberg is zealously noncommercial, digitizes books in the public domain alone, and publishes an accurate rendition of the full electronic text (but not the formatting). The Million Book Project, Internet Archives, and Open Content Alliance are noncommercial, target public-domain books, but also aspire to process copyrighted "orphan" books, and show users page images backed up by full-text searching.

Amazon and Google are commercial. As a bookseller, Amazon deals only with commercially viable books—but has aspirations to expand viability to works with very low sales. Google sells advertising, not books, and plans to offer all three categories of books. For public-domain works, it presents the full text—but you cannot print or save it. You can read books in full, but you must read them in Google. For commercial works, it presents excerpts, as Amazon does, and provides links for you to purchase the book—but not links to local libraries that have copies. For orphan works, it shows snippets and provides links to bookstores and local libraries.

These innovations—particularly the commercial ones—will have enormous repercussions. Publishers will accelerate production of digitized versions of their titles—e-Books—and sell them online through keyword advertising on channels such as Google Book Search. They will continue to rely on conventional retailers for the sale of paper copies. They will experiment with combining e-Books with pre- and post-release paper copies. E-Book technology will be forced to standardize.

Eventually, different sales models for e-Books will emerge. Highly effective search engine advertising will level the market, providing more opportunities for small publishers and self-publishing. Physical bookstores will find themselves bypassed. E-Books will provide preview options (flip through the pages at no cost) and will be rentable on a time-metered, or absolute duration, basis (like video stores), perhaps with an option to purchase. Publishers will experiment with print-on-demand technology.

E-Books present a potential threat to readers. Content owners may adopt technical and legal means to implement restrictive policies governing access to the information they sell. E-Books can restrict access to a particular computer—no lending to friends, no sharing between your home computer and your office, no backing up on another machine. They can forbid resale—no secondhand market. They can impose expiry dates—no permanent collections, no archives. These measures go far beyond the traditional legal bounds of copyright, and the result could immeasurably damage the flow of information in our society.

Can content owners really do this? To counter perceived threats of piracy, the entertainment industry is promoting digital rights management schemes that control what users can do. They are concerned solely with content owners' rights, not at all with users' rights. They are not implementing "permissions," which is what copyright authorizes, but absolute, mechanically enforced "controls." Anti-circumvention rules are sanctioned by the Digital Millennium Copyright Act (DMCA) in the United States; similar legislation is being enacted elsewhere (see Chapter 6, page 201), which gives some background about this act. Control is already firmly established by the motion picture industry, which can compel manufacturers to incorporate encryption into their products because it holds key patents on DVD players.

Commercial book publishers are promoting e-Book readers that, if widely adopted, would allow the same kind of control to be exerted over reading material. Basic rights that we take for granted (and are legally enshrined in the concept of copyright) are in jeopardy. Digital rights management allows reading rights to be controlled, monitored, and withdrawn, and DMCA legislation makes it illegal for users to seek redress by taking matters into their own hands. However, standardization and compatibility issues are delaying consumer adoption of e-Books.

In scholarly publishing, digital rights management is already well advanced. Academic libraries license access to content in electronic form, often in tandem with purchase of print versions. Because they form the entire market, they have been able to negotiate reasonable conditions with publishers. However, libraries have far less power in the consumer book market. One can envisage a scenario where publishers establish a system of commercial pay-per-view libraries for e-Books and refuse public libraries access to books in a form that can be circulated.

SO WHAT?

We live in interesting times. The World Wide Web did not come out of the library world—which has a fascinating history in its own right—but is now threatening to subsume it. This has the potential to be a great unifying and liberating force in the way in which we find and use information. But there is a disturbing side too: the web dragons, which offer an excellent free service to society, centralize access to information on a global scale. This has its own dangers.

Subsequent chapters focus on the web. But as we have seen, the web is taking over our literature. Depending on how the copyright issues (which we return to in Chapter 6) play out, the very same dragons may end up controlling all our information, including the treasury of literature held in libraries. The technical and social issues identified in this book transcend the World Wide Web as we know it today.

WHAT CAN *YOU* DO ABOUT ALL THIS?

- Don't forget your local library when seeking information!
- Learn to use the library catalog.
- Look up the Library of Congress Subject Headings.
- Read about the Bio-Optic Organized Knowledge Device on the web (the acronym hints at what you will find).
- Watch a demo of a 3D book visualizer (e.g., *open_the_book*).
- Download an e-Book from Project Gutenberg (try a talking book).
- Investigate the Internet Archive's Wayback Machine.
- Try searching book contents on Amazon and Google.
- Keep a watching brief on the Open Content Alliance.
- Use Citeseer and Google Scholar to retrieve some scientific literature.

NOTES AND SOURCES

A good source for the development of libraries in general is Thompson (1997), who formulates principles of librarianship, including the one quoted, that it is a librarian's duty to increase the stock of his (*sic*) library. Thompson also came up with the metaphor of snapping the links of the chained book—in fact, he formulates open access as another principle: *libraries are for all*. Gore (1976) recounts the fascinating history of the Alexandrian Library in his book *Farewell to Alexandria*. Some of this chapter is a reworking of material in *How to Build a Digital Library* by Witten and Bainbridge (2003).

The information on Trinity College Dublin was kindly supplied by David Abrahamson; that about the Library of Congress was retrieved from the Internet. Thomas Mann (1993), a reference librarian at the Library of Congress, has prepared a wonderful source of information on libraries and librarianship, full of practical assistance on how to use conventional library resources to find things. The imaginative architectural developments that have occurred in physical libraries at the close of the twentieth century are beautifully illustrated by Wu (1999).

The view of the electronic book in Figure 2.6, earlier in this chapter, is from Chu et al. (2004). The first book on digital libraries was *Practical Digital Libraries* by Lesk (1997), now in an excellent second edition (2005). In contrast, Crawford and Gorman (1995) in *Future Libraries: Dreams, Madness, and Reality* fear that virtual libraries are real nonsense that will devastate the cultural mission of libraries.

The nineteenth-century librarian who "makes time for his fellow mortals" is Bowker (1883), quoted by Crawford and Gorman (1995). The catchphrase "data about data" for metadata is glib but content-free. Lagoze and Payette (2000) give an interesting and helpful discussion of what metadata is and isn't. Our description of bibliographic organization draws on the classic works of Svenonius (2000) and Mann (1993). It is difficult to make books on library science racy, but these come as close as you are ever likely to find.

The Dublin Core metadata initiative is described by Weibel (1999).[13] Thiele (1998) reviews related topics, while current developments are documented on the official Dublin Core Metadata Initiative website run by the Online Computer Library Center (OCLC).[14]

The Internet Archive project is described by Kahle (1997). The factoid that it takes just 15 minutes for the world to churn out an amount of new digital

---

[13] You can download the standard from *www.niso.org*.

[14] *dublincore.org*.

information equivalent to the entire holdings of the Library of Congress is from Smith (2005). The figure dates from 2002; it has surely halved since.[15] We find that Wikipedia (*www.wikipedia.org*) is a valuable source of information, and gleaned some of the details about Project Gutenberg from it. The remark on page 53 about increasing sales by putting books on the web is from Lesk (2005, p. 276).

---

[15] More information on this extraordinary estimate can be found at *www.sims.berkeley. edu/research/projects/how-much-info-2003/execsum.htm.*

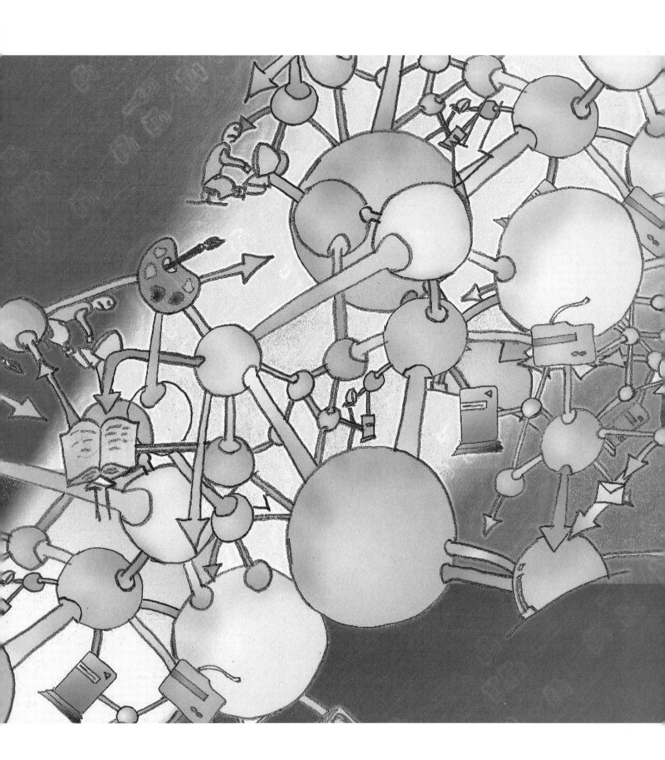

MEET THE WEB

oday the World Wide Web pervades the remotest corners of our
planet. Like water and energy, it has become an invaluable public
resource. Used for countless purposes, in countless contexts, through
countless devices, it's the land of copies and the universe of knowledge. But
like Borges' library with which we opened this book, the web is a deceiver.
It beguiles us into aspiring to understand things by typing in our questions,
trusting that someone, somewhere in this galactic universe (*which others call
the Web*) has already provided the answer. But everything links together in an
infinite loop. The knowledge we glean from the web may be deep, but it may
be illusory. It's a paradox of the infinite.

In this chapter, we examine the web, our precocious teenager, from different viewpoints. We want to see how it works, recognize its strengths, aptitudes,
and skills—and perhaps foretell its future. We normally associate the web with
technical constructs such as the Hypertext Transfer Protocol (HTTP),
Universal Resource Locators (URLs), and the Hypertext Markup Language
(HTML). But it also incorporates stimulating contributions from librarians,
psychologists, economists, linguistics, lawyers, social anthropologists, and

Nodes of the web: everything is here; everything is connected.

humanities scholars. Indeed, they propose ideas that never cross the minds of computer experts.

While it's easy to talk about specific technical issues—you probably already know quite a bit about how the web works—it's hard to arrive at a full understanding of the shape, size, and capabilities of the web. Yet it's of major importance! In terms of components, the web is a collection of documents—more properly of "resources," for it contains much that transcends even the most generous interpretation of "document"—distributed all over the planet. Its resources speak to us in a multitude of expressive forms: text, voice, imagery, animation, movies, and arbitrary interaction styles. All this has been enabled by the convergence of multimedia and network technology, enriched and bound together by hypertext.

Splendid and fascinating as they are, technologies do not by themselves account for the web's extraordinary success. From the outset, the key was the elegant simplicity underlying its document representation and hypertext protocol. Exponential growth in web pages could only be sustained because the barrier to publishing was set very low indeed. Yet—paradoxically—exactly the same ideas open the door to sophisticated technologies for document production and low-key collaborative environments like wikis and blogs. To empower ordinary people to publish what they want and simultaneously provide a platform for continual creative innovation is the genius of the web.

The web obeys the laws of networks. These yield insights into many interesting questions: how many clicks it takes to get from one randomly chosen page to another, the average number of links out of and into a page, and how these figures are growing. Despite its myriad components, the web is seen as an entity in its own right, a sort of "small world"—though not so small! It has a holistic identity that transcends its detailed structure. But, as we will see, the real structure is more complex: the web fragments into "continents" and is strongly organized into communities that directly reflect human struggles and concerns. Moreover, because pages in many major portals emerge only after an extended sequence of queries, there is a huge hidden web that is largely unexplored.

The web is growing fast, and perhaps (for one is never quite sure with teenagers) maturing. Its personality and physiognomy are changing. In order to be sure that we will recognize its face tomorrow, we need a secure understanding of the basic principles by which it operates. The effort will be worthwhile.

BASIC CONCEPTS

In Chapter 1, we related how Tim Berners-Lee created the program that was to become the World Wide Web, and remarked that it is one of the greatest success stories in the history of technology. What are the ingredients of this incredible success? People attribute such things to a combination of luck and genius: luck in thinking about the right things at the right time; genius in recognizing elegance—the right solution, the right degree of functional simplicity. In this case, as we explained in Chapter 1, there was a third factor: the soil had been tilled by philosophers from Socrates to Wittgenstein and fertilized by visionaries from Wiener and Bush to Engelbart and Nelson.

The genius of the web was not recognized immediately. At the time, hypertext was an established field of research with its own experts and academic conferences, and criticisms were raised of the web's implementation of many basic concepts. Berners-Lee's system was too naïve, too simplistic, for hypertext gurus—indeed, it still is. As Steve Jobs, CEO of Apple Computer, put it:

> The Web reminds me of early days of the PC industry. No one really knows anything. There are no exper
> All the experts have been wrong.

The web was born from a paradigm shift: crucial design choices that violated contemporary assumptions of what hypertext should be. First, it did not incorporate Nelson's original idea for a collaborative environment because pages can only be modified by their creator. Second, hyperlinks are directed. They can point to any page without seeking the owner's permission—and the target is not obliged to return the favor by linking back. One-way links are reminiscent of citations in the scientific literature. These two ingredients have been of crucial importance in making the web "world wide." People find it natural to publish information this way, and make such massive use of the linking mechanism that the web is perceived as a unique entity rather than an extension of existing publication media. Last but not least, the simplicity of the underlying HTML language in which documents are expressed has contributed to the enormous diffusion of the web.

The remainder of this section gives a whirlwind tour of the basic concepts underlying the web: HTTP, HTML, URIs and URLs, and crawling. Skip right over it if you already know about these things.

HTTP: HYPERTEXT TRANSFER PROTOCOL

The information on the web is stored in computers referred to as "web servers" and is processed and promptly transmitted upon request. Any computer with a connection to the Internet can be turned into a web server by installing appropriate software. Users access information on the web through programs called "web browsers," which make requests behind the scenes to web servers to obtain the desired information.

The conventions that govern this dialogue constitute the *hypertext transfer protocol* (HTTP). A protocol is a list of rules that define an agreed way of exchanging information. In HTTP, the browser first opens a connection, specifying the address of the desired server. Then it makes its request. After delivering the response, the server closes down the connection. Once the transaction is complete, that is the end of the matter. HTTP is a "stateless" protocol, that is, it does not retain any connection information between transactions. All these operations are expressed in the protocol—indeed, web servers are often referred to as HTTP servers.

Browsers provide the environment that we all use to surf the web and are among the world's most popular computer programs. (But they are not the ones that occupy computers the most. Like automobiles, which spend most of their time stationary, computers are most often at rest—or running screen savers, which is what usually passes as rest. Screen savers are the all-time most popular program in terms of the amount of time computers spend on them.) Browsers let us navigate by following hyperlinks in web pages. Eventually, if we wish, we can return to whence we came by clicking the *Back* button (or selecting *Back* from a menu). The return link is not stored in the web but constructed by the browser, which simply memorizes the path taken as we go. Hyperlinks on the web are not symmetric: a link from page A to page B does not imply a return link, and although return links sometimes exist, they are the exception rather than the rule. Web browsers have a huge variety of capabilities and are among the world's most complex computer programs.

Web servers, like browsers, also have an elaborate structure; they offer a multitude of different services. Like travelers entering a country through immigration, client programs enter the server through a "port" that is able to restrict their visit. In web servers, different ports are used to support different services. For instance, when you surf the web, your browser contacts the HTTP server on port 80 in order to download pages. Sometimes you play an active role by uploading information—for example, when filling out information on a web form. If the information needs to be kept secure, like a credit card number, you will enter through port 443 instead.

There are billions of documents on the web. And it's not just documents: there are millions of other kinds of resources. You can download a pre-stored video (a kind of document). Or you can watch a webcam, a camera integrated into a web server that takes ten to fifteen pictures per second—enough for reasonably smooth motion—and sends them to your browser. You can listen to music, fill out a form for a bank loan, look things up in the Library of Congress catalog, query a search engine, read your e-mail, do your shopping, find the weather in Timbuktu, make a phone call, get a date, or book a hotel.

Given its vast scope, how do we locate the web's resources? Well, how do you find that heartthrob you met in the club last week, or a hotel in an unfamiliar city? You need the address!

URI: UNIFORM RESOURCE IDENTIFIER

A web address could be simply the name of the file containing the information. However, different people might choose the same filename. The best way to avoid confusion is to exploit the structure implicit in the way web servers are organized. Each server is given an address, and the information on it is identified by the pathname of the corresponding file. This yields a structured name called a *Universal Resource Identifier* (URI) because it serves to identify a web resource. For instance, *en.wikipedia.org/wiki/Main_Page* identifies the main page of the Wikipedia encyclopedia. The server that stores this page has the address *en.wikipedia.org* and contains the information in the file *Main_Page* within the folder *wiki*. Following the same path leads to other information in that folder. For instance, current events are at *en.wikipedia.org/wiki/Current_events*, and the Wikipedia search facility is at *en.wikipedia.org/wiki/Special:Search*.

All these are static web pages—even the little one-box form that you fill out when you request a Wikipedia search. They are "static" because the pages are pre-stored. However, portals such as Wikipedia give access to a host of pages that are generated on the fly: they come out when particular queries are submitted from the search page. Dynamically generated pages are also identified by a kind of address. For instance, searching Wikipedia for *World Wide Web* generates a page that can be identified by

```
en.wikipedia.org/wiki/Special:Search?search=World+
                Wide+Web&go=Go
```

If you type this arcane expression into your web browser, you will see exactly the same result as if you entered *World Wide Web* into the Wikipedia search box. It's another kind of URI, constructed from the name of the search page

```
en.wikipedia.org/wiki/Special:Search
```

followed by the query string

```
?search=World+Wide+Web&go=Go
```

The result of the search is not pre-stored but is generated by the Wikipedia web server. It makes it up as it goes along.

Queries are a powerful way of discovering information located deep within the web. Indeed, there is much that can be obtained only in this way. And the mechanism can be very sophisticated, involving a far more complex formulation than the preceding simple example. Basically, whereas a static address gives a path to the information, a dynamic address invokes a program to find the information. The name of the program—*search* in the previous example—is signaled by a preceding question mark. And this program belongs to the web server—Wikipedia's server in this case—not your browser. Wikipedia's search program constructs the answer to your query at the very time you pose it.

The example URIs just given are incomplete. They should also include the name of the protocol that is used to access the resource—in this case HTTP. The full URI for Wikipedia's main page is *http://en.wikipedia.org/wiki/Main_Page*. Other resources use different protocols. When you access your bank account, the bank's web server uses a different protocol that encrypts all transactions. This is signaled by a URI that starts with *https://*—the *s* stands for "secure." It was a brilliant idea to include the protocol name in the URI because it allows the gamut of protocols to be extended later. As well as HTTP and HTTPS, many other protocols are used when surfing the web: for transferring files, dealing with e-mail, reading news feeds, and so on.

Incidentally, people often wonder about the meaning of the mysterious double slash (//). After a lecture on the evolution of the web in London in 1999, Tim Berners-Lee was asked, "If you could go back and change one thing about the design, what would it be?" His characteristically low-key response was that he would use *http:* rather than *http://*. Originally he thought the two slashes looked nice, but now he regrets the countless hours that humanity wastes every year typing them. (And saying them. The BBC used to announce its website over the air as "aitch tee tee pee colon forward slash forward slash double-you double-you double-you dot bee bee cee dot cee oh dot you kay"; recently they dropped the "forward" in favor of simply "slash.") As a concession to human error browsers now accept both // and \\, and *http://* may be omitted entirely.

BROKEN LINKS

The ephemeral nature of resources is a critical issue on the web. During a power cut, the documents on affected web servers disappear from sight. When you reorganize a web server's folders, all the links pointing in are wrong. The same happens when a computer is retired and its files are copied over to a replacement machine. In all these situations, surfers experience an error (perhaps "404 error: page not found," referring to the HTTP error number) instead of the page they were expecting. The link to the resource is broken: at that moment it points nowhere.

Web hyperlinks are attached without seeking permission from the target. Most authors are completely unaware that others have linked to their pages. This is a mixed blessing: it's quick and easy to link, but links can break at any time simply because the target page is moved to a different place or a different server. People call this "link rot": the linkage structure of the web gradually deteriorates over time. But although unidirectional links may cause local breakdowns, they do not compromise the integrity of the web as a whole—which other, more elaborate solutions may risk doing. The system is imperfect but robust. (We return to this issue in Chapter 5.)

Broken links certainly represent a serious problem.[16] As its name implies (*I* stands for "identifier"), the URI is really intended to act as a name rather than an address. The closely related concept URL stands for Universal Resource Locator. In fact, most URIs are also URLs: they show how to locate the file containing the information. However, it is possible to include a "redirect" on the web server that takes you from a URI to a different location, that is, a different URL.

Schemes have been devised for *persistent* identifiers that are guaranteed to survive server reorganizations. One possibility is to register names (URIs) with ultra-reliable servers that record their actual location (URL). Any reference to the resource goes through the appropriate server in order to find out where it is. When a resource is moved, its URL server must be notified. These mechanisms are not widely used: users just have to put up with the inconvenience of link rot.

Another solution that has been proposed is to use associative links. Pages can be identified not just by a name or a location, but also by their content—the very words they contain. A few well-chosen words or phrases are sufficient to identify almost every web page exactly, with high reliability. These snippets—called the page's "signature"—could be added to the URI. Browsers would locate pages in the normal way, but when they encountered a broken link error, they would pass the signature to a search engine to find the page's new location. The same technique identifies all copies of the same page in the web—an important facility for search engines, for they need not bother to index duplicates. The scheme relies on the uniqueness of the signature: there is a trade-off between signature size and reliability.

HTML: HYPERTEXT MARKUP LANGUAGE

Web pages are expressed using the Hypertext Markup Language (HTML), which is designed for visualization of online documents. HTML allows you to lay out text just as typesetters do with paper documents—except that the "page" can be as long as you like. You can include illustrations, and, transcending paper, movie clips, sound bites, and other multimedia objects too. In addition, you can link to other pages on the web.

---

[16] According to Brewster Kahle, who began the Internet Archive in 1997, at that time the average web document lasted only 44 days (Kahle, 1997).

Figure 3.1 shows HTML in action. The code in Figure 3.1(a) generates the web page in Figure 3.1(b). HTML "tags" such as *<html>*, *<body>* and *<p>* give information that affects the presentation of the document. Plain text (e.g., *Felix is looking for inspiration!*) is shown on the page, but tags are not. The opening *<html>* signals the beginning of an HTML document, whose ending

```
<html>
<body>
<img src="felix3.gif" width="230" height="100">
<p>
Felix is looking for inspiration! <br>
<a href="http://www.everwonder.com/david/felixthecat/">
Click here</a> to learn more about Felix.
</p>
</body>
</html>
```

(a) Raw HTML

(b) Resultant web page

```
<html>
<head>
<title>Felix, the cat</title>
<META name="description" content="The best cat around">
<META name="keywords" content="cartoons,cats,VIP">
</head>
<body>
... exactly as above ...
</body>
</html>
```

Figure 3.1
Representation of a document.

(c) HTML with metadata

is marked by the closing tag *</html>*. The second tag indicates the beginning of the "body" of the document, while *<p>* marks the beginning of a paragraph. Most tags have closing versions. The page contains an image that is identified by the tag *<img>* (with no closing tag). Unlike the others, this tag gives further information to specify the image to be shown—its filename (*src*) and dimensions (*width* and *height*). Beneath the image is a paragraph, delimited by *<p>* and *</p>*, with a brief note on Felix. The tag *
* is used to break the line.

You can learn more about Felix by following a hyperlink. This is introduced by the "anchor" tag *<a>*, which, like *<img>*, contains additional information. The incantation *href="http://www.everwonder.com/david/felixthecat/"* indicates the destination of the link. In this example, we use the instruction *Click here* to make it clear how to follow the link. This text is delimited by the *<a>* and *</a>* tags, and the browser underlines it and shows it in a different color. If *</a>* had been placed at the end of the sentence, the entire text *Click here to learn more about Felix* would have been underlined.

This little piece of HTML generates the page shown in Figure 3.1(b). But there's more: when you view the actual page, the cat walks back and forth! The image file, called *felix3.gif*, is not a static picture but contains a sequence of images that give the impression of motion—a so-called animated gif image. Browsers recognize animated gifs and display them appropriately.

Unlike word processors, HTML does not do pagination. You specify a single page by beginning with *<html>* and ending with *</html>*. Long pages are viewed using the browser's scroll bar. This was a crucial design choice that simplifies the development of web pages. Departing from the book metaphor encourages a general notion of "page" that emphasizes content over formatting and reflects the spirit of online resources that reference each other using hyperlinks as opposed to offline ones that use page numbers. It also makes it easier to present the pages in any window, regardless of size.

HTML is one of the prime drivers behind the web's explosive growth. Yet it is a limiting factor for future development because, although it dictates a document's presentation, it does not provide any indication of what the document means. Its development can be traced back to research on document representation in the 1960s. But even in those days, researchers already recognized the importance of describing markup in semantic as well as visual terms. Berners-Lee was not unaware of these issues when he designed the web, but he chose to set them aside for the time being. Behind the scenes, ideas for semantic markup continued to develop, and a simple language for formal specification of document content, the Extensible Markup Language (XML), appeared and became a World Wide Web standard in 1999. We describe it later in this chapter (page 78).

CRAWLING

As the web dawned in the spring of 1993, MIT undergraduate Matthew Gray wondered how big it was. He wrote the World Wide Web Wanderer, a program that counted web servers, and later extended it to capture the actual URLs they served. As we will see in Chapter 4, this was rapidly followed by other programs, embryo ancestors of today's web dragons, that sought to capture the entire web. In keeping with the arachnid metaphor, these systems were called "crawlers" or "spiders," or, because of their autonomous operation, "robots" or simply "bots."

Crawlers work by emulating what you yourself would do if faced with the problem of counting all web pages. Start with one, check its content, and systematically explore all links leading from it. Repeat for each of these pages, and so on, until your time, resources, or patience runs out. The hypertext structure allows the web to be systematically explored, starting from any point.

More formally, a robot crawler starts with an initial seed page, downloads it, analyzes it to identify the outgoing links, and puts these links into a queue for future consideration. It then removes the head of the queue, downloads that page, and appends *its* links to the queue. Of course, it should avoid duplication by first checking whether the link is already in the queue, or whether that page has already been downloaded because it was the target of some other link. (Avoiding duplication is essential, not just for efficiency but to avoid getting into unending cycles.) The process continues until no links remain in the queue. For today's web, this will take a long time and challenge the resources of even the largest computer system.

The crawling process eventually visits all pages that are reachable from the seed. As we will see later, a substantial fraction of pages on the web are all connected to one another (this property holds for many large-scale linked structures, including the brain). Thus, regardless of the seed, the same group of pages is crawled.

The actual crawling strategies used by today's web dragons are more elaborate. They reduce effort by checking to see whether pages have changed since the previous crawl. They take care not to hit individual sites too hard, by restricting the rate at which pages are downloaded from any one server. They visit rapidly changing pages more frequently than static ones. They use many processors operating in parallel. They have high bandwidth connections to the Internet. Today's crawlers can fetch thousands of pages every second, which allows them to visit a good percentage of the web in a few weeks.

Some web crawlers—known as "focused crawlers"—are topic-specific. With a particular topic in mind, they start from a relevant seed page and selectively expand links that appear to be on-topic. To do this, the program must be able to recognize when a particular link refers to an on-topic page, which can only be done by downloading the page and analyzing its content. This is a hard problem! People identify topics by understanding the text, which requires linguistic analysis at syntactic, semantic, and even pragmatic levels—as well as knowledge of the topic itself. Although artificial intelligence techniques have yielded some promising results, automatic text classification, and hence accurate focused crawling, is still a challenging problem.

A critical part of a crawler is how it interacts with web servers when downloading their pages. Pages that are referenced by ordinary URLs are retrieved using the HTTP protocol. But some servers contain dynamic pages that emerge only after specific querying, which is hard to do automatically. These pages belong to what is called the "deep web." Crawlers cannot formulate sensible queries, and so they cannot explore the deep web as a person can. Fortunately, many dynamic pages also belong to the shallow web. As mentioned earlier (page 65), the page that Wikipedia returns in response to the query *World Wide Web* arises dynamically from

```
en.wikipedia.org/wiki/Special:Search?search=World+
               Wide+Web&go=Go
```

Yet that very page is indexed by all major search engines as

```
http://en.wikipedia.org/wiki/World_Wide_Web
```

Crawlers are led to this dynamic page because other web pages, static ones, link to it.

Crawling has its hazards. Web servers can unintentionally contain traps—and if the potential exists, you can be sure that some jokers will try to make life difficult for crawlers by setting traps on purpose. Traps—particularly intentional ones—can be subtle. A dynamic page can refer to itself using an address that is different each time, causing crawlers to fetch it over and over again without limit. Smart crawlers watch out for traps, but they can be concealed, and there is no guaranteed way to detect them automatically. Trap sites typically give themselves away because of the grotesquely large number of documents they appear to contain. The contents of these documents can be analyzed to determine whether they form a natural distribution or are constructed artificially.

Early on it was realized that a mechanism was needed to allow shy websites to opt out of being crawled—for reasons of privacy, computer loading, or bandwidth conservation. Even though the web is public, it is not unreasonable to want to restrict access to certain pages to those who know the URLs. A "robot exclusion protocol" was developed whereby robots look on each site for a particular file (called *robot.txt*) and use it to determine what parts of the site to crawl. This is not a security mechanism. Compliance with the protocol is voluntary, but most crawlers adhere to it.

WEB PAGES: DOCUMENTS AND BEYOND

Charlemagne, whom both France and Germany regard as a founding father of their countries, was a scholar king, significantly better educated than other kings of the early Middle Ages. He learned to read as an adult, but the legend grew that he couldn't write. This isn't surprising, for at the time writing was the province of a trained elite. The tools were difficult to use: parchment, typically goatskin treated with slaked lime, stretched and dried; a goose feather—or, better, a top-quality swan feather, or a crow feather for very fine drawings, preferably, for right-handed writers, from the left wing. The actual process of writing was an art that required small, accurate hand movements and training in calligraphy. In sum, the skills of writing and reading were strongly asymmetric. Publishing was likewise reserved for an elite and had been carefully controlled—and jealously guarded—for centuries.

Computers (jumping quickly over many intermediate technologies) dramatically redress the imbalance between reading and writing in terms of the production of high-quality typeset documents. And the web offers a revolutionary new dissemination method, vastly superior to traditional publishing. Distribution is fast and free. A given URI might yield a static page, the same every time you return, or a form that you can fill out and send back, or a dynamic page that changes with time, or an active page that shows a program-driven visualization. The web supports different methods of publishing, some simple and widely accessible and others requiring hard-won technical skills. It promotes cooperation by allowing people to share documents and contribute articles to electronic journals and weekly or daily—even hourly—newsletters. All this greatly facilitates scholarship and the rapid growth of ideas.

It is now easy to produce and publish information with high standards of presentation quality. But retrieval is still in its infancy. The web explosion has been fueled by documents whose strengths lie more in visual presentation than in natural, human-like retrieval of information. The XML language (see page 78) offers expressive mechanisms to declare the content of the document, and this is crucial when trying to lace queries with a modicum of semantics.

STATIC, DYNAMIC, AND ACTIVE PAGES

Your browser is your web surfboard. You type a URL, and the HTML file at that address is downloaded and rendered on your screen. Unless the page's owner updates it, you find the same information every time you visit. You might (unusually) see something move, like Felix—but (at least in Felix's case) all you get is a preprogrammed motion repeated over and over. In short, most web documents show a static electronic publication that remains there until someone updates the content. It's like writing a newsletter with a word processor and presenting it to the world on electronic paper.

The web also offers something more dynamic. You might find different information at the same address, like the Wikipedia search page (whose operation was explained on page 65). This mechanism ends up executing a program that belongs to the web server in order to come up with the information to display. Dynamic information such as this goes well beyond traditional means of publication. An ordinary HTML description completely defines the content and presentation of the page, the same at every visit. Dynamic pages are defined by a linguistic description as well, but they also specify some processing that the server must undertake before returning the page to the browser as an HTML document description. When you view a static page, what you see is produced entirely by your browser on the basis of stored information sent by the server. But when you view a dynamic one, the server does some processing too.

Consider our well-worn example of entering *World Wide Web* as a Wikipedia search. The resulting URI contains *?search=World+Wide+Web&go=Go*, and this is interpreted by the server at *en.wikipedia.org/wiki/Special:Search*. The server produces the appropriate information and uses it to construct an HTML page, which it then transmits to your browser, which in turn shows it on your screen. Dynamic pages, plus the possibility of transmitting information from browser to server (in this case, your query is coded as *World+Wide+Web*), transcend what is possible with static presentations.

Dynamic web pages are capable of many useful things. A particular page can show the number of times that people have visited by keeping a counter on the server and increasing it at every access—like a book that counts its readers. Alternatively, and much more surprisingly, it can show how many times you—yes, just *you*, not all the others—have visited. This requires a counter just for you, accessible to the server. This can be arranged using a mechanism called "cookies." A cookie is a packet of information sent to your browser by a web server the first time you visit it. Your browser stores it locally, and later, when you revisit the site, it sends the cookie back unmodified. One thing the server can do with this is keep track of the number of times you have visited, by storing the information in the cookie, updating it, and sending it back at each visit. It's a sort of user profile.

Cookies are powerful—and dangerous. Earlier we explained that HTTP is a stateless protocol: it does not retain information between transactions. But the cookie *does* retain information, and web servers often use cookies to store user profiles. For instance, if you leave your name on a web server, don't be surprised if it greets you personally next time you visit. According to the HTTP protocol, every return to a page is exactly the same as the first visit. This can be annoying: the server might repeatedly ask you to identify yourself and reset preferences that you already specified last time. Cookies solve the problem: the server stores your identity and user profile in a cookie which it leaves on your computer. On the other hand, cookies might compromise your privacy by revealing your profile. Don't leave your bank account number and password on a machine in an Internet café! We return to this in Chapter 6.

Cookies allow servers to execute programs that know about your previous interactions. But web resources can be interactive in an even more powerful sense. Visiting a given page can cause a program to be downloaded and executed on your own computer rather than the server. Such programs are called "applets" (small applications) and are written in the Java programming language: they are embedded into HTML using an *<applet>* metatag. Applets are popular for online demos that interact with the user directly, without having to wait for responses from across the Internet.

Web pages go far beyond the paper documents that flood our desk and the books that have lurked in libraries for centuries. They are living entities that evolve. They can contain multimedia. They can cause programs to run on the server, programs that can use data recalled from past interactions. They can even cause programs to run on your own computer, the one running your web browser. Not only is more information published as time goes by, but as technology evolves, existing information can be represented in different ways—like intellectual spirits reincarnated in new bodies.

AVATARS AND CHATBOTS

According to Hindu lore, the Avatara descends from Heaven as a material manifestation of God in a particular form, an incarnation of the Godhead. In computer animation, avatars have a more prosaic interpretation which can be traced back to 1985 when George Lucas of *Star Wars* fame catapulted animated cartoon figures, humanoid in appearance, into a popular chat system. These figures could move around, manipulate objects, and converse with one another. In the future avatars will be used to facilitate access to websites.

Imagine being guided around a field of knowledge by a wise, omniscient, and infinitely patient teacher, who can speak your language—and everyone else's. Among the many ways that existing information can be reincarnated in a new body, avatars represent a sort of platonic perfection, a divine teacher who offers an ideal presentation—Socrates on your laptop. (The reality may fall short of the dream, however.) Avatars lend their humanoid appearance to chat robots or *chatbots*, programs capable of providing guidance by maintaining a conversation with a person. Some chatbots can talk to one other, creating a framework for autonomous interaction.

Research on chatbots has a checkered history, success mingling with failure. The challenge of natural language understanding seems to be inseparable from the whole of human intelligence. Intensive research at the height of the Cold War in the 1950s, when the U.S. government regarded automatic translation from Russian to English as a strategic national problem, bore little fruit apart from a sharper realization of just how difficult it is. Ten years later, a chatbot posing as a psychotherapist called Eliza created a minor sensation in computer circles. Early in the conversation, Eliza could fool even careful observers, but the interchange eventually degenerated into a bizarre charade because she didn't understand questions at all. Instead, the program detected simple linguistic patterns and produced canned responses that cleverly interpolated words from prior input. Today, after decades of research, chatbots can behave impressively on a few examples but eventually make stupendous blunders. To behave like people, they need to acquire a vast store of knowledge and use it as a basis for reasoning, which is very difficult—particularly for conversation in unrestricted domains.

Nevertheless, chatbots, personalized as avatars, will play a significant role in the evolution of the web. They work well in certain domains and can offer personalized, user-friendly guidance in navigating websites to obtain useful information. They represent a new frontier in human-computer interaction and multimedia information presentation. But true semantic information retrieval is still way beyond reach, and today's chatbots, like their great-grandmother Eliza, are limited to cooperative conversations on particular, well-defined topics.

COLLABORATIVE ENVIRONMENTS

As we learned in Chapter 1, a quest for congenial and effective environments for collaboration was part of the heady atmosphere that led to the web. However, Berners-Lee's decision to allow free hyperlinking to other pages, without notification or request, was inimical to the kind of support being envisaged at the time. Of course, the web's explosion—due in some measure to that very decision—has greatly facilitated information sharing through the Internet. But the thirst for more intimately collaborative environments continues unquenched, and as technology develops, they are emerging in different guises.

Wiki—*wiki wiki* is Hawaiian for "quick"—is one of today's most popular collaboration systems. Devised in 1995, it is server software that allows you to use your browser to create and edit web pages. Many people can contribute to a wiki, and the system helps them organize their contributions as well as create and edit the content. Wikis are widely used, particularly by nontechnical people, thereby contributing to democracy on the web. In the last few years, this technology has supported community-based collaboration in countless companies and research institutes. It has also given rise to Wikipedia, an online encyclopedia to which anyone can contribute, which represents a fascinating social experiment in its own right. Wikipedia crosses community boundaries and has become a respected—though controversial—repository of information that some regard as library quality.

In blogging, the emphasis is on individual publication rather than coordinated collaboration. A *blog* (short for *weblog*) is an electronic journal that is frequently updated and usually intended for a broad readership. Unlike most websites, blogs are based on templates that govern the presentation of content from a database. New pages can be created very quickly, since content is entered in raw form and the template takes care of the presentation and how the entry links to existing material. Templates include metadata, so content can be filtered by category, date, or author. Blogs can be found on any subject under the sun, but the initial driving spirit was to promote democracy by giving a public soapbox for minority points of view. Blogging has emerged as a cultural process that affects nearly every field.

Typical blogs consist of title, body—which can include text, hyperlinks, and often photos, video, music—and comments added by readers. They're far easier to create than ordinary web pages. They differ from forums like newsgroups because authors can introduce any subject for discussion; follow-up postings comment on that subject. Blogs are defined by the article's URL or "permalink"; the date of posting is also commonly used as a search criterion. Some blogs are maintained by software on the user's own computer; others are supported by tools provided by web hosting companies, who also store the documents.

Blogs, like wikis, have become popular because of their versatility. Their uses range from professional journalism, to teenage diaries intended to keep friends up to date with events and thoughts. The idea of minute-by-minute updating is affecting schools of journalism and having a profound impact on social and political life. Blogs often bring key information to the attention of the mainstream media. They gain popularity through word of mouth and citations (permalinks) that reveal who their readers are. Some people criticize the quality of this kind of journalism with its occasional disregard of proper attribution.

Wikis and blogging exemplify rapid publication par excellence. Charlemagne's quill and parchment presented a formidable barrier to writing and publication, but software eliminates that barrier almost entirely. Of course, quick-fire production of articles in blogs means that they tend to be opinion pieces and commentary rather than carefully reasoned arguments and in-depth analyses. On the other hand, rapid expression and cross-linking of many different viewpoints provides a sort of cultural mirror. Blogs permit collaborative growth of individual ideas and thoughts in a public space, and are emerging as an important new cultural phenomenon.

ENRICHING WITH METATAGS

Chapter 2 argued that metadata plays a central role in organizing libraries. Though HTML was conceived primarily for presentation, it allows supplementary information to be included with a document. This is done using special tags that are not intended for presentation but for describing the content of the page. These "metatags" are included at the beginning of the page in an area delimited by *<head>* … *</head>*. Figure 3.1(c) shows an example where two metatags are used, one to describe Felix's page, and the other to include suitable keywords (see page 68). This content is not shown on the web page but is available for information retrieval or other automatic processing. While the *keywords* metatag offers a compact description of Felix's page, the *description* metatag enriches the textual description on the page. A *<title>* tag also appears within the head area; browsers show the title in the top border of the web page.

Metadata can be extremely useful for retrieval. The designer might flag one page as containing "adult content" to facilitate the filtering of pornography, and another as one containing informed medical recommendations. However, self-assessment is obviously suspect—particularly since the information is not displayed but used solely for automatic processing. While almost everyone would disagree with a "VIP" keyword attached to Felix, machines are more gullible. Of course, Felix might pose as a VIP just for fun, but, to be useful, metadata must be taken seriously.

Metadata is essential when it comes to image retrieval. Automatic understanding of both text and images falls far below human levels, but whereas text in some sense describes itself, images give few clues. When someone creates a web page that comprises an image, they can insert metatags that describe it, but this raises the nasty question of duplicity—and while machines can do some sanity checking of textual pages, with images they are completely at the tagger's mercy.

Here's an imaginative way to exploit the web to provide accurate image metadata. Two strangers play a collaborative game, just for fun (it's called the ESP game; you can find it on the web and play it yourself). They don't know anything about each other: the server pairs each user randomly with an opponent, perhaps in another country, whose identity is completely unknown. The server chooses an image from the web, shows it to both partners simultaneously, and asks them to label it. Each player's goal is to guess what the other is typing, without any communication. As soon as you both type the same phrase, the system offers a new image and you play again. Meanwhile, behind the scenes, that phrase is recorded as metadata for the image. This is a simple yet effective means of producing reliable metadata. Random pairing and anonymity eliminate any opportunity to spoof the system by colluding with a friend or bribing your partner. All parties win: the players have fun—for the machine displays scores, providing a constant challenge—and the system gathers metadata. This is a creative use of anonymity and real-time communication on the web.

XML: EXTENSIBLE MARKUP LANGUAGE

HTML describes the visual form of web documents, not their content. The *M* is for markup, which applies to the format—just as copyeditors mark up manuscripts in traditional publishing. This emphasis on visual aspects contrasts with database representations, which are rich in expressing content in terms of well-structured data records but impoverished in expressing presentation.

Database records are interpreted with respect to a schema, which gives a complete definition of the fields that constitute each record. Personal records, for example, contain separate fields (first and last names, birth data, address, and so on), some of which—such as "birth data" and "address"—are themselves structured into further fields. This kind of organization makes it possible to answer complex queries, because meanings are attached to each field of the record. Whereas databases were conceived for automatic processing and born in computers, documents were conceived for human communication. Documents are difficult to process automatically simply because it is hard to interpret natural language automatically. The schema is the key to interpreting database records, but no corresponding semantic description is available for documents.

The Extensible Markup Language, XML, is a systematic way of formulating semantic document descriptions. It's neither a replacement for HTML nor an evolution of it. Whereas HTML was designed to display information, XML focuses on describing the content. It's a declarative language: it doesn't actually *do* anything. Figure 3.2 shows a note that the CatVIP club sent to Felix begging him to stop pacing back and forth across the screen, expressed in XML.

When interpreted by a web browser, the HTML in Figure 3.1(a) produces the web page in Figure 3.1(b). In contrast, the XML in Figure 3.2 produces … nothing. It focuses on content, not presentation. There's a message header (*<heading>* … *</heading>*) and a body (*<body>*... *</body>*), preceded by some auxiliary information using other tags (*<date>*, *<day>*, etc.). Unlike HTML, XML tags are not predefined—you make them up as you go

```
<note id="B110">
  <date>
    <day>2</day>
    <month>3</month>
    <year>2006</year>
  </date>
  <to>Felix</to>
  <from>CatVIP</from>
  <heading>Reminder</heading>
  <body>Please stop pacing back and forth across the
        screen!</body>
</note>
```

Figure 3.2
Representation of a message in XML.

along. The assumption is that you choose them to provide a useful semantic description.

The whole note is embraced within a *<note>* tag. Attributes can accompany tags (as with HTML), and this note has the identifier *B110* as an attribute, which could be used to refer to it. Another way of specifying the date would be to make it an attribute too, like

```
<note date = "March 2, 2006">
```

The advantage of using separate elements, as Figure 3.2 does, is that it's more suitable for computer interpretation, just like database records.

In addition to the date, the description in Figure 3.2 also specifies the sender and the receiver. Of course, these could be further decomposed into subfields if appropriate. The body is the truly textual part, which is typically unstructured. As this simple example shows, XML yields semi-structured representations that lie somewhere between database schema and free text.

XML documents have a hierarchical organization. A collection of notes like the one in Figure 3.2 could be framed within an enclosing *<messages>*... *</messages>* construct, so that individual notes were identifiable by their *id* attribute. It is possible to define a formal schema—like a database schema—that precisely expresses constraints on the structure of the document in terms of the elements and their nesting, and the attributes that can occur with each element. Furthermore, elements are extensible. We could later decide to add a new item *<weather>* . . . *</weather>* to the note, indicating whether it was written on a sunny or a cloudy day.

XML offers new opportunities for document processing by exploiting the semantics associated with the tags. Everyone is free to define his or her own tags, and only the page author (or the author of the corresponding XML schema) knows what they are supposed to mean. XML doesn't help others to understand the meaning of the tags. In Chapter 4, we'll see that the semantic web, another creation of Tim Berners-Lee's fertile mind, is moving in the direction of removing this obstacle too.

METROLOGY AND SCALING

William Thomson (1824–1907), better known as Lord Kelvin, was a renowned Scottish mathematician who made many major discoveries, including the formulation and interpretation of the second law of thermodynamics. An infant prodigy, he was renowned for his self-confidence and strongly held views. He was a passionate advocate of the importance of measurement in physics.

I often say that when you can measure what you are speaking about, and express it in numbers, you know something about it; but when you cannot measure it, when you cannot express it in numbers, your knowledge is of a meager and unsatisfactory kind; it may be the beginning of knowledge, but you have scarcely in your thoughts advanced to the state of Science, whatever the matter may be.

– Thomson (1883)

For example, he studied the fascinating problem of calculating the age of the earth. Unfortunately, the figure he came up with, 25 million years, is a gross underestimate—for reasons he couldn't have known (concerned with radioactive elements, which produce heat at the earth's core and significantly enhance the geothermal flux). That unlucky prediction is a salutary reminder of the fallibility of even the most expert reasoning.

The importance of expressing knowledge with numbers, so dear to Kelvin's heart, goes well beyond physics. The universe that we know as the web—like the one we actually live in—is huge and expanding. No one can see it all: we can only comprehend it secondhand, through the misty glass of measuring instruments. How big is the web? How fast is it growing? Is the growth sustainable by computer and communication technologies? What does it take to crawl the web and make a copy? How many links separate any two pages? The answers to these questions might help us anticipate the web's future.

ESTIMATING THE WEB'S SIZE

Counting the pages on the web seems almost as daunting as counting the books in the Library of Babel. Fortunately, hypertext links—something librarians do not have—come to our aid, and we have already learned how they can be used to crawl the web. In June 1993, the pioneer World Wide Web Wanderer estimated its size to be 100 servers and 200,000 documents, an average of 2,000 pages per site.

Today's search engines, operating in essentially the same way, give an estimate four orders of magnitude larger. They report how many pages they crawl and index, and compete for the greatest coverage. But the web is clearly even bigger than any of these figures. For one thing, pages are added continuously, whereas search engines' figures are based on their last crawl. More importantly, it is easy to find pages indexed by one search engine that have been overlooked by another.

Different search engines use different crawling strategies. If two turn out to have a high proportion of pages in common, the web is probably not much larger than the greater of the two. On the other hand, a small overlap would suggest that the actual dimension significantly exceeds both numbers. This simple idea can be operationalized by submitting random queries to different search engines, analyzing the overlap, and repeating the procedure many times. From the results, simple probabilistic reasoning leads to a lower bound on the web's dimension.

Counting how many pages two search engines have in common is not quite as simple as it sounds. Any particular page might have a replica that is indexed with a different URL. This situation occurs frequently, and unless care is taken to detect it, common pages might be excluded from the overlap, leading to an overestimate of the lower bound. It is better to check the pages' content than simply inspect their URL.

Using these techniques, the number of pages in the indexable web was estimated to be at least 11.5 billion in early 2005. The estimate was made by creating 440,000 one-term test queries in a systematic way and submitting them to four major search engines (Google, MSN, Yahoo, and Ask). Care was taken to ensure that the queries contained words in many different languages (75). The four individual search engines had coverages ranging from 2 billion to 8 billion pages. The estimated intersection of all four was 3 billion pages, and their union was 9 billion. At that time, even the most comprehensive search engine covered only 70 percent of the indexable web. And as we will see, the web contains many pages that cannot be found by crawling and are therefore not indexable.

In practice, different crawlers do not yield independent samples of the web. Though they act independently, they share many design principles. Moreover, the fact that the web has a few huge sites biases the crawling process. This lack of independence is the reason why the estimate is a lower bound. An upper bound would allow us to pin down how big the haystack really is. Unfortunately, there is no credible procedure for bounding the size of the web, for when pages are generated dynamically, there is really no limit to how many there can be. We return to this question when discussing the deep web.

RATE OF GROWTH

In 1997, Mathew Gray, who had introduced the World Wide Web Wanderer four years earlier, confirmed that the web was growing exponentially, doubling every six months. Growth had slowed since the heady days of 1993, when it doubled in just three months. Other studies have confirmed a relentless exponential trend, though the magnitude of the exponent is tailing off. Table 3.1 shows the growth of the web in terms of sites, in both tabular and chart form.

What are the limits to growth? One relates to the protocol underlying the Internet, called TCP/IP, which provides addresses for only 4 billion web servers. However, a new version, the Next Generation Internet Protocol, overcomes this restriction. In any case, a technique called "virtual hosting" allows you to place an essentially limitless number of unique sites at a single Internet address. Only a small percentage of computer disk space is used for web pages, and anyway disk capacity will grow significantly over the next few years.

Table 3.1
Growth in Websites

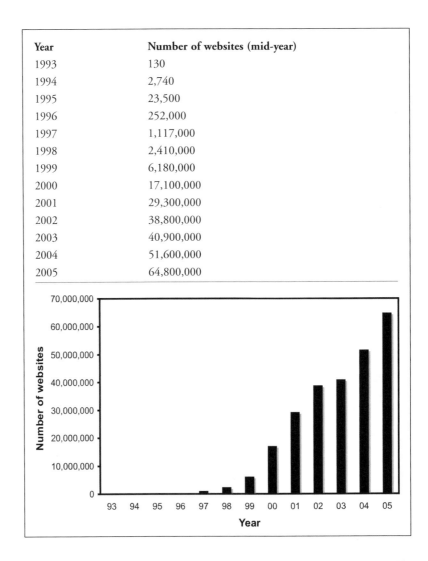

Year	Number of websites (mid-year)
1993	130
1994	2,740
1995	23,500
1996	252,000
1997	1,117,000
1998	2,410,000
1999	6,180,000
2000	17,100,000
2001	29,300,000
2002	38,800,000
2003	40,900,000
2004	51,600,000
2005	64,800,000

The scale of objects in nature is governed by natural laws. The bodily proportions of elephants are not just those of ants scaled up. If they were, it would be hard to explain why ants easily drop from a tree while a far lesser fall will injure an elephant. Imagine scaling an ant up 500 times, bringing it to the dimensions of a large African elephant. Volume grows with the cube of linear dimension and would increase 125 million times. The same goes for weight (if it were still made of ant-stuff, which is not all *that* different from elephant-stuff). But leg strength depends on cross-sectional area, not volume, and increases with the square of the linear dimension, so the legs could only bear a weight increase of 250,000. The giant ant's skinny legs couldn't carry its gargantuan body.

Similar laws govern the growth of artifacts. Laptop designers take no special precautions to dissipate heat from the power supply, whereas transformers in power stations need refrigeration. The heat generated by a transformer is proportional to its volume, but heat dispersion is proportional to area. This imposes limits to growth. Engineers understand this: when more power is required, they employ more units rather than scaling up a single one.

In the field of electronics and communication, huge improvements in processing and transmission technologies have produced a vast increase in the number of intercommunicating devices on our planet. Like ants, elephants, and transformers, these networks must obey laws that govern growth. However, whereas engineers are familiar with the scaling issues that surround physical devices, the effects of scaling in information technology are far less well understood.

In Chapter 2, we met what is commonly called "Moore's law": the number of transistors on a chip doubles about every 18 months. The ant-chips of the 1960s, whose bodies contained just a few transistors, have become gigantic. Moore's is not a natural law like those of physics, but an empirical observation coupled with a strong intuition of how things will evolve in the future—and so far it has turned out to be amazingly accurate. Exponential growth also holds for disk storage, whose capacity is growing even faster than processing power.

To analyze the sustainability of web growth, we must also consider the evolution of communication technology. In 1998, Jacob Nielsen, who the *New York Times* calls the "guru of web page usability," predicted that users' connection speeds would grow by 50 percent per year on average. Though large, this rate is nowhere near as high as for processing and disk technologies. And doubling the capacity of your local connection might not double the speed at which web pages arrive. The Internet is a complex infrastructure, and you don't necessarily benefit from upgrading the local connection.[17]

COVERAGE, FRESHNESS, AND COHERENCE

Predictions of developments in Internet bandwidth suggest that even though it is growing exponentially (at perhaps 50 percent per year) it will fall behind the web itself, which is also growing exponentially but with a greater exponent.[18] The time taken to download the entire web depends on the capacity of all its individual sites. Regardless of a crawler's effectiveness, download time increases with the size of the web—which is increasing exponentially.

The *coverage* of a particular engine can be expressed as the percentage of pages that it indexes. Once a page has been processed, the crawler can keep it in its entirety or discard it (but retain the URL, which is needed to avoid

---

[17] Slow web content delivery inspires cynical surfers to call the WWW the "World Wide Wait."

[18] When two exponential growths compete, the one with the larger exponent wins. In fact, the effect is equivalent to exponential web growth (with exponent equal to the difference between web and bandwidth exponents) under *fixed* bandwidth.

reprocessing the page). If it is kept, the search engine can offer its cached copy to users—which means they can access the page even when the original source is unreachable, either because it has been removed or the server is temporarily down.

Early search engines took several weeks to crawl the entire web. Today, as we shall see, the situation is more complex. In any case, because of the time needed to complete the crawl, search engines' cached versions aren't necessarily identical to the actual pages themselves. The *coherence* of a copy of the web is the overall extent to which it corresponds to the web itself, and the *freshness* of a particular page can be defined as the reciprocal of the time that elapses between successive visits to it.

Coverage, freshness, and coherence are three key properties of a web crawler. If pages are crawled uniformly—that is, if they all have the same freshness—then doubling coverage implies halving freshness. This is a kind of uncertainty principle. But unlike Heisenberg's celebrated result in quantum mechanics, it can be ameliorated by tuning the freshness to the nature of the page. A good strategy is to classify pages into categories with different freshness, and crawl the web accordingly. Of course, this isn't easy because it requires predicting the times at which web pages will be updated.

Search engines don't crawl the web uniformly, visiting every page equally often. A university web page might be updated a few times a year, whereas most news channels change their information daily—or hourly—and should be captured more frequently. To optimize coherence, crawlers visit volatile pages more often than static ones. Depending on the crawling policy, the freshness of different pages can be very different and might also change with time.

Given a perfectly accurate crystal ball, a crawler should download each page as soon as it is created or updated, ensuring optimum coherence within the constraints of available bandwidth. This would achieve the same effect as automatically notifying search engines of every change. Unfortunately, crystal balls are hard to come by. Instead, one can take into account the page's usage and the time between its last updates, preferring popular pages that change frequently. It is not easy to find a good recipe for mixing these ingredients.

Even using a crystal ball, the uncertainty principle holds and becomes critical if the web's exponential growth outpaces the growth in bandwidth. One solution is to increase the overall quality of the index by paying frequent visits only to important pages. Of course, this raises the difficult question of how to judge the quality of a document automatically.

If we regard the web as a repository of human knowledge, once the initial target of collecting everything is accomplished, one would only have to keep up with its rate of increase. Exponential growth in our planet's population cannot be sustained over the long run, and the same must surely hold for worthwhile web pages. Growth has to saturate eventually. If this is true, in the long run all will be well: computer and communication technologies will ultimately be in good shape to sustain the growth of the web. We will eventually have the technology to create the building of the Library of Babel and house all its books. But there is far more to it than that: we need to sort the wheat from the chaff and provide useful access to the content.

STRUCTURE OF THE WEB

Borges' library, with its countless floors, labyrinthine galleries, lustrous mirrors, and infinite repetitions of myriad books, seems designed to demoralize and confuse. In contrast, real librarians organize books so as to facilitate the retrieval process. They proceed in careful and measured ways. They design and implement well-defined structures for information seeking. They promote standardization so that they can cooperate effectively with other libraries. They plan their acquisitions according to clearly stated policies.

The web does not grow in accordance with any plan or policy—far from it. Growth arises from a haphazard distributed mechanism which at first glance appears virtually random. Whereas other striking engineering achievements—bridges, airplanes, satellites—are fully documented by the design team in the form of technical drawings, Berners-Lee drew no map of the web. Of course, if you had enough resources, you could make yourself one by crawling it and reconstructing the linkage structure on the way. Simple in principle, this exercise in cartography calls for all the infrastructure of a major search engine. And for reasons explained before, a complete and up-to-date map will always elude you.

Notwithstanding its distributed and chaotic nature, structure does play a central role in the web. Surprising insights can be obtained from the network induced by the hyperlinks, insights that also apply to other large-scale networks, whether natural or artificial. The fact that links are directed implies further structure that many other networks do not share. A good approximation to the web's gross structure can be obtained from elegant models of random evolution. Structure emerges out of chaos. As for the fine details, they reflect the social behavior of users and their communities. The organization of parts of the web is recorded in manually created hierarchies. Finally, the web that search engines know is just the tip of the iceberg: underneath lurks the deep web.

SMALL WORLDS

Stanley Milgram was one of the most important and influential psychologists of the twentieth century. Notwithstanding his scientific achievements, his professional life was dogged by controversy. To study obedience to authority, he conducted experiments in which people were asked to administer severe electric shocks (up to 450 volts) to victims. In fact—as the subjects were informed later—the victims were actors and the shocks were simulated. Astonishingly, most people deferred to the authority of the experimenter and were prepared to inflict apparently severe pain on another human being. Needless to say, this work raised serious ethical concerns.

In 1967, Milgram published in *Psychology Today* a completely different but equally striking result which he called the "Small World Problem." He selected people in the American Midwest and asked them to send packages to a particular person in Massachusetts—the "target." They knew the target's name and occupation, but not the address. They were told to mail the package to one of their friends, the one who seemed most likely to know the target. That person was instructed to do the same, and so on, until the package was finally delivered. Though participants expected chains of hundreds of acquaintances before reaching the target, the astonishing result was that the median was only 5.5. Rounded up, this gave rise to the widely quoted notion of "six degrees of separation."[19] It's a small world after all! In their own specialized milieu, mathematicians boast of their "Erdös number," which is the number of degrees they are separated from Paul Erdös, a famously prolific mathematician, in the chain defined by joint authorship of published papers.

The idea of six degrees of separation has emerged in different guises in other contexts. And unlike Milgram's study of blind obedience to authority, it has strong mathematical foundations in an area known as graph theory. Mathematical graphs—which are not the same as the quantitative plots used in empirical science—comprise elements called "nodes," connected by links. In Milgram's experiment, nodes are people and links are to their friends. In the web, nodes are web pages and links are hyperlinks to other pages. The amount of connectedness determines how easy it is to reach one page from another, and affects the operation of the crawlers that dragons use to make copies of the web to index.

Computer scientists often employ abstract devices called "trees"—not the same as biological trees—which are nothing more than special graphs with a root node and no cycles in the link structure. A family tree is a familiar example. Factor out the complication of sexual reproduction (if only real life were so easy!) by restricting the tree to, say, females. At the top is the root node, the matriarch—Eve, perhaps. There can be no cycles because biology prevents you from being your own mother or grandmother. Trees occur in all kinds of problems in computer science: they first appeared in 1846 in a paper on electric circuits.

The number of nodes in a tree grows exponentially with its height. This is easy to see. For simplicity, suppose each node has exactly two children. If there is but a single node (the root), the height is 1. If the root has children

---

[19] The basic idea had been proposed forty years earlier by the Hungarian writer Frigyes Karinthy in a short story called "Chains." However, Milgram was the first to provide scientific evidence.

(height 2), there are two of them, and whenever you pass to the next generation, the number of children doubles: 4, 8, 16,.... This is an exponential sequence, and it means that the number of nodes in the tree grows exponentially. Conversely, height grows logarithmically with the number of nodes. If the number of children is not two—indeed, if different generations have different numbers—growth is still exponential, the exponent depending on the average branching factor. For example, if the number of children ranges randomly from 0 to 2, it can be shown that the average height grows to about 40 percent of the figure for two children. If there are 32 children per node and the tree represents seven generations, the tree will contain 32 billion nodes.

Similar results hold for graphs, except that they lack the concept of height because there is no root. Instead, the height of a tree corresponds to the length of the longest path connecting any two nodes in the graph, which is called the graph's "diameter." Sometimes the average path length is used instead of the longest.

Studies of the web reveal a structure that resembles Milgram's original discovery. In an early experiment, a single domain about 3000 times smaller than the web was crawled and analyzed. Its average degree of separation was found to be 11. To scale the result to the entire web, experiments were carried out on smaller portions to determine the rate of growth, and then the actual value for the entire web was extrapolated. Using a 1999 estimate of the web size, the average degree of separation was predicted to be 19.

This result indicates that, despite its almost incomprehensible vastness, the web is a "small world" in the sense that all its pages are quite close neighbors. However, the value found for the average degree of separation is biased by the special connection structure of the small sample that was used. Full-scale experiments are difficult to conduct because the entire web must be crawled first—and even then the magnitude of the graph challenges ordinary computer systems. Later studies using data from a major search engine painted a more subtle picture. Many pairs of websites are simply not connected at all: with random start and finish pages, more than 75 percent of the time there is no path between. When a path exists, its length is about 16. However, if links could be traversed in either direction, a far larger proportion of random pairs would be connected, and the distance between them would be much smaller—around 7. These figures are all astonishingly small, considering that the web contains many billions of pages.

If you could construct an intelligent agent that traversed the web following only the most relevant links, as Milgram's subjects did, you could get to any target that was reachable in just a few judicious clicks. The previous section closed with some reassurance about the sustainability of the web by electronic and communication technologies. And now we know that, immense as it is, even the web is a fairly small world! Once again, however, we have fetched up on the same rocky shore: the intransigent problem of finding good ways to access the relevant information.

SCALE-FREE NETWORKS

Organizing things in the form of networks seems to be a principle that nature adopts to support the emergence of complex systems. The idea of connecting basic building blocks applies from the molecular structure of benzene to neural pathways in the brain. The blocks themselves are not the principal actors because, at a finer scale, they can be regarded as networks themselves. What is primarily responsible for both molecular reactions and human behavior? It's not so much the nodes as the pattern of connections.

Complex human artifacts also adopt the network organization. Roadmaps, airline routes, power grids, VLSI chip layouts, the Internet, and, of course, the web are all characterized by their interconnection patterns. Amazingly, these systems obey laws that are independent of the particular domain, and applying knowledge that is standard in one field to another field can yield valuable new insights. A crucial feature of all networks is the number of links per node and the distribution of this number over all the nodes in the network. For example, a quick glance at an airline routing map shows that the network is characterized by a few important airports—hubs—that are massively connected.

Despite their underlying organization, most large networks, including the web, appear to be largely random. You could model the web as a graph in which links emanate from each page randomly. Given a particular page, first determine the number of outgoing links by rolling dice. Then, for each link, figure out its destination by choosing a random page from the entire web. This strategy distributes the number of links emanating from each page uniformly from 1 to the number of faces on a die (6, in most casinos).

In scientific domains, quantities are commonly distributed in a bell-shaped or Gaussian curve around a particular average value. Indeed, in the preceding experiment, it can be shown that the number of links into a node is distributed in an approximately Gaussian manner.[20] However, the number of outbound links is uniform, not Gaussian, because it is determined by throwing a die, which gives an equal probability to 1, 2, 3, 4, 5, and 6 links. An alternative method of construction is to randomly choose start and end pages and connect them, repeating the process over and over again until sufficiently many links have been created. Then the links emanating from each node will have a Gaussian distribution whose average is determined by dividing the total links by the number of nodes—the link density.

---

[20] The distribution of the number of links is technically not Gaussian but Poisson. Gaussian distributions are symmetric. The number of links into a particular node could be very large, but cannot be less than 0, which makes the distribution asymmetric. However, the Poisson distribution shares many Gaussian properties. It has an approximate bell shape (though asymmetric) whose peak is close to the mean, and for large mean and relatively small variance, it is indistinguishable from the Gaussian distribution. We loosely refer to it as "Gaussian" throughout.

How are the numbers of inbound and outbound links distributed in the web itself? The first experiments were performed on the Internet, which is the computer network that supports the World Wide Web (and many other things as well), not just the web, which links documents rather than computers. The results disagreed substantially with both the Gaussian and uniform models. It turns out that most Internet nodes have few connections, while a small minority are densely connected. As we will learn, this is not what the Gaussian model predicts. Subsequent experiments on the number of links to and from websites revealed the same behavior.

Measurements of everyday phenomena usually exhibit the bell-shaped Gaussian distribution sketched in Figure 3.3(a). Values cluster around a particular average value. The average conveys a tangible sense of scale. For example, people's heights have a distribution that is fairly narrow. Although height differs from one person to the next, there is a negligible probability that an adult's height is twice or half the average value. The average depends (slightly) on sex and ethnic origin and is quite different for other species (ants and elephants). Values deviate from the average to some extent depending on whether the bell is broad or narrow, but there are no radical departures outside this general variation.

Figure 3.3(b) shows a statistical distribution called the power law, which is a far better fit to the empirical distribution of links in the web (and the Internet too) than the Gaussian distribution. According to it, the most common number of links is the smallest possible number, and pages with more links become rarer as the number of links increases.[21] Unlike the Gaussian distribution, the number of links doesn't cluster around the average. Also, radical departures aren't so rare. Compared to Gaussian, the power law has a heavy tail: it drops off far less quickly as you move to the right of the graph.

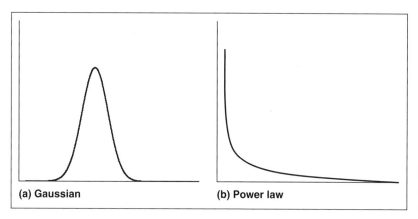

(a) Gaussian   (b) Power law

Figure 3.3 Gaussian and power-law distributions.

---

[21] With the power law, the probability that a randomly selected page has k links is proportional to $k^{-\gamma}$ for large k, where γ is a positive constant.

If people's heights followed the power law, most of us would be very short, far shorter than the average, but some would be very tall—and it would not be too surprising to find someone five or ten times taller than the average. Another way of looking at the difference is that in the Gaussian distribution, the mean (average value) is the same as the mode (most popular value), whereas with the power law, the mode is the smallest value and the mean is skewed well above it.

Power-law distributions are unusual in daily phenomena. Because they don't cluster around a particular value, they convey no sense of scale. If you pick a few samples from a Gaussian distribution, they will all be pretty well the same as the mean, where the interpretation of "pretty well" is determined by the variance. Just a few samples give a good idea of scale—they'll tell you whether you're looking at ants or elephants. But if you pick a few samples from the power-law distribution, they do not convey a sense of scale. You can still calculate the mean and variance, but these are abstract mathematical constructs without the same visceral interpretation as their Gaussian counterparts. Regardless of whether a network is large or small, the power-law distribution of links always has the shape of Figure 3.3(b).

Whereas Gaussian distributions do not exhibit radical outliers (10-meter giants), power-law distributions do. In networks, an outlier is a hub, a node with far more links than average. This is an attractive feature for many practical purposes, as travel agents who plan airplane journeys will confirm. Hubs, though rare, are plainly visible because they attract a large number of links.

EVOLUTIONARY MODELS

In the web, the process of attaching links is inherently dynamic. Nodes that turn out to be popular destinations are not defined in advance but emerge as the network evolves. Earlier we described how to generate a web randomly, but unrealistic distributions resulted—Gaussian for the number of inbound links, and uniform or Gaussian distributions for the outbound links. In these scenarios, we began with all pages in place and then made links between them. However, in reality, pages are created dynamically and only link to then-existing pages. If the random-generation model is adjusted to steadily increase the number of pages and only attach links to pages that already exist, the Gaussian peaks disappear. However, the result is not quite a power law, for the probability of a certain number of links decays exponentially with the number.

This generation model favors old nodes, which tend to become more frequently connected. In the web, however, it seems likely that popularity breeds popularity. Regardless of its age, a node with many inbound links is a more likely target for a new link than one with just a few. Destinations are not chosen randomly: strongly connected nodes are preferred. If the model is altered so that new links are attached to nodes in proportion to the number of existing links, it turns out that a power-law distribution is obtained for inbound links, just as occurs in the web. This state of affairs has been metaphorically (though inaccurately) dubbed "winners take all." A few popular pages with many inbound links tend to attract most of the attention, and, therefore, most of the new links. Meanwhile, most pages suffer from poor visibility and have difficulty attracting attention—and new links.

This elegant evolutionary model provides an excellent explanation of the distribution of inbound links in the web. It turns out that the number of outbound links is distributed in the same way.[22] The web is a scale-free network. It can evolve to any size whatsoever and the power-law link distribution still holds. Although you can work out the mean number of links per page, the actual figures do not cluster around the mean.

The model, though quite accurate, is still rather simplistic. First, nodes that have been around for a long time are more likely targets of links—in fact, nodes are favored in proportion to their age. But this aging effect is inconsistent with reality: venerable web pages are not popular purely by virtue of their longevity. The model can be improved by introducing a fitness measure for every node, chosen randomly, so that it is possible for a latecomer to vie in popularity with old nodes. The probability of attaching a new link is the product of the number of already attached links and this fitness measure.

Second, in large networks like the web, generating links independently of nodes does not always yield a satisfactory approximation. In some circumstances, the distribution departs from the power law, especially among pages on the same topic. For example, if you take all university home pages, or all company home pages, the distribution is an amalgamation of the peaked distribution of Figure 3.3(a) and the heavy tail of Figure 3.3(b).[23] Most company home pages were observed to have between 100 and 150 inbound links (in 2002), whereas the power-law distribution predicts that the most popular number of links is 1. Yet despite local variations, the overall distribution for all web pages does respect the power law.

BOW TIE ARCHITECTURE

Milgram's studies of the small world phenomenon remind us that our society is a strongly connected network: that is, one that links everyone to everyone else. Nature has produced many such networks—most notably the human brain. This contains 100 billion neurons with 10,000 connections each, and the growth mechanism clearly favors a strongly connected organization over a fragmented structure. The web is also, in large measure, strongly connected

---

[22] The exponent γ has been empirically determined as 2.1 for inbound links and 2.7 for outbound links (Broder et al., 2000).

[23] Technically, the body of the distribution is log-normal while the tail fits a power law.

rather than broken up into a multitude of fragments. This is important to its success, since a disconnected structure would not support crawling, and consequently searching.

What accounts for the development of single, large, connected structures as opposed to many fragmented clusters? In the web, it emerges from a bottom-up process of connecting pages all over the world, without any centralized control. In other fields, different reasons apply. In physics, insight into the phenomenon has been gained through the study of percolation—gravity-driven movement of water between soil and rock layers. It turns out that under weak assumptions, a random distribution of connections yields a single, holistic, connected component, which is essentially what happens in the network of human relationships. Randomness helps to create connected components.

In the web, things are more complicated, as the above-mentioned estimates of the average degree of separation showed. It's clear that the degree of separation in the web is significantly higher than the magic number 6. And, as it happens, at the time these estimates were made, there were fewer web pages than people on earth. One explanation is that real people have more friends than web pages have links. However, this only partially explains the discrepancy.

A more significant difference is that the web's links are directed. Unlike relationships between people, which by and large (ignoring unrequited love) are symmetric, a page can receive a link from another without returning the favor. It's the mixed blessing of one-way roads: security, in that you have to make fewer decisions about which way to turn, yet tortuous paths to the target, as everyone who has been lost in a one-way system can testify. The reason that web links are one-way is precisely to simplify the publication of pages. You can attach a link wherever you want without asking the permission of the target page.[24] The fact that links are directed makes paths to targets longer than in Milgram's experiment and gives the network a more complex structure.

Figure 3.4 shows a chart of the web, produced during a systematic study of the overall linkage structure in 1999. Its shape is reminiscent of a bow tie. The central knot is a giant connected subnet that we call "Milgram's continent," a large, strongly connected structure in which all pages are linked together. Here you can travel from one page to any other by following the links—just as when surfing with a browser. This continent is Milgram's "small world." It's where most surfing takes place. Crawlers explore it all. It's the dominant part of the web.

The directed links create other regions, also shown on the chart. There are three, each the same size or slightly smaller than the main continent. The *new archipelago* is a large group of fragmented islands; Milgram's continent can be

---

[24] Of course, it is always possible to implement a symmetric relationship, if the target page does the source page the favor of returning the link.

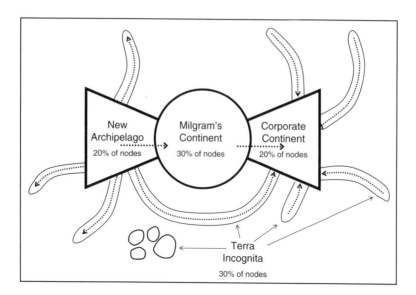

Figure 3.4 Chart of
the web.

reached from each island by following links. Most pages here are likely to be quite new and haven't received many links. The archipelago's youth explains its fragmentation. The fact that it contains no large strongly connected components reflects its recent evolution—it's like the dawn of the web. It does nevertheless contain some old pages to which no one in Milgram's continent has thought fit to link.

The corporate continent comprises a large collection of pages that can all be reached from Milgram's. Some of its members are sinks, pages without any outward links at all (for example, most Word documents and PDF files). However, these are a minority. This continent is highly fragmented and comprises an immense number of connected islands. Although it contains the second largest strongly connected component in the web (not shown on the chart), this component is hundreds of times smaller than Milgram's continent. The corporate continent includes company websites that do not link out to Milgram's continent. Though relatively small compared with Milgram's continent, these islands are significantly larger than those of the new continent.

Terra incognita is the rest of the universe. The distinctive feature of its pages is that surfers who reach them haven't come from Milgram's continent and won't get there in the future—though they may have traveled from the new archipelago, and they may end up in the corporate continent. Linked trails in terra incognita do not cross the main part of the web: the pages here are simply disconnected from it. However, as shown in the chart, pages in terra incognita can be connected to the new or corporate continents, giving rise to tendrils of two different kinds. Some tendrils only receive links from pages in the new continent, whereas others send links to the corporate continent. Like those in the new archipelago, pages in terra incognita are likely to be new.

The web is bigger and more complex than we had imagined. The seemingly innocuous decision to make links directed implies the chart in Figure 3.4. If links were bi-directional, the chart's complexity would evaporate into one large connected region, leaving only the few small islands shown near the bottom left. As it is, search engines explore Milgram's and the corporate continent. They encounter the rest of the universe only if someone submits a page directly as a new seed for exploration. Without explicit notification, the other two regions are invisible.

COMMUNITIES

The English word *community*, which can be traced back to the fourteenth century, derives from Middle French *comuneté*, from the Latin root *comunis*. Today the term is used to refer to a state of organized society, the people living in a district, a sense of common identity, and the quality of sharing something in common—like goods, and also interests. A community is

a group of people who share a common sense of identity and interact with one another on a sustained basis. While traditionally communities have existed in geographically defined areas, new telecommunications technology allows for the creation of communities with members spread throughout the world.
— *Elmer Social Science Dictionary (2003)*

The web, with its links from one page to another, is a good place to locate communities that share interests and enjoy a common sense of identity. It not only includes technological counterparts to established communities (people in the same university or the same company), but also encourages the creation of new communities from the ground up. The organization that emerges is not just of interest to sociologists, but can inspire new ways of searching. In the web, communities significantly enrich the general structure inherited from the science of networks described before. In addition to hubs that accumulate links and the fragmented bow tie structure induced by directed links, many features of the interconnection pattern arise out of relationships established by the people who inhabit the web.

The notion of "community" as just a set of members is simplistic: in reality the concept that emerges from social interactions is far more complex. Not all members are equal, and rather than partition the universe into members and non-members, it might be more accurate to talk of *degree* of membership. However, the degree of membership is not explicitly stated, but must be induced from the interactions between community members.

On the web, an extreme example of a community is a collection of pages that each link to each other (they may also link to pages outside the community). Mathematicians call this a "clique," the word for a small, exclusive circle of people. In general, communities are characterized by different patterns of links and are not necessarily easily detectable. One definition is a set of pages that link (in either direction) to more pages within the community than to pages outside it. This makes the clique a strong community. For any page, the ratio between the number of links within and outside the community give a measure of its degree of membership.

HIERARCHIES

Hierarchies are a classic way of organizing large amounts of information—or anything else. Beginning in the early days of the web, enthusiasts created hierarchical directories, structures that computer operating systems have used for organizing files since the 1960s. Web directories are intuitive, easy to use, and a natural way to locate resources. But, being hand-crafted, they are expensive. The web is so large that it is hard to achieve good coverage even when the work is distributed among volunteers, and quality control is difficult to enforce as the operation scales up. In fact, today's directories cover only a small portion of web resources, and their organization reflects the personal view of a new generation of web librarians.

Many individual users produce their own directories using the bookmarking facility that web browsers provide. Related bookmarks are placed in folders, and folders can be nested to reflect subtopics at any level of refinement. Bookmarks identify a microcosm of the web that corresponds to the user's personal view. Again they are constructed entirely by hand, which greatly restricts their coverage. Manual classification schemes, which are exemplified by the organization of traditional libraries, were ineffective in the Library of Babel, and the web shares the same problem: scaling up to the seemingly infinite.

The web does contain some natural hierarchical structure. Individual sites are organized hierarchically. Top-level descriptions are located at or near the root, while pages dealing with specific topics lie deep within the structure. There is evidence that this hierarchy is to some extent reflected in the structure of the links, although the effect is less apparent when considering links between pages of different domains.

It would be nice to be able to organize pages into a sensible hierarchy automatically, and even to tag nodes in the hierarchy with metadata. Joint analysis of the links and the page content offers a rich source of information for this kind of enterprise, and we return to this topic in Chapter 7. In addition, the social relationships between users, and their browsing behavior, are useful sources of information that can be profitably explored.

THE DEEP WEB

The quasi-random evolution of the web and its links makes it a "small world," like the sphere of human relationships that Milgram studied. However, as we have seen, directed links give the web a more complex geography by fragmenting it into four continents. Links imply further structure—the presence of communities—which is also reflected to some extent in the content of the pages. All these properties are clear signs that there's order in the web: in fact, they give it a rich and fascinating aspect. But that's not the whole story. The web is even richer, because many of its pages are inaccessible to the robots that crawl it and map out its structure. "There are finer fish in the sea that have ever been caught," declares an Irish proverb. Untold gold is buried in the web, untrawled by today's search engines.

Somewhere in the deep Atlantic lies a casualty of World War II, a Japanese submarine code-named Momi that is believed to carry tons of gold. The movie *Three Miles Down* recounts the gripping tale of an attempt to recover the treasure. Never before had anyone risked depths four times greater than the Titanic's watery grave. A story of courage, it also tells of surprising intuitions and clever discoveries—though not enough to complete the mission by reaching the submarine.[25]

Like the deep sea, there's a deep web. It contains treasure that you can't harvest just by dragging a net across the surface, as crawlers do. Crawlers will never find pages that are dynamically created in response to a direct query issued to a searchable database. Portals for electronic commerce provide examples galore—from booking flights to making domestic purchases. The web servers on these systems deliver the appropriate page to the user only after a dynamic query, that is, an interaction through a web interface that garners specifications for one or more database retrieval operations. Other treasures are hard to reach because you need privileged information to track them down, like the Momi submarine. For instance, all projects sponsored by the Italian Ministry of Research and Education are described on the web, but to access them you need a password. In fact, however, only a small fraction of the deep web (estimated at 5 percent) requires a password to access.

It is difficult to find automatic ways of discovering information in the deep web that are capable of working independently of the portal. As in *Three Miles Down*, the deeper you delve, the greater the difficulties you face. For the web, depth corresponds to the amount of interaction required to select the page. What's the problem? Suppose your robot reaches a portal for finding apartments

---

[25] That was finally achieved by Paul Tidwell, shipwreck salvager and decorated Vietnam veteran. He headed an expedition that was less well funded and equipped, but perhaps luckier.

in Boston. First, it must understand the interface the portal offers. Unless you decide to limit crawling to a finite list of portals whose interfaces have previously been mapped, the robot needs to be intelligent enough to understand the intermediate pages and formulate appropriate queries, one by one, until the required depth is reached.

Digital libraries are a prime example of the deep web. A digital library is a focused collection of digital objects, including text, audio, and video, along with methods for access and retrieval, and for selection, organization, and maintenance of the collection. They differ from the web at large because their material is selected and carefully organized. In addition to large collaborative efforts such as the Gutenberg and Million Book projects mentioned in Chapter 2, countless smaller, more focused digital library collections are created and maintained by individual institutions and national or international associations. Some are closed: only accessible from within a particular institution or with the necessary authorization; but most are open. Some are served up to crawlers and become part of the indexable web, but most remain hidden.

The deep web is controlled by organizations that run the underlying databases. As a rule—though there are many exceptions—their owners take care of the content because it affects their corporate image. This means that it is likely to be well checked: quality tends to be higher than on the open web. And it's huge. In September 2001, based on the same kind of overlap analysis described earlier (page 80), the deep web was estimated to be 400 to 550 times larger than the surface web. Though automatic exploration of the deep web is hard, efforts to mine the treasure will be amply rewarded. Progress in the field of artificial intelligence is likely to provide useful tools for mining.

SO WHAT?

This chapter has equipped you with the technical background to the web and the way it works: the acronym-laden world of HTML, HTTP, HTTPS, XML, URIs and URLs; new meanings for cookies and crawling; mysterious-sounding avatars and chatbots, blogs and wikis. And not just the technical background: there's a mathematical side too. The web is a huge network that, viewed from afar, shares the properties of scale-free random networks. The pattern of links does not give a sense of scale: it doesn't make much sense to talk about the "average" number of links into or out of a node. The connectivity imparted by links breaks the web up into distinct regions or continents. Zooming in, the details start to come into focus: the connection pattern is not random at all but reflects the myriad communities that have created the web.

How can you possibly find stuff in this gargantuan information space? Read on.

WHAT CAN *YOU* DO ABOUT ALL THIS?

- Estimate what proportion of broken links you've encountered recently.
- How many cookies are on your computer? Find out the consequences of deleting them (*be careful*—some may be more important than you think).
- Search the *wikiHow* to learn how you can safely delete your usage history.
- Play with image search and figure out what's being searched.
- Donate some metadata—play the ESP game on the web.
- Talk to a chatbot (the chatbot George won the illustrious Loebner Prize for the most convincing conversational program in 2005).
- Surf around the deep web. Why is this hard for search engines?
- Comment on the book using the blog at *www.blogger.com/home*.
- Watch Felix walk: try out Figure 3.1(a) in a web browser.
- Surf around to find an example of static, dynamic, and active pages.
- What properties do the Internet and web share with biological structures?

NOTES AND SOURCES

The development of the web is regulated by the World Wide Web Consortium,[26] of which Berners-Lee is a founding member. It continues to define new specifications and refine existing ones—including HTML, HTTP, and XML. The term *hypertext* was coined by Ted Nelson long before the web was born. Markup languages such as HTML originated even earlier when Charles Goldfarb, an attorney practicing in Boston, joined IBM in 1967 and began to work on a document markup language with Edward Mosher and Raymond Lorie. They defined a language called GML (their own initials) which many years later, in 1986, became the Standard Generalized Markup Language (SGML), a general concept of which HTML is a particular application. SGML also spawned XML, a far simpler version. The quote from Steve Jobs on page 63 is from a 1996 interview in *Wired Magazine* (Wolf, 1996).

The idea of countering the brittleness of the web by using associative links to identify pages by a few well-chosen rare words and phrases was suggested by

---

[26] *www.w3.org*

Phelps and Wilensky (2000). Two Carnegie Mellon University graduate students, von Ahn and Dabbish (2004), developed the ESP game for providing accurate image metadata.

The 2005 estimate of the size of the indexable web was obtained by Gulli and Signorini (2005). The continued growth of the web shown in Table 3.1 is documented by Hobbes's Internet Timeline,[27] which confirms a relentless exponential trend. Bharat and Broder (1999) and Lawrence and Giles (1999) worked on quantifying the number of pages that are indexed by inventing random queries and sending them to different search engines.

The estimate of 19 for the degree of separation on the web is due to Albert et al. (1999), who studied the Notre Dame University website. Based on data crawled by the (now-defunct) AltaVista search engine, researchers at IBM and Compaq estimated that the average degree of separation exceeds 500 (Broder et al., 2000).

The classic way of generating a random graph by allocating a given number of links to randomly chosen pairs of nodes is due to Erdös and Reny (1960). This predicts Gaussian distributions for the number of links. In 1999, an analysis of links in the Internet came up with the power-law distribution instead (Faloutsos et al., 1999). Barabási and Albert (1999) devised the elegant explanation of the generation of power laws in the web; Bianconi and Barabási (2001) improved the model by introducing a fitness measure for every node. Pennock et al. (2002) found that the distribution exhibits significant local departures from the power law, especially among competing pages on the same topic.

The bow tie model of the web is due to Broder et al. (2000); Barabási (2002) introduced the continent metaphor. Dorogovtsev et al. (2001) discuss algorithms for calculating the size of the strongly connected components.

The Elmer Social Science Dictionary, the source of our definition of community, is online.[28] Flake et al. (2002) came up with the notion of a web community as a set of pages that link (in either direction) to more pages in the community than to pages outside it.

The estimate that the deep web is 400 to 550 times bigger than the surface web is due to *BrightPlanet.com*, who believe that only a small fraction (say 5 percent) requires a password for access. Digital libraries are discussed by Witten and Bainbridge (2003) and Lesk (2005).

---

[27] *www.zakon.org/robert/internet/timeline*

[28] *www/elissetche.org*

CHAPTER 4

HOW TO SEARCH

In 1828, at the age of 19, Mary Novello married the 41-year-old writer and publisher Charles Clarke. He was a Shakespeare scholar, and the next year Mary embarked on a monumental task: to produce a systematic concordance of all Shakespeare's plays. Today we are so used to machines doing all our clerical work that it's hard to imagine the scale of her undertaking—and she probably had no idea what she was letting herself in for, either. At the start, she was an enthusiastic amateur, brought up in the company of the Regency literati. It took her twelve years to extract and order the data, then another four to check it against current editions and prepare it for the press. After sixteen years of toil—almost half her young life—the concordance's 310,000 entries appeared in eighteen monthly parts in 1844–45. This was the first concordance to any body of secular literature in English.

Every word that Shakespeare wrote was arranged alphabetically, along with the play, scene, and line numbers in which it appeared. The preface proudly proclaimed that "to furnish a faithful guide to this rich mine of intellectual treasure...has been the ambition of a life; and it is hoped that the sixteen years' assiduous labour...may be found to have accomplished that ambition."

The dragon stands guard over a treasure chest.

It certainly saved users labor: they could now identify half-remembered quotations, make exhaustive surveys of chosen themes, and undertake systematic studies of Shakespeare's writing. It laid a foundation that today we would call an enabling technology.

Comprehensive indexes to many other books—such as the Bible and the writings of famous authors and classical philosophers—were produced by hand in the nineteenth and early twentieth centuries. The prefaces of these works tell of years of painstaking toil, presumably driven by a belief in the worthiness of the text being indexed. The word *concordance* originally applied just to biblical indexes. Its root, *concord*, means "unity," and the term apparently arose out of the school of thought that the unity of the Bible should be reflected in consistency between the Old and New Testaments, which could be demonstrated by a concordance.

The task of constructing concordances manually is onerous and time consuming. Sometimes it was passed on from father to son. A concordance for the Greek version of the New Testament, published in 1897, has since undergone several revisions, and responsibility for the task has passed down through three generations of the same family. Figure 4.1 shows part of the entry for the word 'εραυνα'ω, a Greek verb for *search*. The task is not entirely mechanical, since several inflections of the verb are recorded under the one heading.

Technology improved. In 1911, a concordance of William Wordsworth's poetry was published. The 1,136-page tome lists all 211,000 nontrivial words in the poet's works, from *Aäaliza* to *Zutphen's*, yet took less than seven months to construct. The task was completed so quickly because it was undertaken by a highly organized team of 67 people—three of whom had died by the time the concordance was published—using three-by-five-inch cards, scissors, glue, and stamps.

Of course, the biggest technological improvement came when computers were recruited to work on the task. In the beginning, computer resources were

Figure 4.1 A concordance entry for the verb *to search* from the Greek New Testament (Moulton and Geden, 1977).

Reprinted by permission from T & T Clark, Ltd.

'ΕΡΑΥΝΑ'Ω   2037.5

Jo   5 39 ἐραυνᾶτε τ. γραφάς
     7 52 ἐραύνησον κ. ἴδε
Ro   8 27 ὁ δὲ ἐραυνῶν τ. καρδίας οἶδεν
I Co 2 10 τὸ γὰρ πνεῦμα πάντα ἐραυνᾷ
I Pe 1 11 ἐραυνῶντες εἰς τίνα ἢ ποῖον καιρὸν ἐδή-
          λου τὸ ἐν αὐτοῖς πνεῦμα Χριστοῦ
Re   2 23 ἐγώ εἰμι ὁ ἐραυνῶν νεφροὺς κ. καρδίας

```
SHEEPFOLD
        THE SHEEPFOLD OF MICHAEL SURVIVES     .  .  .  .  .  .   228 YOUTH OF NATURE       21

SHEET
        OER THE BLANCHD SHEET HER RAVEN HAIR  .  .  .  .  .  .   146 TRISTRAM 2           107
        AND REACH THAT GLIMMERING SHEET OF GLASS  .  .  .  .  .  310 OBERMANN             119

SHEETS
        THERE WHERE DOWN CLOUDY CLIFFS THROUGH SHEETS OF FOAM    262 SCHOLAR-GIPSY        248
        IN SHEETS OF SCATHING FIRE      .  .  .  .  .  .  .  .   319 OBERMANN MORE        202
        FAR OER THE GLISTENING SHEETS OF WINDY CORN      .  .   473 CROMWELL              36

SHELF
        AND FROM SOME SWARDED SHELF HIGH UP THERE CAME    .  .    25 DREAM                11

SHELL
        THE WIND IS DOWN BUT SHELL NOT COME TO-NIGHT    .  .   139 TRISTRAM 1           300
        SHELL LIGHT HER SILVER LAMP WHICH FISHERMEN    .  .   151 TRISTRAM 3            79
        AND TAKE HER BROIDERY-FRAME AND THERE SHELL SIT   .  .   152 TRISTRAM 3            82
        WHOSE STRIPED SHELL FOUNDED    .  .  .  .  .  .  .  .   392 MEROPE              1628
```

Figure 4.2 Entries from an early computer-produced concordance of Matthew Arnold (Parrish, 1959).

scarce: in 1970, an early pioneer blew most of his computer budget for the entire year on a single run to generate a concordance. Early works were printed on a line printer, in uppercase letters, without punctuation. Figure 4.2 shows some entries from a 1959 concordance of Matthew Arnold: note that *she'll* is indistinguishable from *shell*. As computers became cheaper and more powerful, it became easier and more economical to produce concordances, and print quality improved. By the 1980s, personal computers could be used to generate and print concordances whose quality was comparable to that of handmade ones—possibly even better.

Technology now makes it trivial. Today you can generate a concordance for any document or corpus of documents on your laptop or home computer in a few seconds or minutes (perhaps hours, for a monumental corpus). You only need an electronic version of the text. They might be your own files. Or a set of web pages. Or a public-domain book somewhere on the web, perhaps in the Gutenberg or Internet Archives corpus. But you probably needn't bother, for the web dragons have already done the work and will let you use their concordance for free. Just one hundred years after Mary Clarke died, search engines were regularly churning out a concordance of the entire web every few months. A few years later, they brought within their ambit massive portions of our treasury of literature—including, of course, Shakespeare's plays, over which she had labored so hard. It is hard to imagine what she would have made of this.

Today a concordance is usually called a "full-text index." With it, not only can you examine all the contexts in which a word appears, but you can also search for any part of a text that contains a particular set of words that interest you. You might include phrases; specify whether all the words must appear or just some of them; or determine how far apart they may be. You might restrict your search to a particular work, or website. You might control the order in which results are presented, sorted by some metadata value like author, or date, or in order of how well they match the query. If you work with information, you probably use full-text retrieval every day.

SEARCHING TEXT

Searching a full text is not quite as simple as having a computer go through it from start to finish looking for the words you want to find. Despite their reputation for speed and blind obedience, an exhaustive search is still a lengthy business for computers. Even a fast system takes several minutes to read an entire CD-ROM, and on the enormous volumes of text managed by web search engines, a full scan would take longer than any user would be prepared to wait.

FULL-TEXT INDEXES

To accomplish searching very rapidly, computers use precisely the same technique that Mary did: they first build a concordance or full-text index. This lists all the words that appear in the text, along with a pointer to every occurrence. If the text were Hamlet's famous soliloquy "To be or not to be, that is the question...," the index would start as shown in Figure 4.3(a). Here, pointers are numbers: the 2 and 6 beside *be* indicate that it is the second and sixth word in the text, as shown in Figure 4.3(b). Words are ordered alphabetically, and in reality the list will contain many more—from *aardvark* to *zygote*, perhaps. Alongside each word are several pointers, sometimes just one (for unusual words like these) and sometimes a great many (for *a, and, of, to,* and *the*). Each word has as many pointers as it has appearances in the text. And the grand

be	2 6 ...
is	8 ...
not	4 ...
or	3 ...
question	10 ...
that	7 ...
the	9 ...
to	1 5 ...

(a) The beginning of the index.

```
1  2  3   4   5  6   7  8   9   10
to be or not to be that is the question . . .
```

(b) The text.

Figure 4.3 Making a full-text index.

total number of pointers is the number of words in the text. In this example, there are ten words and therefore ten pointers.

Mary Clarke's Shakespeare concordance recorded pointers in terms of the play, scene, and line number. Our example uses just the word number. In reality, one might use a document number and word within the document, or perhaps a document number, paragraph number, and word within the paragraph. It really depends on what kind of searches you want to do.

How big is the index? Any large corpus of text will contain a host of different words. It is surprisingly hard to estimate the size of the vocabulary. It isn't useful to simply count the words in a language dictionary, because each inflected variant will have its own entry in the list (we discuss this further soon). For English, around 100,000 to 200,000 words seems a plausible ballpark figure. But bulk text contains far more than this, because of neologisms, proper names, foreign words, and—above all—misspellings. A typical collection of a billion web pages—equivalent to about 2,000 books—will include as many as a million different words (assuming they're in English). Google's text base is several orders of magnitude larger and contains many billions of *different* words—only a tiny fraction of which are bona fide ones that would appear in a language dictionary. Fortunately, computers can quickly locate items in ordered lists, even if the lists are very long.

The size of the list of pointers that accompanies each word depends on how many times that word appears. Unique words, ones that occur only once in a corpus of text, are referred to by the Greek term *hapax legomena*, and their list contains just one pointer. It turns out that around half of the terms in a typical text are *hapax legomena*: for example, around 45 percent of the 31,500 different words in *The Complete Works of Shakespeare* occur just once. At the other extreme, Shakespeare used 850 words more than 100 times each. At the very extreme, today Google says it indexes 21,630,000,000 pages that contain the word *the*, and it surely appears many times on the average page. There will probably be 100 billion pointers for this one word.

How much space does the index occupy? As we saw earlier, it contains as many entries as there are words in the text, one pointer for every word appearance. In fact, the space needed to store a pointer is not all that different from the amount needed to store the word itself: thus the size of the index is about the same as the size of the text. Both can be compressed, and practical compression techniques reduce the index slightly more than they reduce the text. Search engines keep both a full-text index and a text-only version of all documents on the web, and in broad terms they are about the same size as each other. That's not surprising, for they store exactly the same amount of information: from the text you can derive the index and vice versa.

USING THE INDEX

Given an index, it's easy to search the text for a particular word: just locate it in the ordered list and extract its associated list of numbers. Assuming that each appearance position comprises both the document number and the word within the document, a search will find all the documents that contain the word. Although computers cannot scan quickly all the way through large amounts of text, they can rapidly locate a word in an ordered list (or report that it doesn't appear).

To process a query that contains several terms, first locate them all and extract their lists of document and word numbers. Then scan the lists together to see which document numbers are common to them—in other words, which documents contain all the query terms. Merging the lists is easy because each one is sorted into ascending order of position. Alternatively, to locate those documents that contain any (rather than all) of the words, scan along the lists and output all the document numbers they contain. Any logical combination of words can be dealt with in like manner.

So far we have only used the document numbers, not the word-within-document numbers. Word numbers become important when seeking phrases. To see where the phrase *to be* occurs in Hamlet's soliloquy, retrieve the lists for *to* and *be* and check whether they contain any adjacent numbers. *To* is word 1 and *be* word 2, which indicates an occurrence of the phrase *to be*. Scanning to the next item on both lists indicates a second occurrence. On the other hand, although the words *is* and *not* both appear, the phrase *is not* does not, since their respective positions, 8 and 4, are not consecutive. Instead of phrase searching, it is sometimes useful to find terms that occur within a certain distance of each other—a *proximity* search. To do this, instead of seeking consecutive words, look for positions that differ by up to a specified maximum.

These techniques return the documents that match a set of query terms in the order in which the documents appear in the collection. In practice, documents are encountered haphazardly—perhaps by crawling the web—and this ordering is not meaningful. It is better to try to return documents in relevance order, beginning with those that are most closely related to the query.

Computers cannot comprehend the documents and determine which is really most relevant to the query—even human librarians have a hard time doing that. However, a good approximation can be obtained simply by counting words. A document is more relevant

- if it contains more query terms
- if the query terms occur more often
- if it contains fewer non-query terms

When evaluating these factors, you should give more weight to terms that seldom occur in the document collection than to frequent ones, for rare terms like *martini* are more important than common ones like *the*.

These rules lead to a simple method for estimating the relevance of a document to a query. Imagine a very high-dimensional space, with as many dimensions as there are different words in the collection—thousands (for Shakespeare), millions (for a small library), or billions (for the web). Each axis corresponds to a particular word. A document defines a certain point in the space, where the distance along each axis corresponds to the number of times the word appears. But the scale of the axis depends on the word's overall popularity: to move one inch along the *woman* axis requires more appearances of that term than to move the same distance along the *goddess* axis simply by virtue of the relative frequency of these words (for most collections). The intuition is that words that occur frequently in a particular document convey information *about it*, while words that appear rarely in the collection as a whole convey more information *in general*.

The position of a document in this high-dimensional space depends greatly on its size. Suppose that from document A we construct a new document B that contains nothing more than two copies of A. The point corresponding to B is twice as far from the origin, in precisely the same direction, as that for A—yet both documents contain exactly the same information. As this illustrates, what really characterizes a document is not its position in the space, but the direction of the line to it from the origin. To judge the similarity of two documents, we use the angle between their vectors. To judge the relevance of a document to a query, we treat the query as a tiny little document and calculate the similarity between it and the document. Technically, the cosine of the angle is used, not the angle itself, and this is called the *cosine similarity measure*. It ranges from 1 if the documents are identical to 0 if they have no words in common.

The cosine similarity measure treats each document as though its words are completely independent of one another—documents are just a "bag of words." A scrambled document will match the original with a 100 percent similarity score! This is a gross oversimplification of real language, where *John hit Mary* differs radically from *Mary hit John*. Nevertheless, it seems to work quite well, since word order rarely affects what should be returned as the result of a query. You are more likely to be looking for documents about John and Mary's aggression in general, rather than who was the aggressor—and in that case, you could always use a phrase search.

WHAT'S A WORD?

Where does one word end and the next begin? There are countless little decisions to make. Basically, each alphabetic or alphanumeric string that appears in the text is a potential query term. Numbers should not be ignored: queries often contain them, particularly in the form of dates or years. Punctuation is ignored, but embedded apostrophes (and unmatched trailing apostrophes) should be retained. Ideally, so should periods that indicate abbreviations. Hyphens should sometimes be ignored and sometimes treated like a space: usage is inconsistent. Other punctuation, like white space, is a word separator. Probably a maximum word length should be imposed, in case there is a very long string—like the expansion of π to a million digits—that could choke the indexing software.

Case "folding" replaces uppercase characters with their lowercase equivalents. For example, *the*, *The*, *THE*, *tHe*, and four other combinations would all be folded to the representative term *the*. We assumed case folding in the example of Figure 4.3 by combining the entries for *To* and *to*. If all terms in the index are case folded, and the query terms are as well, case will be ignored when matching. This is not always appropriate—when searching for *General Motors*, you do not want to be swamped with answers about *general repairs to all kinds of motors*.

"Stemming" gives leeway when comparing words with different endings— like *motor*, *motors*, *motoring*, *motorist*. It involves stripping off one or more suffixes to reduce the word to root form, converting it to a stem devoid of tense and plurality. In some languages, the process is simple; in others, it is far more complex. If all terms in the index are stemmed, and the query is too, suffixes will be ignored when matching. Again, this is sometimes inappropriate, as when seeking proper names or documents containing particular phrases.

Another common trick is to ignore or "stop" frequently occurring terms and not index them at all. The ignored words are called *stop words*. In an uncompressed index, this yields a substantial saving in space—billions of pages contain the word *the*, which translates into a list of tens of billions of numbers in a full-text index. However, such lists compress very well, and it turns out that if the index is compressed, omitting stop words does not save much space— perhaps 10 percent, compared with a 25 percent saving for uncompressed indexes (since roughly every fourth word is a stop word).

If you create an index that ignores words, you are assuming that users will not be interested in those terms. In reality, it is not easy to predict what will attract the attention of future scholars. Mary Clarke omitted common words in her concordance of Shakespeare. But because *when*, *whenever*, and *until* were excluded, the concordance could not be used to investigate Shakespeare's treatment of time; the exclusion of *never* and *if* ignored crucial terms in *Lear* and *Macbeth*; and studies of Shakespeare's use of the verb *to do* were likewise precluded. A further problem is that many common stop words—notably *may*, *can*, and *will*—are homonyms for rarer nouns: stopping the word *may* also removes references to the month of May.

These effects combine. After special characters, single-letter words, and the lowercased stop word *at* have been removed from the term *AT&T*, there is nothing left to index!

DOING IT FAST

Constructing a full-text index for a large document collection, and using it to answer queries quickly is a daunting undertaking—almost as daunting as Mary Clarke's production of the Shakespeare concordance. It is accomplished, of course, by breaking the problem down into smaller parts, and these into smaller parts still, until you get right down to individual algorithms that any competent computer science student can implement. The student's advantage over Mary is that he or she can rerun the procedure over and over again to fix the bugs and get it right, and once the program is complete, it can process any other document collection without additional labor.

Building an index is a large computation that may take minutes for Shakespeare's complete works, hours for a small library, and days for a vast collection. The problem is to read in the text word by word, and output it dictionary word by dictionary word (*aardvark* to *zygote*) in the form of pointers. This is easy in principle—so easy it is often set as an introductory undergraduate student computing assignment. The snag is that for a large collection, all the information—the input text and the output word list—will not fit into the computer's main memory. Simply putting it on disk won't work because access is so much slower that the operation would take literally centuries (and the disk drives would wear out).

Making an indexing program work is just a matter of detail. First, you partition the collection—do a slice at a time, where each slice fits into main memory. Then you must solve the problem of putting the bits back together. Second, compress the data, so more fits into main memory at once. In fact, those lists of pointers compress well if you use the right technique. Third, fiddle with the algorithms to make them read information off disk sequentially as much as possible, which is far faster than random access. The result is a complex system whose components are all carefully optimized, involving a great deal of mathematical theory.

The second part is doing the searching. Whereas the index only has to be built once, or perhaps periodically whenever the collection is updated, searching is done continually—and a multiple-user system must respond to different queries simultaneously. The fundamental problem is to look up each query term, read its list of pointers off disk, and process the lists together. Computers consult entries in alphabetical dictionaries by "binary searching," checking the middle to narrow the search down to one half or the other, and repeating. This is very fast, because doubling the size of the dictionary only adds one more operation. Dealing with the lists of pointers is more challenging because it seems necessary to scan through them in order, which is excessively time-consuming for long lists. However, if there is only one query term, you don't need to look through the list: just present the first 10 or 20 documents to the user as the search results. If you are looking for documents that contain all the query terms, you can start with the rarest term and, for each occurrence, look it up in the other term lists using binary search.

These operations can be done extremely efficiently. And there is no reason at all why queries should be restricted to the one or two words that are typical when searching the web. Indeed, when documents are required to include all the query terms (rather than just some of them), which is normally the case with a web search, it is far more efficient to seek a complete paragraph—even a full page of text—than a couple of words. The reason is that, when merging, you can start with the rarest word, immediately pruning the list of document numbers down to just a few entries. Search engines have tiny query boxes purely for aesthetic reasons, not for efficiency, and because most users issue only tiny queries.

Returning results in order of relevance, estimated using a similarity measure, is more challenging. If there are many matches, even sorting the documents into order can be a substantial undertaking. However, you don't need all the results at once, just the top 10 or 20, and there are ways of finding the top few documents without sorting the entire list. But we do need to compute all the similarity values to find the best ones—or do we? Having found a few good ones, there are ways of quickly ruling out most of the others on the basis of a partial computation. These are things you might learn in a graduate computer science course.

Building an efficient, web-scale, robust, industrial-strength full-text indexing system is a substantial undertaking—perhaps on a par with the sixteen person-years it took to produce a concordance of Shakespeare manually. Once done, however, it can be applied again and again to index new bodies of text and answer simultaneous full-text queries by users all over the world.

EVALUATING THE RESULTS

A good indexing system will answer queries quickly and effectively, be able to rebuild the index quickly, and not require excessive resources. The most difficult part to evaluate is the effectiveness of the answers—in particular, the effectiveness of relevance ranking.

The most common way to characterize retrieval performance is to calculate how many of the relevant documents have been retrieved and how early they occur in the ranked list. To do this, people adopt the (admittedly simplistic) view that a document either is or is not relevant to the query—and this judgment is made by the human user. We consider all documents up to a certain cutoff point in the ranking—say, the first 20 of them (typically the number that appears in the first page of search results). Some documents in this set will be relevant, others not. Retrieval performance is expressed in terms of three quantities: the number of documents that are retrieved (20 in this case), the number of those that are relevant, and the total number of relevant documents (which could be far larger). There are two measures that depend on these quantities:

$$Precision = \frac{Number\ of\ retrieved\ documents\ that\ are\ relevant}{Total\ number\ retrieved}$$

$$Recall = \frac{Number\ of\ relevant\ documents\ that\ are\ retrieved}{Total\ number\ relevant}$$

The number on the top is the same in both cases. For example, if 20 documents are retrieved in answer to some query, and 15 of them are relevant, the precision is 75 percent. If, in addition, the collection contained a total of 60 relevant documents, the recall is 25 percent. The two quantities measure different things. Precision assesses the accuracy of the set of search results in terms of what proportion are good ones, while recall indicates the coverage in terms of what proportion of good ones are returned.

There is a tradeoff between precision and recall as the number of documents retrieved is varied. If all documents in the collection were retrieved, recall would be 100 percent—but precision would be miniscule. If just one document were retrieved, hopefully it would be a relevant one—surely, if asked for just one document, the search system could find one that was certainly relevant—in which case precision would be 100 percent but recall would be miniscule.

You can evaluate precision by looking at each document returned and deciding whether it is relevant to the query (which may be a tough decision). You probably can't evaluate recall, for to do so you would have to examine every single document in the collection and decide which ones were relevant. For large collections, this is completely impossible.

SEARCHING IN A WEB

Given a query and a set of documents, full-text retrieval locates those documents that are most relevant to the query. This now-classic model of information retrieval was studied comprehensively and in great detail from the 1960s onward. The web, when it came along, provided a massive, universally accessible set of documents. For computer scientists, this was a new adventure playground, and many eagerly rushed off to apply information retrieval techniques. The web presented an interesting challenge because it was huge—at the time, it was not easy to get hold of massive quantities of electronic text. There was also the fun of downloading or "crawling" the web so that inverted indexes could be produced, itself an interesting problem.

This kept scientists busy for a couple of years, and soon the first search engines appeared. They were marvelous software achievements that faithfully located all web pages containing the keywords you specified, and presented these pages to you in order of relevance. It was a triumph of software engineering that such huge indexes could be created at all, let alone consulted by a multitude of users simultaneously.

Prior to the inception of search engines, the web was of limited practical interest, though aficionados found it fascinating. Of course, it was great that you could easily read what others had written, and follow their hyperlinks to further interesting material. But if you didn't already know where it was, seeking out information was like looking for needles in haystacks. You could spend a lot of time getting to know where things were, and early adopters became real experts at ferreting out information on the web. But it was an exhausting business because the haystack kept changing! You had to invest a lot of time, not just in getting to know the web, but also in maintaining your knowledge in the face of continual evolution.

Search engines changed all that. They finally made it worthwhile coming to grips with the baby World Wide Web. When academics and researchers learned about search engines (for this was before the web's discovery by commerce), they started to learn more about the web.

While most were playing in this new sandbox and marveling at its toys and how easily you could find them, a perspicacious few noticed that something was slightly wrong. Most web queries were—and still are—very short: one or two words.[29] Incidentally, by far the most common web query is...nothing, the empty string, generated by users who reach a search engine and hit the Enter key. If a particular word occurs at most once in each document, a one-word query with the cosine ranking algorithm returns documents in order of length, shortest first, because brevity enhances the apparent significance of each word. In an early example from Google's pioneers, the word *University* returned a long but haphazard list of pages, sorted in order of occurrence frequency and length, not prestige. (The pioneers were at Stanford and were probably irked that it appeared way down the list, outranked by minor institutions.)

---

[29] This is just what people do. We have already noted on page 110 that there is no good *technical* reason to restrict queries to a few words.

DETERMINING WHAT A PAGE IS ABOUT

There were other problems. One arose when people started to realize how important it was to get noticed and began putting words into their pages specifically for that purpose. Traditional information retrieval takes documents at face value: it assumes that the words they contain are a fair representation of what they are about. But if you want to promote your wares, why not include additional text intended solely to increase its visibility? Unlike paper documents, words can easily be hidden in web pages, visible to programs but not to human readers.

Here's a simple idea: judge people by what others say about them, not by their own ego. And judge what web pages are about by looking at the "anchor text"—that is, the clickable text—of hyperlinks that point to them. Take the book you're reading now. If many people link to the publisher's web page and label their links "great book about the web," that's a far more credible testament than any self-congratulatory proclamation in the book itself, or in its web page.

This insight suggests an advantage in including the words on all links into a page in the full-text index entries for that page, as though the anchor text were actually present in the page itself. In fact, these words should be weighted more highly than those in the page because external opinions are usually more accurate. All this is very easy to do, and in a world tainted with deceit, it substantially improves retrieval effectiveness.

MEASURING PRESTIGE

Suppose we want to return results in order of prestige, rather than in order of density of occurrence of the search terms, as the cosine rule does. Dictionaries define *prestige* as "high standing achieved through success or influence." A metric called PageRank, introduced by the founders of Google and used in various guises by other search engine developers too, attempts to measure the standing of a web page. The hope is that prestige is a good way to determine authority, defined as "an accepted source of expert information or advice."

In a networked community, people reward success with links. If you link to my page, it's probably because you find it useful and informative—it's a successful web page. If a whole host of people link to it, that indicates prestige: my page is successful and influential. Look at Figure 4.4, which shows a tiny fraction of the web, including links between pages. Which ones do you think are most authoritative? Page **F** has five incoming links, which indicates that five other people found it worth linking to, so there's a good chance that this page is more authoritative than the others. **B** is second best, with four links.

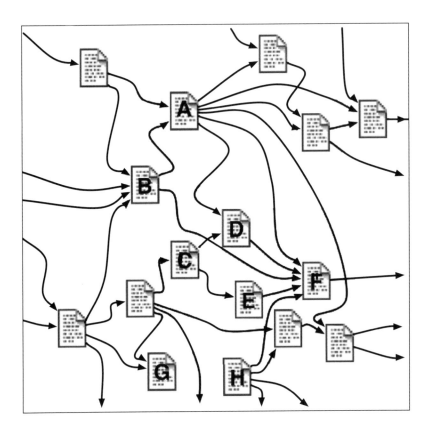

Figure 4.4 A tangled web.

Merely counting links is a crude measure. We learned earlier that when rank-ing retrieval results, some words should count more than others because they are rarer and therefore more informative. Likewise, some web pages have thou-sands of outgoing links whereas others have just one or two. Rarer links are more discriminating and should count more than others. A link from your page to mine bestows more prestige if your page has few outlinks; less if it has many. In Figure 4.4, the many links emanating from page **A** mean that each link carries less weight, simply because **A** is a prolific linker. From **F**'s point of view, the links from **D** and **E** may be more valuable than the one from **A**.

There is another factor: a link is more valuable if it comes from a presti-gious page. The link from **B** to **F** may be better than the others into **F** because **B** is more prestigious. At first sight, this smacks of the English "old school tie" network of political elite, which bestows a phony and incestuous kind of pres-tige. But here it's different: prestige is not an accident of breeding, but must be earned by attracting links. Admittedly, this factor involves a certain circu-larity, and without further analysis it's not clear that it can be made to work. But indeed it can.

Underlying these ideas is the assumption that all links are bona fide ones. We fretted earlier that deceitful authors could insert misleading words into their pages to attract attention and ensure that they were returned more often as search results. Could they not also establish a fake kind of prestige by establishing phony links to their page? The answer is yes—and we will discuss this issue extensively in the next chapter. But arranging phony links is not as easy as editing the page to include misleading words. What counts are links *in* to the page, not links from it to others. And placing thousands of links from another page does not help much because inlinks are not just counted—their influence is attenuated by the host of outlinks from the linking page.

To summarize: We define the PageRank of a page to be a number between 0 and 1 that measures its prestige. Each link into the page contributes to its PageRank. The amount it contributes is the PageRank of the linking page divided by the number of outlinks from it. The PageRank of any page is calculated by summing that quantity over all links into it. The value for **D** in Figure 4.4 is calculated by adding one-fifth of the value for **A** (because it has five outlinks) to one-half the value for **C**.

Calculating PageRank

The definition is circular: how can you calculate the PageRank of a page without knowing the PageRanks of all the other pages? In fact, it's not difficult: we use what mathematicians call an "iterative" method. Start by randomly assigning an initial value to each page. Each value could be chosen to be different, or they could all be the same: it doesn't matter (provided they're not all zero). Then recompute each page's PageRank by summing the appropriate quantities, described earlier, over its inlinks. If the initial values are thought of as an approximation to the true value of PageRank, the new values are a better approximation. Keep going, generating a third approximation, and a fourth, and so on. At each stage, recompute the PageRank for every page in the web. Stop when, for every page, the next iteration turns out to give almost exactly the same PageRank as the previous one.

Will this converge? And how long does it take? These are questions for mathematicians. The answer is yes (subject to a couple of modifications discussed later). And the number of iterations depends on the desired accuracy (and other more technical factors). The relevant branch of mathematics is called *linear algebra*, and the web presents the largest practical problem in linear algebra that has ever been contemplated.

Mathematicians talk of the "connection matrix," a huge array of rows and columns with each cell containing either 1 or 0. A row represents the links out of a particular web page, and a column represents the links into another web page. A 1 (one) is placed at the intersection if the row's page contains a link to the column's page; otherwise a 0 is written there. The number of rows and columns are both the same as the number of pages in the web. Most entries are 0 since the probability of one randomly chosen web page having a direct link to another randomly chosen page is very small.

Mathematicians have studied matrix computations for 150 years and have come up with clever methods for solving just the kind of problem that PageRank presents. One day, out of nowhere, along came the web, bearing the largest, most practical matrix problem ever encountered. Suddenly mathematicians found themselves in demand, and their expertise is at the very core of companies that trade for billions of dollars on the stock exchange.

The iterative technique described earlier is exactly what search engines use today, but the precise details are only known to insiders. The accuracy used for the final values probably lies between 10^{-9} and 10^{-12}. An early experiment reported 50 iterations for a much smaller version of the web than today's, before the details became a trade secret; several times as many iterations are probably needed now. Google is thought to run programs for several days to perform the PageRank calculation for the entire web, and the operation is—or at any rate used to be—performed every few weeks.

As we have seen, a random starting point is used. You might think that the current values of PageRank would be an excellent choice to begin the iteration. Unfortunately, it turns out that this does not reduce the number of iterations significantly over starting from scratch with a purely random assignment. Some pages—for example, those concerning news and current events—need updating far more frequently than once every few weeks. Incrementally updating the PageRank calculation is an important practical problem: you somehow want to use the old values and take into account changes to the web—both new pages (called *node updates*) and new links on old pages (*link updates*). There are ways of doing this, but they don't apply on a sufficiently large scale. Perhaps an approximate updating is good enough? This is an active research area that you can be sure has received a great deal of attention in search engine companies.

The Random Surfer

There are two problems with the PageRank calculation we have described, both relating to the bow tie structure of the web depicted in Figure 3.4. You probably have a mental picture of PageRank flowing through the tangled web of Figure 4.4, coming into a page through its inlinks and leaving it through its outlinks. What if there are no inlinks (page **H**)? Or no outlinks (page **G**)?

To operationalize this picture, imagine a web surfer who clicks links at random. If he (or she, but perhaps young males are more likely to exhibit such obsessive behavior) is on a page with a certain number of outlinks, he chooses one at random and goes to that link's target page. The probability of taking any particular link is smaller if there are many outlinks, which is exactly the behavior we want from PageRank. It turns out that the PageRank of a given page is proportional to the probability that the random surfer lands on that page.

Now the problem raised by a page with no outlinks (**G**) becomes apparent: it's a PageRank sink because when the surfer comes in, he cannot get out. More generally, a set of pages might link to each other but not to anywhere else. This incestuous group is also a PageRank sink: the random surfer gets stuck in a trap. He has reached the corporate continent.

And a page with no inlinks (**H**)? The random surfer never reaches it. In fact, he never reaches any group of pages that has no inlinks from the rest of the web, even though it may have internal links, and outlinks to the web at large. He never visits the new archipelago.

These two problems mean that the iterative calculation described earlier does not converge, as we earlier claimed it would. But the solution is simple: *teleportation*. With a certain small probability, just make the surfer arrive at a randomly chosen web page instead of following a link from the one he is on. That solves both problems. If he's stuck in the corporate continent, he will eventually teleport out of it. And if he can't reach the new archipelago by surfing, he will eventually teleport into it.

The teleport probability has a strong influence on the rate of convergence of the iterative algorithm—and on the accuracy of its results. At the extreme, if it were equal to 1, meaning that the surfer always teleported, the link structure of the web would have no effect on PageRank, and no iteration would be necessary. If it were 0 and the surfer never teleported, the calculation would not converge at all. Early published experiments used a teleportation probability of 0.15; some speculate that search engines increase it a little to hasten convergence.

Instead of teleporting to a randomly chosen page, you could choose a predetermined probability for each page, and—once you had decided to teleport—use that probability to determine where to land. This does not affect the calculation. But it does affect the result. If a page were discriminated against by receiving a smaller probability than the others, it would end up with a smaller PageRank than it deserves. This gives search engine operators an opportunity to influence the results of the calculation—an opportunity that they probably use to discriminate against certain sites (e.g., ones they believe are trying to gain an unfair advantage by exploiting the PageRank system). As we will see in Chapter 6, this is the stuff of which lawsuits are made.

COMBINING PRESTIGE AND RELEVANCE

For a one-word query, we have suggested locating all pages that contain the word and returning them in order of prestige, that is, PageRank. But what about the number of occurrences of the word: shouldn't that be taken into account? And, more importantly, what about multiword queries? Ordinary ranked retrievals treat multiword queries as OR queries and calculates the cosine measure for each document to determine its relevance. The prestige model suggests sorting retrieved documents by PageRank instead.

Because the web is so vast, popular search engines treat all queries as AND queries, so that every returned page contains all the search terms. However, that does not solve the problem: there is still the question of how many times the search terms appear in each page. Moreover, search engines modulate the influence of terms in the page using a number of heuristics. A word appearance is more important if it

- occurs in anchor text
- occurs in the title tag
- occurs in the document's URL
- occurs in an HTML heading
- occurs in capital letters
- occurs in a larger font than the rest of the document
- occurs early on in the document
- occurs in an HTML metatag

And a set of query terms is more influential if the terms

- appear close together
- appear in the right order
- appear as a phrase

Actually, this is all guesswork. No one knows the precise set of factors used by search engines. Some guesses are likely to be wrong, or change over time. For example, in an ideal world, words in HTML metatags ought to be especially important, because they are designed to help characterize the content of the document. But in the web's early days, tags were widely misused to give an erroneous impression of what the document was about. Today's search engines may treat them as more influential, or less, or ignore them, or even use them as negative evidence. Who knows? Only insiders.

All these factors are combined with the PageRank of the returned document—which clearly plays a dominant role—into a single measure, and this is used to sort documents for presentation to the user. The recipe is a closely guarded secret—think of it as the crown jewels of the search engine company—and, as we will learn in the next chapter, changes from one month to the next to help fight spam.

HUBS AND AUTHORITIES

The PageRank concept was invented by Google founders Larry Page and Sergey Brin in 1998, and its success was responsible for elevating Google to the position of the world's preeminent search engine. According to the Google website, "the heart of our software is PageRank...it provides the basis for all of our web search tools." An alternative, also invented in 1998, was developed by leading computer science academic Jon Kleinberg. Called HITS, for Hypertext-Induced Topic Selection, it has the same self-referential character as PageRank, but the details are intriguingly different. Though their work proceeded independently, Page/Brin's and Kleinberg's papers cite each other.

Whereas PageRank is a single measure of the prestige of each page, HITS divides pages into two classes: hubs and authorities. A hub has many outlinks; a good hub contains a list of useful resources on a single topic. An authority has many inlinks and constitutes a useful source document. Good hubs point to good authorities; conversely, good authorities are pointed to by good hubs. In Figure 4.4, page **F** looks like a good authority, while **A** may be a good hub.

In this model, each page has two measures, hub score and authority score. The hub score is the sum of the authority scores of all the pages it links to. The authority score is the sum of the hub scores of all the pages that link to it. Although—like PageRank—this sounds circular, the solution can be formulated as a problem in linear algebra based on the web's connection matrix, that gargantuan array of 1s and 0s mentioned earlier.

FINDING HUBS AND AUTHORITIES FOR A QUERY

The HITS method uses the formulation in a rather different way from PageRank. Instead of applying it once and for all to the whole web, it computes hub and authority scores that are particular to the query at hand. Given a query, a set of related pages is determined as follows. First, all pages that contain the query terms are located and placed in the set. Next, the pages that are linked to by these original set members (that is, have inlinks from them), and the pages that the original set members link to (the ones they have outlinks to), are added to the set. The process could be continued, adding neighbors linked in two steps, three steps, and so on, but in practice the set is probably quite large enough already. Indeed, it may be too large: perhaps, though all query-term pages were included, only the first 100 pages that each one points to should be added, along with the first 100 pages that point to each query-term page.

The result is a subgraph of the web called the *neighborhood graph* of the query. For each of its pages, hub and authority scores are derived using the same kind of iterative algorithm that we described earlier for PageRank. Mathematical analysis shows that division into hubs and authorities sidesteps some of the PageRank algorithm's convergence problems—problems that the teleportation option was introduced to solve. However, lesser convergence problems can still arise, and similar solutions apply. Of course, the computational load is far smaller than the PageRank calculation because we are dealing with a tiny subset of the web. On the other hand, the work must be redone for every query, rather than once a month as for PageRank.

A nice feature of HITS is that it helps with synonyms. A classic problem of information retrieval is that many queries do not return pertinent documents, merely because they use slightly different terminology. For example, search engines like Google do not return a page unless it contains all the query terms. HITS includes other pages in the neighborhood graph—pages that are linked to by query-term pages, and pages that link to query-term pages. This greatly increases the chance of pulling in pages containing synonyms of the query terms. It also increases the chance of pulling in other relevant pages. To borrow an example from Kleinberg, there is no reason to expect that Toyota's or Honda's home pages should contain the term *automobile manufacturers*, yet they are very much authoritative pages on the subject.

USING HUBS AND AUTHORITIES

The user will find the list of hubs and authorities for her query very useful. What the algorithm has computed is a hub score and an authority score for every page in the neighborhood graph—which includes every page containing all the query terms. Those with the highest authority scores should be the best authorities on the query, even though they do not necessarily contain all (or indeed any) of the query terms. Those with the highest hub scores will be useful for finding links related to the query. Depending on the application, hubs may be even more useful than authorities. Sometimes there is nothing more valuable than a good reading list.

One obvious drawback of HITS is the computational load. Whereas PageRank is query-independent, HITS is not. It seems far easier to undertake an offline calculation of PageRank every few weeks than to compute hubs and authorities dynamically for every query. And PageRank, a general measure of the prestige of each page, is useful for many other purposes—for example, it's an obvious yardstick for deciding which sites to crawl more frequently in an incremental update. On the other hand, HITS does not need incremental updates: hubs and authorities are computed afresh for every query. (In practice, though, caching is used for frequent queries.)

HITS is easier to spam than PageRank. Simply adding to your web page outlinks that point to popular pages will increase its hub score. From a web page owner's point of view, it is far easier to add outlinks than inlinks, which are what PageRank uses. For a more systematic spam attack, first you create a good hub by linking to many popular pages. Then, you populate it with lots of different words to maximize its chance of being selected for a query. Having created a few good hubs, you create a good authority by pointing the hubs at them. To make matters worse (or, depending on your point of view, better), HITS does not offer the search engine operator the opportunity to combat spam by tweaking the teleportation probability vector. However, an advantage of HITS is that it is more transparent than PageRank because it doesn't involve a secret recipe for combining relevance with prestige.

HITS suffers from a problem called *topic drift*. If the pages selected for a query happen to contain a strikingly authoritative document on a cognate topic, its rating may rise above that of more relevant documents. Suppose the query is for Sauvignon Blanc (a fine New Zealand wine). A high-quality hub page devoted to New Zealand wine might have links to Chardonnay and Pinot Noir too. If the page is a universally good hub, the pages about Chardonnay and Pinot Noir will be good authorities and will occur high up the list of search results, even though they are not really relevant to the query. In the HITS algorithm, once the neighborhood graph has been built, the query plays no further role in the calculations.

HITS can be extended with heuristics to address this problem. One might insist that returned pages be a good match to the query terms independent of their status as authorities, or identify interesting sections of web pages and use these sections to determine which other pages might be good hubs or authorities.

DISCOVERING WEB COMMUNITIES

Within a fair-sized subset of the web, it seems plausible that you could identify several different communities. Each one would contain many links to the web pages of other community members, along with a few external links. Scientific communities are a good example: biologists will tend to link to web pages of other biologists. Hobbies provide another: the home pages or blog entries of people interested in, say, skateboarding might exhibit similar link targets.

It has long been known that a simple mathematical technique—simple, that is, to mathematicians—can be used to identify clusters of self-referential nodes in a graph like the web. People call this "social network analysis," but the details involve advanced mathematical concepts that we will not explain here (eigenvalues and eigenvectors). It would be fascinating to apply these techniques to the web graph, but because of its immense size, this is completely impractical.

The fact that HITS works with a far more manageable matrix than the entire web opens the door to new possibilities. The hub and authority scores found by the iterative algorithm we have described represent the structure of just one of the communities—the dominant one. Other techniques can be used to calculate alternative sets of hub/authority scores, many of which represent particular identifiable subcommunities of the original set of web pages. These might give more focused results for the user's query.

Consider the neighborhood graph for the Sauvignon Blanc query mentioned earlier, and recall that pages containing the query terms have been augmented by adding linking and linked-to pages as well. It might include many pages from a New Zealand wine community, as well as subcommunities for

Sauvignon Blanc, Chardonnay, and Pinot Noir—and perhaps for individual wine-growing regions too. Each community has its own hubs and authorities. Rather than simply returning a list of search results, a query gives an entrée into the entire space, created on the fly by the search engine. The original broad topic is distilled—an appropriate metaphor for this example—into subtopics, and high-quality pages are identified for each one.

Is it really feasible for a search engine to do all this work in response to a single user's query? Are social network algorithms efficient enough to operate on the fly? A 1999 research project reported that it took less than a minute of computation to process each query—fast, but nowhere near fast enough to satisfy impatient users, and far beyond what a mass-market search engine could afford. Of course, just how search engines work is a closely guarded secret. This is why mathematicians expert in matrix computation suddenly became hot property.

The Teoma search engine, at the core of the Ask web search service, organizes websites relevant to a query into naturally occurring communities that relate to the query topic.[30] These communities are presented under a *Refine* heading on the results page, and allow users to further focus their search. According to Teoma's website, a search for *Soprano* would present the user with a set of refinement suggestions such as *Marie-Adele McArthur* (a renowned New Zealand soprano), *Three Sopranos* (the operatic trio), *The Sopranos* (a megapopular U.S. television show), and several other choices. In practice, however, many of the subcommunities that Teoma identifies are not so clear-cut.

As with any HITS-based technique, the search results include hubs and authorities for the query. Authorities are listed in the form of conventional search results—documents that satisfy the query. Hubs are portrayed as a set of resources: sites that point to other authoritative sites and give links relating to the search topic. The Teoma website mentions an example of a professor of Middle Eastern history who has created a page devoted to his collection of websites that explain the geography and topography of the Persian Gulf. That page would appear under the heading *Resources* in response to a Persian Gulf–related query.

There has been a great deal of discussion about how well the method described earlier works. Does it really discover good and useful communities? Examples of anomalous results abound. For instance, at one time a search for *jaguar* reputedly converged to a collection of sites about the city of Cincinnati, because many online articles in the local newspaper discuss the Jacksonville Jaguars football team, and all link to the same *Cincinnati Enquirer* service pages. The HITS method ranks authorities based on the structure of the neighborhood graph as a whole, which tends to favor the authorities of tightly

---

[30] Teoma is Gaelic for "expert."

knit communities. An alternative is to rank authorities based on their popularity in their immediate neighborhood, which favors authorities from different communities.

BIBLIOMETRICS

Some of the ideas underlying both PageRank and HITS echo techniques used in bibliometrics, a field that analyzes the citation or cross-reference structure of printed literature. Scientists are ranked on the basis of the citations that their papers attract. In general, the more citations your papers receive from highly ranked scientists, the greater your prestige. But citations carry more weight if they come from someone who links to a few select colleagues. Even a mention by a Nobel Prize winner counts for little if that person tends to cite copiously. There's also a parallel to teleporting: scientists with no citations at all still deserve a nonzero rank.

The *impact factor*, calculated each year by the Institute for Scientific Information (ISI) for a large set of scientific journals, is a widely used measure of a journal's importance. Impact factors have a huge, though controversial, influence on the way published research is perceived and evaluated. The impact factor for a journal in a given year is defined as the average number of citations received by papers published in that journal over the previous two years, where citations are counted over all the journals that ISI tracks. In our terms, it is based on a pure counting of inlinks.

More subtle measures have been proposed, based on the observation that not all citations are equally important. Some have argued that a journal is influential if it is heavily cited by other influential journals—a circular definition just like the one we used earlier for "prestige." The connection strength from one journal to another is the fraction of the first journal's citations that go to papers in the second. In concrete terms, a journal's measure of standing, called its *influence weight*, is the sum of the influence weights of all journals that cite it, each one weighted by the connection strength. This is essentially the same as the recursive definition of PageRank (without the problem of pages with no inlinks or no outlinks). The random surfer model applies to influence weights too: starting with an arbitrary journal, you choose a random reference appearing in it and move to the journal specified in the reference. A journal's influence weight is the proportion of time spent in that journal.

What about HITS? The scientific literature is governed by quite different principles than the World Wide Web. Scientific journals have a common purpose and a tradition of citation (enforced by the peer review process), which ensures that prestigious journals on a common topic reference one another extensively. This justifies a one-level model in which authorities directly endorse other authorities. The web, on the other hand, is heterogeneous, and its pages serve countless different functions. Moreover, the strongest authorities rarely link directly to one another—either they are in completely different domains, or they are direct competitors. There are no links from Toyota's website to Honda's, despite the fact that they have much in common. They are interconnected by an intermediate layer of relatively anonymous hub pages, which link to a thematically related set of authorities. This two-level linkage pattern exposes structure between the hubs, which are likely unaware of one another's existence, and authorities, which may not wish to acknowledge one another for commercial reasons.

LEARNING TO RANK

Analyzing huge networks containing immense amounts of implicit information will remain a fertile research area for decades to come. Today it is bubbling with activity—which is not surprising, considering that the search engine business is populated by a mixture of mathematicians and multimillionaires. The only thing we can be sure of is that radical new methods will appear, perhaps ousting today's megadragons. The book is by no means closed on search engine technology.

One way of tackling the problem of how to rank web pages is to use techniques of machine learning. First, create a "training set" with many examples of documents that contain the terms in a query, along with human judgments about how relevant they are to that query. Then, a learning algorithm analyzes this training data and comes up with a way to predict the relevance judgment for any document and query. This is used to rank queries in the future.

There is no magic in machine learning: these are perfectly straightforward algorithms that take a set of training data and produce a way of calculating judgments on new data. This calculation typically uses numeric weights to combine different features of the document—for example, the features listed earlier (page 118) when discussing how prestige and relevance are combined into a single page rank value. It might simply multiply each numeric feature value by its weight and add them all together. The weights reflect the relative importance of each feature, and training data are used to derive suitable values for them, values that produce a good approximation to the relevance judgments assigned to the training examples by human evaluators. Of course, we want the system to work well not just for the training data, but for all other documents and queries too.

We cannot produce a different set of weights for each query—there are an infinite number of them. Instead, for each document, a set of feature values is calculated that depends on the query term—for example, how often it appears in anchor text, whether it occurs in the title tag, whether it occurs in the document's URL, and how often it occurs in the document itself. And for multiterm queries, values could include how often two different terms appear close together in the document, and so on. The list mirrors that on page 118. There are many possible features: typical algorithms for learning ranks use several hundred of them—let's say a thousand. Given a query, a thousand feature values are computed for every document that contains the query terms and are combined to yield its ranking. They may just be weighted and added together. Some machine learning techniques combine them in ways that are a bit more complex than this, but the principle remains the same.

The trick is to derive the one thousand weights from the training data in a way that yields a good approximation to actual human judgments. There are many different techniques of machine learning. Microsoft's MSN search engine uses a technique called RankNet which employs a "neural net" learning scheme. Despite its brainy anthropomorphic name, this need not be any more complex than calculating a weight for each feature and summing them up as described earlier.

Although the actual details of how MSN employs RankNet are a commercial secret, the basic idea was described in a 2005 paper by Microsoft researchers. Given a query, they calculated 600 features for each document. They assembled a training set of 17,000 queries, with almost 1000 documents for each one. Human evaluators judged the relevance of a few of the documents that contained the query terms on a scale of 1 ("poor match") to 5 ("excellent match"), but for each query an average of only about 10 documents were labeled. The majority of queries and documents were used for training, and the remainder were kept aside for independent testing. Evaluation focused on assessing the quality of ranking on the top 15 documents returned, on the basis that most users rarely examine lower-ranked documents. The authors conclude that, even using the simple weighted linear sum described earlier, the system yields excellent performance on a real-world ranking problem with large amounts of data. If more complex ways were used to combine the features, performance was better still.

The clever part was the way the training data were used. Given a query and a document, values are calculated for all 600 features. The set of 600 numbers is a single training example. The innovative feature of the learning method was to take pairs of training examples with the same query but different documents. Each example has a relevance judgment between 1 and 5, and the essential feature of an example pair is not the particular values—after all, they are on an arbitrary scale—but which of the pair is ranked higher than the other. Pairing up examples had the twin effect of greatly multiplying the number of different inputs, and eliminating the arbitrariness of the rating scale. Although the details are beyond the scope of this book, this ingenious idea allowed the researchers to thoroughly train the neural net on what was, compared with the size of the web, a puny example set.

Learning techniques have the potential to continually improve their performance as new data are gathered from the users of a search engine. Suppose a query is posed, and the user picks some of the documents that are returned and indicates "I like these ones," perhaps even giving them a score, and picks others and clicks a button to say "These are red herrings." This provides new training data for the learning algorithm, which can be used offline to improve the ranking method by altering the weights to give better performance.

Judgments of which documents are approved and disapproved gives a rich set of additional information for the search engine to use. In practice, harried users are hardly likely to give explicit feedback about every document in the search results. However, information can be gleaned from the user's subsequent behavior. Which documents does he click on, how long does he dwell on each one? Are her needs satisfied, or does she return to search again? There is a lot of information here, information that could be used to improve search performance in general. It could also be used to improve results for specific searches. As we will learn shortly, typical queries are not unique but are issued many times—sometimes hundreds of thousands of times—by different users. The subsequent behavior of each user could be integrated to provide an enormous volume of information about which documents best satisfy that particular query.

You might object that once you have made a query, search engines do not get to see your subsequent behavior. However, they could very well intercept the clicks you make on the search results page: it's not hard to arrange to return information about which link is clicked by redirecting the link back through the search engine's own site. Still, it seems hard for them to determine information about your subsequent behavior: how long you spend with each document, or what you do next. But that depends. Who wrote the web browser? Have you downloaded the Google toolbar (a browser add-on)? If the outcome improves the results of your searches, you might well be prepared to share this information with the dragons. After all, you're sharing your queries.

Full-text search, the classic method of retrieval, uses information supplied by authors—the document text. Link analysis, the innovation of Google and company, uses information supplied by other authors—the links. User feedback, perhaps the next wave, uses information supplied by users—readers, not writers. It's potentially far more powerful because it is these end users, not the authors, who are actually doing the searching.

DISTRIBUTING THE INDEX

How search engines deliver the goods is one of the marvels of our world. Full-text search is an advanced technology, the kind you learn about in computer science graduate school. Although the concepts are simple, making them work in practice is tricky. Leading search engines deal with many thousands of queries per second and aim to respond to each one in half a second or less. That's fast! Though computers may be quick, this presents great challenges. Leading search engines deal with many terabytes—even petabytes—of text. That's big! Though disks may be large and cheap, organizing information on this scale is daunting. But the real problem is that with computers, time and space interact. If you keep everything in main memory, things go fast. If you put it on disk, they can be big. But not both together.

Couple full-text searching with link analysis: searching in a web. We have already seen the general idea, but heavy theory lurks behind. This involves a different set of skills, the kind you learn about in math graduate school. Calculating PageRank is hard enough, but building the neighborhood graph's connection matrix and analyzing it to determine communities require sophisticated techniques. Combining prestige and relevance, and finding good ways to take into account the various types and styles of text, involve tedious experimentation with actual queries and painstaking evaluation of actual search results. All these variables will affect your company's bottom line tomorrow, in a hotly competitive market.

An even greater technical marvel than fast searching and web analysis is the standard of responsiveness and reliability set by search engines. They involve tens or hundreds of thousands of interlinked computers. In part, speed and reliability are obtained by having separate sites operate independently. If the lights go out in California, the site in Texas is unaffected. Your query is automatically routed to one of these sites in a way that balances the load between them, and if one is down, the others silently share its burden.

At each site, the index and the cached web pages are divided into parts and shared among many different computers—thousands of them. Specially designed supercomputers are uneconomical; it's cheaper to buy vast arrays of standard machines at discount prices. Each one resembles an ordinary office workstation, loaded with as much memory and disk as it can hold in the standard way without going to special hardware. But the machines are not boxed like office workstations; they are naked and mounted en masse in custom-designed racks.

Creating and operating the network presents great challenges. Most search engine companies (except Microsoft) probably use the Linux operating system—Google certainly does. Wherever possible, they use open source software—for databases, for compressing the text, for processing the images, for the countless routine tasks that must be undertaken to maintain the service to users.

When you have ten thousand computers, you must expect many failures. One calendar day times ten thousand corresponds to 30 years, a human generation. How many times does your computer fail in a generation? With so many machines, you must plan for a hundred failures every day. The system monitors itself, notices wounds, isolates them, and informs headquarters.

Its human operators are kept busy swapping out complete units and replacing them with new ones. Since you must plan for failure anyway, why not buy cheaper, less reliable machines, with cheaper, less reliable memory?

DEVELOPMENTS IN WEB SEARCH

There are many developments in the air that could radically affect the search process. Web pages are beginning to be expressed in different ways. The HTML and XML languages described in the last chapter, and the way that servers can process them, have turned out to be extraordinarily flexible and are beginning to be employed in new ways as web usage evolves. We will briefly introduce three trends that are affecting (or will affect) how search works: blogs, a lightweight way of supporting commentary and collaboration intro- duced in Chapter 3 (page 76); AJAX, a new technical way of making web pages more interactive by breaking them down into small pieces; and—by far the most ambitious—the semantic web, a vision of how automated computer "agents" could be provided with the same kind of web services as human users are today. These are just examples of forthcoming changes in how the World Wide Web will work.

SEARCHING BLOGS

Searching the "blogosphere"—for that's what bloggers call their information environment—is similar to searching the web, with two exceptions. First, freshness of information plays a crucial role. Most blog retrieval systems allow users to indicate whether to sort results by relevance or by date. In this domain, only recent entries are regarded as important information.

Second, blog authors usually attach metadata tags to their entries to describe the subject under discussion. (Blog entries also include *trackbacks*, which are links to other sites that refer to that entry, and a *blogroll*, which is a list of other blogs read by the author.) This metadata can be exploited when searching to make it easier to retrieve relevant blogs on a particular topic.[31] However, as blogging spreads, so does the lack of agreement on the meaning of tags. Free and easy tagging is becoming a mixed blessing: on one hand, the simplicity of annotation encourages the assignment of metadata, while on the other, tags become ineffective at retrieval time because there is no standardiza- tion of terms. We return to this dilemma when discussing folksonomies in Chapter 7 (page 231).

---

[31] For example, Technorati (*www.technorati.com*) performs retrieval on author-defined subject tags.

AJAX TECHNOLOGY

AJAX, an acronym for "asynchronous JavaScript and XML," is growing ever more popular as we write. While the details are shrouded in technospeak, think of it as a way of updating little bits of web pages without having to re-download the whole page. When you click on links in websites today, whole new pages are downloaded—and web crawlers emulate this in order to find pages to index. However, if the link is an internal one, much of the page content may remain the same and shouldn't have to be retransmitted—such as all the branding and navigation information. With AJAX, the web server can arrange to download just that little piece of information that does change, and slot it into the right place on the existing page. Web browsers are powerful pieces of software, quite capable of doing this. The result is a far more reactive system, with faster access—it feels as though things are happening locally on your machine instead of remotely over the web.

This idea is likely to be widely adopted: we return to it in Chapter 7, when we talk about future developments, and predict that you will ultimately use the web as a global office. (Google already uses AJAX in its GMail system.) AJAX has immense implications for the search environment. Websites will send information to your browser in little nuggets, not as fully contextualized pages. Should nuggets be indexed individually, or in the context of the page in which they occur? Which would you prefer? These are issues for the search engine gurus to ponder.

THE SEMANTIC WEB

The web was made for people, conceived as a universal library in which we read, write, and organize our thoughts. It is not a congenial environment for machines that aspire to work alongside humans. Again and again in this book, we have come up against the same limitation. The dragons, and other systems that mediate access to knowledge on the web, simply do not understand what you are talking about. More to the point, they don't understand what the web page you are reading is talking about either.

Remember that delicious dessert you ate when you visited the Tyrol? If you asked your landlady or concierge there—or any person of a certain age—how to make the popular local pastry, they would immediately know you were talking about apple strudel and give you the recipe. Try that on the web! No problem if you remember the name, but otherwise you must rely on luck, perseverance, and considerable skill.

This is a situation that requires you to make an inference to come up with the answer. First, find the name of the most popular Tyrolean dessert; then, seek the recipe. Today's dragons do not perform reasoning, even at this modest level of sophistication. The first part is the hard bit, but the web's resources can be brought to bear on this kind of problem. An agent connects to a search engine through a back door, poses a query, downloads the responses, and processes the text to ascertain the necessary information. Just as people access web applications over the Internet to obtain and process information, so can machines, through what are called *web services*. For this to succeed in general on a large scale, we must clarify how the machines are to exchange knowledge.

The *semantic web* is an attempt to enrich web pages so that machines can cooperate to perform inferences in the way that people do. Computers find human inference hard to emulate because of the difficulty of processing natural language—anyone who has written a program to extract information from text knows this all too well. On the other hand, there is a compelling motivation to equip machines to perform tasks by exploiting the treasure of information on the web. The idea behind the semantic web is to give information a well-defined meaning specifically in order to enable interaction among machines. Today's web is for people; tomorrow's semantic web will be for machines too.

We have explained in Chapter 3 (page 78) how the extensible markup language (XML) can be used to embed structured data in a document, alongside the unstructured text. This is the first step toward incorporating information specifically aimed at facilitating mechanical interpretation. The second is to exploit the flexibility of the web's mechanism for identifying resources. A Universal Resource Identifier (URI) can be given to anything, not just web pages, and anything with a URI can become the subject of reasoning on the semantic web. A further level of abstraction is achieved by describing relationships between resources in a way that can be processed by machines.

Consider this three-part statement:

```
<http://www.everwonder.com/david/felixthecat/>
<http://love.example.org/terms/reallyLikes>
<http://fishhead.homestead.com/>
```

It's not difficult to guess its meaning. The first URI is the subject of the statement, namely, the web page on Felix the cat. The second is a predicate that relates the subject to the object, represented by the third. The predicate expresses the meaning, which is that Felix likes fish. This way of describing relations between resources is called the Resource Description Framework, or RDF, and provides a simple way to express statements about web resources.

RDF statements can claim nearly anything—even contradictions. The preceding example was expressed as a triple, in which URIs identify the subject, predicate, and object. Unlike web pages, a collection of statements expressed in this way presents a clear structure. When browsing pages about Felix, people readily learn that the cat likes fishing. Although machines cannot interpret the text, the RDF statement expresses the same information. However, just as the page's text does not explain the meaning of the terms it employs, neither does the RDF. To make use of the information, we must describe what subject, predicate, and object mean.

The semantic web accomplishes this using *ontologies*. The word derives from Greek *onto* and *logia*, meaning "being" and "written or spoken discourse." An ontology is a formal description of the concepts and relationships that can exist for a community of agents. Recall from Chapter 1 Wittgenstein's obsession with the social nature of language, the fact that language is inseparable from community. Now the community includes computers—programmed agents. A formal description is what is needed to allow machines to work with concepts and relationships, and build bridges among related concepts. Machines can then interpret these statements and draw conclusions—perhaps putting the result of their deliberations back on the web.

The semantic web is a huge challenge, conceived by Tim Berners-Lee, the father of the web. If successful, it will open the door to a panoply of new web applications. However, its growth has been throttled by the effort needed to create RDF statements and ontologies. The web's new form may not share the elegant simplicity that underpins the original design and fuelled its explosion into our lives.

The semantic web envisions a paradigm shift. The emphasis is no longer on documents alone, but on documents backed up with fragments of data arranged to support automated reasoning. The new web will not be for people only, but for machines too, which will join with people in new partnerships. If the dream comes to fruition, its impact will extend far beyond the dragons and into our daily lives. It will bring the web one step closer to real life—or vice versa.

BIRTH OF THE DRAGONS

The Internet opened for business in 1973 when the U.S. Defense Advanced Research Projects Agency (DARPA) began a research program designed to allow computers to communicate transparently across multiple networks. The early Internet was used by computer experts, engineers, and scientists. There were no home or office computers, and the system was arcane and complex to use. You could only access a computer on the network if you had an account on it, in which case you could log in remotely. As a goodwill gesture, many sites provided guest accounts that were open to all, but these had few privileges and there was little you could do.

The first modern file transfer protocol (FTP) was defined in 1980, following early efforts dating back to the beginning of the Internet. At first, you needed an account on the remote computer to transfer files from it, but in another friendly gesture, an "anonymous" variant was developed. Anyone could open up anonymous FTP on a remote computer that supported it and take a look at what files it made available. (For resource reasons, you couldn't transfer files *to* sites anonymously.)

There was no way to find anything unless you already knew where it was, and what the file was called. Nevertheless, at last this vast network of computers was able to do something useful for people who were not affiliated with the big projects that provided accounts on remote computers. You could put your files up under anonymous FTP on your computer, tell your friends, and they could download them. But it wasn't easy: the commands for using the file transfer protocol were (and still are) arcane and nerdy.

THE WOMB IS PREPARED

Now all the structure was in place to support the automatic creation of an index, and there was a growing need for one—for there was no way to find anything in the FTP jungle except by asking people. In 1989, a group at McGill University in Canada wrote a program that automatically connected to FTP sites, which were commonly called "archives," and built up a directory of what files were there. They supplied it with a set of sites and let it loose. It updated the directory by reconnecting to each site once a month, politely avoiding soaking up excessive resources on other people's computers. The program was called Archie, an abbreviation for *archives*—although it did not download or archive the files themselves, but only listed their names. To search the directory for a file of a particular name, or whose name matched a particular pattern of characters, you again had to use arcane commands. But with patience and computer expertise, you could now find things.

Two years later, a more usable substrate was developed for the files that were proliferating on the publicly accessible Internet. Originally designed to give access to information in files on the University of Minnesota's local network, it was called Gopher, after the University mascot. Built on a simple protocol that allowed distributed access to documents on many servers, Gopher presented users with a menu of items and folders much like a hierarchical file system. Menu items could point to resources on other computers. At last, you could look at the Internet without being a computer expert: you just typed or clicked on a number to indicate the desired menu selection. Selecting a file downloaded it; selecting a folder took you to its files—which could be on another computer.

This software was distributed freely and became very popular. Within a few years, there were more than 10,000 Gophers around the world. But in 1993, the University of Minnesota announced that they would charge licensing fees to companies that used it for commercial purposes, which some believe stifled its development. (They later relented, relicensing it as free, open-source software.)

Archie had to be provided with an explicit list of sites to index. But Gopher links could point to other computers, paving the way for an automatically produced directory of files on different sites. And the ease that Gopher brought to navigation inspired a similar menu-based scheme to access the directory. A radical and whimsically named scheme called Veronica—ostensibly an acronym for "Very Easy Rodent-Oriented Netwide Index to Computerized Archives" but actually the name of Archie's girlfriend in the well-known comic strip—crawled Gopher menus around the world, collecting links for the directory. It was a constantly updated database of the names of every menu item on thousands of Gopher servers. News of Veronica spread like wildfire from the University of Nevada at Reno, where it was created. The service rapidly became so popular that it was difficult to connect to—the first of many "flash crowds" on the Internet—and sister sites were developed to spread the load. Meanwhile, acronym creativity ran rampant, and Archie's best friend Jughead entered the arena as Jonzy's Universal Gopher Hierarchy Excavation And Display, providing a Veronica-like directory for single sites.

Across the Atlantic Ocean, the World Wide Web was in the crucible at CERN, the European Laboratory for Particle Physics. Sir Tim Berners-Lee, knighted in 2004 by Queen Elizabeth for his services to the global development of the Internet, proposed a new protocol for information distribution in 1989, which was refined and announced as the World Wide Web in 1991. This was an alternative to Gopher's menu-oriented navigation scheme, and it eradicated the distinction between documents and menus. Menus could be enriched with free text and formatting commands, making them into documents. Conversely, links to other documents could be embedded within a document. Hypertext was an active research area at the time, and the web was a simple form of hypertext that exploded onto the scene like a supernova in left field, blinding every player and all but obliterating the hypertext research community.

Uptake was slow at first, because Berners-Lee's software only worked on the soon-to-be-obsolete NeXT computer, and although browsers for other platforms soon appeared, the early ones did not allow images to be displayed. Its rapid uptake in the mid-1990s is attributed to the emergence of the Mosaic web browser, followed by Netscape Navigator, a commercial version.

THE DRAGONS HATCH

As the World Wide Web became established, a clutch of search engines hatched, built mostly by creative students who were just playing around. The first crawler was the World Wide Web Wanderer in 1993, whose purpose was not to index the web, but to measure its growth. It caused controversy by hogging network bandwidth, downloading pages so rapidly that servers crashed. In response to these problems, Aliweb—whose expansion, "Archie-Like Index of the Web," betrays its inspiration—was created and still lives today. Instead of automatic crawling, Aliweb invited users to submit web pages along with their own description. By year's end, these two were joined by JumpStation, which gathered the title and header from web pages and used a simple linear search to retrieve items. (The part-time product of a junior systems administrator at Stirling University in Scotland, JumpStation was abruptly terminated when some prestigious U.S. institutions complained to the university's Director of Computing Services about mysterious downloads.) The World Wide Web Worm built a proper search index and so became the first scalable search engine. These early systems all listed search results in whatever order they had crawled the sites.

In 1994, full-text indexing began. The first to index entire web pages was WebCrawler. Soon followed Lycos, which provided relevance ranking of search results and other features such as prefix matching and word proximity. An early leader in search technology and web coverage, by late 1996 Lycos had indexed a record 60 million pages. Begun at Carnegie Mellon University, Lycos went commercial in 1995 and public in 1996. Infoseek also began in 1994. The search engine Hotbot was introduced in 1996 using software from Inktomi, written by two Berkeley students. In 1997, Ask Jeeves and Northern Light were launched.

OpenText, another early system, taught search operators a sharp lesson. It quickly sank into obscurity when it introduced a "preferred listings" scheme that allowed you to gain exposure by purchasing the top spot for a query. You chose a term and it guaranteed your website priority listing whenever a user sought that term. Ever since, most search engines have taken great care to distinguish advertisements from search results and to make it clear to the public that placement in the search results cannot be bought. Of course, users have no way of checking this: search engine companies trade on trust. Did you know that publishers pay Amazon to have their books listed first in response to user's queries?

Unlike most search engines, AltaVista ("a view from above") did not originate in a university project. It was developed by the computer manufacturer Digital Equipment Corporation and was designed to showcase their new Alpha range of computers. A public advertisement of the product, it was engineered for extreme responsiveness and reliability, a hallmark of the search engine business today. AltaVista was backed up by computing resources of unprecedented size and an exceptionally fast Internet connection. It opened its doors to the public in December 1995 with an index of 16 million web pages. Its astounding speed immediately made it the market leader, a favorite of information professionals and casual users alike—a position it held for years. It started to decline with the advent of Google and with changes in its parent company's business direction. Eventually spun off as an independent company intending to go public, it was instead acquired by an Internet investment company. Relaunched in 2002, it offered some innovative features—including BabelFish, an automatic translation service for web pages. It was purchased in 2003 for a small fraction of its valuation three years earlier and is now part of the Yahoo empire.

Google led a second generation of search engines that adopted the revolutionary new idea of looking beyond a document's text to determine where to place it in the search results. Until Google's appearance in 1998, search engines followed the classic model of information retrieval: to see whether a document is a good match to a query, you need only look inside the document itself. The new insights were that you can help determine what a page is about by examining the links into it, and—even more importantly—you can assess its prestige by analyzing the web matrix.

THE BIG FIVE

Search engines were the brightest stars in the Internet investing frenzy of the late 1990s. Several companies made spectacular market entries with record gains during their initial public offerings. Now, most have dismantled their public search engine and concentrate on behind-the-firewall search products for large companies. From this market shakedown, five major players remained in 2005: Google, Yahoo, MSN Search, AOL, and Ask. This list is in order of their mid-2006 popularity in searches per day in the United States: Google with 49 percent, followed by Yahoo with 23 percent, MSN with 10 percent, AOL with 7 percent, and Ask with 2 percent, leaving 9 percent for others. At the time Google's dominance was even more apparent in the international market, with more than 60 percent of searches according to some reports.

As we mentioned when discussing PageRank, Google was founded by Stanford graduate students Larry Page and Sergey Brin. The name is a play on the word *googol*, which refers to the number represented by the digit 1 followed by 100 zeros. Google began in September 1998 in the time-honored manner of a high-tech startup, with two geeks in a garage—literally—and three months later was cited by *PC Magazine* as one of its Top 100 Web Sites and Search Engines. The news of its revolutionary PageRank technology and trademark spartan web pages spread by word of mouth among academics everywhere. Its clean, cool image was enhanced by funky colors and the cocky *I'm feeling lucky* button. Google did everything right. Once they discovered Google, people stayed with it—most still use it today. From the outset, it cultivated a trendy, quirky image, with specially designed logos to celebrate public holidays, and April Fool's jokes about pigeons pecking PageRank and a new office on the moon. During 2000, their index climbed to a billion pages, the first to reach this size, and at that time Google provided the search facility for Yahoo—as it does for AOL today. Google held on until 2004 before going public, and did so in a blaze of publicity.

Yahoo was also founded by two Stanford Ph.D. students, David Filo and Jerry Yang, who, like Larry and Sergey, are still on leave of absence from their Ph.D. program. It started in 1994 as a collection of their favorite web pages, along with a description of each one. Eventually the lists became long and unwieldy, and they broke them into categories and developed a hierarchy of subcategories. The name is a goofy acronym for "Yet Another Hierarchical Officious Oracle." Yahoo was incorporated in 1995 and went public in 1996. It acquired a team of website reviewers who visited hundreds of Internet sites daily. As the collection grew, Yahoo had to continually reorganize its structure and eventually became a searchable directory. In 2002, it acquired Inktomi and, in 2003, AltaVista. Previously powered by Google, in 2004 Yahoo launched its own search engine based on the combined technologies of its acquisitions, and provided a service that now focuses as much on searching as on the directory.

After years of planning, Microsoft finally launched its own web search service at the beginning of 2005 and stopped using Yahoo's Inktomi search engine on its main portal pages. MSN Search is a home-grown engine that allows you to search for web pages, news, products, MSN Groups, images, and encyclopaedia articles; it also offers local search with a *Near Me* button. It sports its own text ads, designed to compete directly with Google and Yahoo. Microsoft offers the 40,000 articles in its own encyclopaedia (Encarta) free with the service, in addition to 1.5 million other facts contained in Encarta. The search method is based on the machine learning approach using neural nets that was described earlier (page 125).

AOL relies on others to provide its searching. Excite, an early search engine company, bought out WebCrawler, the first full search engine, in 1997, and AOL began using Excite to power its NetFind. Since 2002, AOL Search has used Google for searching, with the same advertisements, and today a search on both systems comes up with similar matches. One operational difference is that AOL Search has an internal version that links to content only available within the AOL online service, whereas the external version lacks these links. On the other hand, it does not offer many of Google's features (such as cached pages).

Ask (which used to be called "Ask Jeeves" after Jeeves the Butler) was launched in 1997 as a natural-language search engine that sought precise answers to users' questions. After going public in 1999, the company suffered badly in the dot-com bust. However, it survived and has reinvented itself as a keyword-triggered search engine using the Teoma technology mentioned earlier, which it acquired in 2001. In July 2005, Ask Jeeves was bought by Internet media conglomerate InterActiveCorp, who renamed it by dropping *Jeeves* and rebranding its core search technology to ExpertRank.[32]

---

[32] The butler-as-personal-servant metaphor was totally missed by some users. Children see a picture of this old guy but have no idea that Jeeves is a butler, or what a butler is.

These are the leading search engines as we write. Other systems (such as Dogpile) perform metasearch by combining their results: if you pose a query, a combination of results from various search engines is returned, tagged with where they came from. There is intense interest in comparing performance; pundits speculate who is edging ahead as the dragons constantly tweak their algorithms in an ongoing multibillion-dollar competition.

One way to achieve an unbiased comparison is for a metasearch engine to route queries to a random search engine and display the results without showing their origin. The user is invited to select any of the results and rate their relevance on a scale from (say) 1 to 5. Figure 4.5(a) shows the overall scores for four search engines, displayed by such a system (in early 2006).[33] Figure 4.5(b) gives a histogram of the five rating values and shows that people tend to use the extreme ends of the scales. It is unusual to be indifferent about the quality of a search result.

The search engine business is extremely volatile. Some predict that today's big five will be ousted next week by upstarts with names like Wisenut and Gigablast—or, more likely, by something completely unheard of. Expect seismic shifts in the structure of the whole business as media giants wade in— for today, as much money is spent on web advertising as on TV advertising. Fortunately, the actual players are of minor concern to us in this book: our aim is to tease out the implications of the change in how people access information—whatever search system they use.

INSIDE THE DRAGON'S LAIR

It is hard for mortals to comprehend the scale of usage of search engines. The book you are reading contains 100,000 words. The *Complete Works of Shakespeare* is nearly 10 times as big, with 885,000 words. Taken together, the 32 volumes of the 2004 *Encyclopedia Britannica* are 40 times bigger again, with 44 million words. How many queries do large search engines process per day? Although the exact figures are not public, Google was reported to process around 100 million U.S. queries per day by mid-2006.[34] The actual number will be far larger when international traffic is taken into account. But even this figure amounts to 150 million words *per day*, assuming most queries are one or two words. Over three times the complete *Encyclopedia Britannica* every day, day after day, week after week, month after month. Throughout this section, we continue to use Google as an example, mainly because its website provides the public with some fascinating glimpses into its operation.

---

[33] RustySearch, at *www.rustybrick.com/search-engine-challenge.php*

[34] Figures from Nielsen NetRatings search engine ratings.

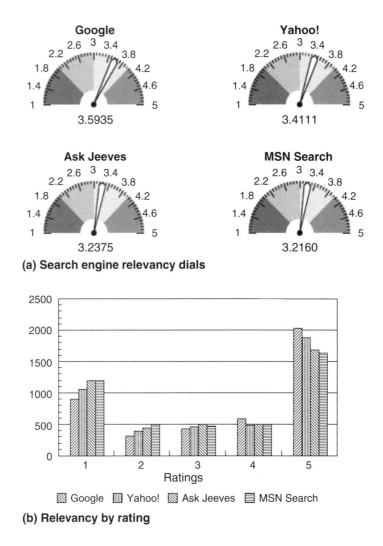

(a) Search engine relevancy dials

(b) Relevancy by rating

Figure 4.5 A comparison of search engines (early 2006).

In a typical month some years ago, according to its website, Google received 200,000 queries for *Britney Spears*. The number is staggering—that's nearly half a million words, enough to fill five full-length novels (not very interesting ones) in a month, one book a week. And these are old figures, from a time when Google was still taking off. Table 4.1 shows a few misspellings of the query, along with the number of users who spelled it this way. Each variation was entered by at least forty (!) different users within a three-month period, and was corrected to *britney spears* by Google's spelling correction system. If we had included variations entered by two or more different users, the list would

Table 4.1

Misspellings of *Britney Spears* Typed into Google

			488941	britney spears			
40134	brittany spears	544	brittaney spears	121	britainy spears	73	pritney spears
36315	brittney spears	544	brittnay spears	121	britmey spears	66	brintany spears
24342	britany spears	364	britey spears	109	brietney spears	66	britnery spears
7331	britny spears	364	brittiny spears	109	brithny spears	59	briitney spears
6633	briteny spears	329	brtney spears	109	britni spears	59	britinay spears
2696	britteny spears	269	bretney spears	109	brittant spears	54	britneay spears
1807	briney spears	269	britneys spears	98	bittney spears	54	britner spears
1635	brittny spears	244	britne spears	98	brithey spears	54	britney's spears
1479	brintey spears	244	brytney spears	98	brittiany spears	54	britnye spears
1479	britanny spears	220	breatney spears	98	btitney spears	54	britt spears
1338	britiny spears	220	britiany spears	89	brietny spears	54	brttany spears
1211	britnet spears	199	brittnney spears	89	brinety spears	48	bitany spears
1096	britiney spears	163	britnry spears	89	brintny spears	48	briny spears
991	britaney spears	147	breatny spears	89	britnie spears	48	brirney spears
991	britnay spears	147	brittiney spears	89	brittey spears	48	britant spears
811	brithney spears	147	britty spears	89	brittnet spears	48	britnety spears
811	brtiney spears	147	brotney spears	89	brity spears	48	brittanny spears
664	birtney spears	147	brutney spears	89	ritney spears	48	brttney spears
664	brintney spears	133	britteney spears	80	bretny spears	44	birttany spears
664	briteney spears	133	briyney spears	80	britnany spears	44	brittani spears
601	bitney spears	121	bittany spears	73	brinteny spears	44	brityney spears
601	brinty spears	121	bridney spears	73	brittainy spears	44	brtitney spears

have been eight times as long. Data for the correctly spelled query is shown at the top.

From the cataclysmic to the trivial, from the popular to the arcane, from the sublime to the ridiculous, the web dragons silently observe our requests for information. Nothing could be more valuable than our treasury of literature, the intellectual heritage of the human race, to which web dragons are the gate-keepers. But there is another treasure that is potentially valuable, at least in commercial terms, which the dragons hoard in their lair and guard jealously: their query logs. They certainly do not provide access to these. For one thing, people wouldn't search the web if they thought their queries were not private. Your record of requests for information reveals what you are thinking about.

It would be incredibly valuable to advertisers, private investigators, and nosy governments (we return to this in Chapter 6).

A search engine's record of all queries reveals what *everyone* is thinking about. At regular intervals, Google updates its Zeitgeist, a word that combines the German *Zeit* (time) and *Geist* (spirit) to denote the general intellectual, moral, and cultural climate of an era. At year's end, they record the most popular queries (*Janet Jackson* in 2005), popular men (*Brad Pitt*), popular women (in 2005 *Janet Jackson* overtook *Britney Spears*), popular events (*Hurricane Katrina* and *tsunami*), popular tech stuff (*xbox 360*), popular consumer brand names, television shows, sports topics, news outlets, companies, ... the list goes on. And that's just for text search. They give popular image queries, popular queries to their electronic shopping service, local search, and so on. And not just for the year: for the week and month too.

Google calls its Zeitgeist a "real-time window into the collective consciousness . . . that showcases the rising and falling stars in the search firmament as names and places flicker from obscurity to center stage and fade back again." In fact, you can now go to Google Trends and find out search trends for any query you choose.[35] On their website, Google thanks its users for their contribution to these fascinating bits of information, which, as they put it, "perhaps reveal a little of the human condition." They add that "in compiling the Zeitgeist, no individual searcher's information is available to us." Though, of course, Google has this information. The point is that it's not available *to anyone else*.

The proportion of queries in the English language has steadily dropped over the years; today over half are in other languages. Web dragons don't know only what America is thinking, they know what the whole world is thinking. Google publishes Zeitgeists for Australia, Brazil, Canada, Denmark, ... even little New Zealand. We can tell you that *muttertag* was up among the top in Germany in May, indicating Mother's Day there, and that in New Zealand *trade me*—the name of a popular electronic store there—was the top query.

When dramatic events happen across the world, they are reflected in people's requests for information. In the days after September 11, 2001, search engines were overwhelmed by queries for *World Trade Center, New York skyline, Statue of Liberty, American flag, eagle*—the last ones presumably from people seeking images for their web pages. The 2004 Boxing Day tsunami evoked a tsunami of requests for information about tidal waves and the various places struck by the tragedy. Of course, it doesn't take a search engine to learn about such cataclysmic events.

---

[35] *http://www.google.com/trends*

Smaller events—ones you would never know about—are also noticed by search engine companies. A huge flurry of people posing the four-word query *carol brady maiden name* was prompted when the million-dollar question on the popular TV show *Who Wants to Be a Millionaire?* asked, "What was Carol Brady's maiden name?" The same peak was observed one, two, and three hours later as the show aired in later time zones; another peak occurred when it finally reached Hawaii. In February 2001, Google engineers noticed a plethora of queries for the curious phrase *all your base are belong to us*. The target was a cult video game, execrably translated from the original Japanese, which swept like wildfire through an Internet subculture.

Web dragons find out what's going on, and they find it out first. They have a virtual monopoly on this information. Whereas websites and our treasury of literature reflect what the literati, the reporters, the columnists, and the academics are thinking and writing about, search engine query logs show what ordinary people—the readers—want to know. They give an objective, quantitative record of our society's concerns, day by day, week by week, month by month, year by year. This is immensely valuable information, to which only the dragons are privy.

What do they do with it? Aye, there's the rub. No one outside knows.

We can make some guesses. One practical application is to save the results of common queries to avoid having to repeat the search when they are asked again. Answering a query from scratch is far more onerous than looking up the answer in a cache. Search engines probably reap enormous benefits from this—and the ones with most to gain are those that do query-specific processing using the HITS algorithm to discover web communities. In 2001, a trivia game called "Google-whacking" appeared in which users playfully sought obscure two-word queries that could only be found in a single, unique web page. It was rumored that Google was dismayed: whereas the vast majority of ordinary queries were answered from its cache, all the obscure ones posed by Google-whackers required a full search, making them inordinately expensive.

Another application of live queries is to improve the performance of spell correction. When the user is presented with a possible alternative, success can immediately be judged by whether or not the user accepts it by clicking it.

Query logs are a veritable mine of information. Gleaning meaningful information from natural-language text is often referred to as *text mining*; the process of analyzing text to extract information that is useful for particular purposes. For example, one could segment text into sentences and cluster the words in each one to automatically induce associations between words. Mining large query logs is a wide-open area, and the nuggets found will be immensely valuable. But alas, the data are only accessible to the dragons.

SO WHAT?

In the beginning, scientists developed large-scale full-text search techniques that work by counting words, weighing them, and measuring how well each document matches the user's query. This was an appropriate way of finding information in a set of unrelated documents. However, pages on the web are not unrelated: they are densely hyperlinked. Today's search engines acknowledge this by counting links as well as words and weighing them too. This is an appropriate way of measuring the objective reality that is the web. However, the dragons do not divulge the recipe they use to weigh and combine links and words. It's not a science open to public scrutiny and debate. It's a commercial trade secret.

More fundamentally, as we will learn in the next chapter, secrecy is an unavoidable side effect of the need to maintain the illusion of an objective reality—an illusory reality that the bad guys, the spammers, are trying to distort.

WHAT CAN *YOU* DO ABOUT ALL THIS?

- Be a random surfer and see where you get.
- Find some hubs for your hobby.
- Investigate spelling correction on a major search engine. Does context matter?
- Play with a metasearch engine.
- What happened last week? Check Google's Zeitgeist.
- Find out which are the biggest dragons today.
- List the stop words in the quotation that begins Chapter 1.
- Explain why most pages returned for a query such as *using Google* don't contain the query term (Hint: Consider anchor text).
- Use the same query in different search engines and compare the results.
- Find examples of useful things the semantic web will do.

NOTES AND SOURCES

The earliest Bible concordance was constructed in the thirteenth century by Frère Hewe of S. Victor (also known as Hugo de St. Caro, or Cardinal Hugo). The Shakespeare concordance with which this chapter opened was finally published in 1875 (Clarke, 1875); coincidentally another Shakespeare concordance, in this case of his poems, was published in the United States in the same year (Furness, 1875). More information about Mary Clarke's life and times can be found in Bellamy et al. (2001). The Greek concordance edited by three generations of the same family was originally published in 1897 (Moulton and Geden, 1897) and was revised most recently in 1977 (Moulton and Geden 1977); Figure 4.1 is from the latter. The concordance of Wordsworth was published by Cooper (1911). One of the first to use computers for concordancing was Todd Bender, professor of English at the University of Wisconsin, who produced nine concordances single-handedly and contributed to a further 22. The remark about using a year's computing budget for one run is from one of his later works (Bender and Higdon, 1988). Figure 4.2 is from Parrish (1959).

A technical description of full-text searching from which some of the material in this chapter is distilled can be found in Witten et al. (1999); Berry and Browne (2005) provide another perspective on this subject. The Google founders' early paper introducing PageRank is Brin and Page (1998); Kleinberg (1998) wrote a paper on the HITS algorithm. At the same time, Gibson et al. (1998) introduced the idea of identifying communities from the topology of the web. Borodin et al. (2002) discuss these ideas further and identify some deficiencies of HITS: they came up with the *jaguar* example in the text. Davison et al. (1999) applied these ideas to the web, and it was their system that took one minute to process each query. Langville and Meyer (2005, 2006) produced excellent surveys of algorithms for web information retrieval. Microsoft's RankNet technology is described by Burges et al. (2005); a related algorithm is described by Diligenti et al. (2003). For more information about machine learning techniques, including the neural net method, see Witten and Frank (2005). The impact factor in bibliometrics was introduced by Garfield (1972); a more recent account of citation structures is Egghe and Rousseau (1990).

You can read about AJAX technology in Crane et al. (2005). The semantic web is the brainchild of Tim Berners-Lee, who penned his vision for *Scientific American* in 2001 (Berners-Lee et al., 2001). Wikipedia is an excellent source of information about the development of indexing. The information about Google comes from its website. A rich mine of information about search engines can be found at *http://searchenginewatch.com*.

THE WEB WARS

The web is a sort of ecosystem and, like other ecosystems, is exposed to risks. Its body, the Internet, inevitably suffers occasional glitches in the physical hardware. The programs that support the communication protocols contain the logic bugs that plague every large-scale software system. There are external threats too: software invasions created with the specific intention of damaging the system.

Like any ecosystem, the web reacts. It differs from other human artifacts, which collapse entirely when trivial faults occur. Its network structure bestows a robustness that is familiar to biologists and shared by many scale-free networks. During the gloomy days of the dot-com boom-and-bust cycle, you might be forgiven for wondering whether the web is just another nine-day wonder, another zany computer project that will enjoy its fifteen minutes of fame and then sink into obscurity over the years ahead. But you would be wrong. With its almost biological structure, the web will surely evolve, but it certainly won't disappear.

The most serious threats to biological ecosystems are often not external but come from within. In the early 1990s, the killer lobster arrived in the Versilia area

Trawling for fish while battling a spam attack.

of Italy, off the coast of Pisa. With an extraordinarily prolific rate of reproduction, it invaded the ecosystem and overwhelmed everything else. In an emergency of Hitchcock proportions, lobsters arose from the sea and entered people's gardens—even their houses.[36] Soon this was the only species around. Fishermen seeking to fill their nets with a seafood cornucopia were doomed to disappointment. Likewise, those trawling the web for information will meet nothing but disappointment if it becomes infested with low-quality documents that stifle everything else with their overwhelming rate of reproduction.

To neutralize the risk of the web being invaded, we must encourage and preserve a panoply of biological diversity. But we must do more. In *The Name of the Rose*, Umberto Eco describes an abbey whose library seems to have been inspired by Borges' Library of Babel. It's a labyrinth whose twisting paths are known only to the librarian; before he dies, he communicates the secret plan to the assistant who is to succeed him. According to the abbot, there's a good reason for this: "Not all truths are for all ears, not all falsehoods can be recognized as such by a pious soul"—for as well as truth, the library holds many books that contain lies. The mission of untold generations of abbey librarians is to protect the monks from corruption.

The explosion of low-quality documents on the web is reminiscent of the abbey library, except that the abbot and his trusty librarian have gone missing. To find information, we monks are forced to rely not on inspired human judgment, but on machines, the web dragons, to make the right kind of documents visible. It is they who fight spam, the killer lobsters of the web. And it's a tough battle. At least Umberto Eco's abbot, in trying to recognize falsehood, could aspire to perfection by invoking the divine. In our story, web spam might be the devil. But who is the abbot?

PRESERVING THE ECOSYSTEM

WebCrow is a program that is capable of cracking crosswords in any language, using the web as its source of knowledge. It reads the clues, converts them into a search engine query, and fits the answers into the puzzle. Devised in 2004, after a few months of intensive development it entered a competition with 25 university students. Four puzzles were posed, with one hour to solve them all; the students worked individually through a well-crafted interactive web application. Only three of them achieved performances comparable with the program.

For a novice like WebCrow, this was a great achievement. Of course, it was possible only because it inhabits the web, an ecosystem in which the food

---

[36] Read about it at *www.uniurb.it/giornalismo/lavori2002/fedeli* (in Italian).

is information. The students could also use the web during the competition—indeed, they were encouraged to do so. In effect, they acted as *cyborgs* natural organisms whose human intelligence is enhanced by artificial technology. What the experiment showed was that the constraints posed by crosswords can be more effectively exploited by computer programs than by humans. Although only a game, for both WebCrow and the cyborgs the process of cracking crosswords was an adventurous mix of discovery and dialogue with the web.

The web is a living ecosystem that supplies information. It isn't just a passive repository. It's a fertile breeding ground that supports a continual process of dialogue and refinement. As we learned in Chapter 1, this process has been at the very center of knowledge creation since before Plato's time. Despite its teenage immaturity, this artificial ecosystem has already become so crucial to our work and lives that most of us question how we could possibly operate without it.

As with other ecosystems, sustaining and preserving the web is a noble and important mission. We need to consider how it is being used—what we ask of it—and establish conventions, or perhaps even enact legislation, to help protect its resources. For example, the access demanded by crawlers might have to be restricted. We also need to preserve the network's ecosystem from natural damage. Broken links are defects that, as we have seen (page 66), are inherently related to basic web design choices. Other damage stems from failure of the underlying Internet communication infrastructure. Still more arises from software bugs, which neither defensive programming practices nor redundant and introspective machines will ever completely eradicate.

More serious problems have begun to emerge from deliberate attacks. If the web is regarded as the natural home for the knowledge repository of the future, we must take care to safeguard it from malign influences—and from collective madness. Alexandria's library was eventually destroyed by zealots, the seeds of destruction having been sown by Julius Caesar's rampage. Nearly two millennia later, in May 1933, the same tragic story was echoed in Berlin's Babelplatz, where a convulsive mass of screaming humanity participated in a gigantic book burning, promoted by the Nazis, and incinerated 20,000 volumes. The burning of the web might arise out of different emotions, in another context, and with flames in bizarre and unconventional form, yet it behooves us not to ignore the possibility.

PROXIES

As in any great city, the movement of information around the web creates heavy traffic that compromises the efficiency of the overall system. A surprisingly large volume of traffic comes when a particular user or group of users repeatedly downloads the same pages. People in the same institution often seek the same information: they have the same interests, track the same trends, and hear rumors through the same grapevine. It turns out that traffic can be greatly reduced if institutions retain on their own computers a *cache* containing local copies of the pages their members download.

In order for this to work, users' browsers must first consult the institutional computer to check whether the page they seek is in the cache, before venturing out onto the web to fetch it. In webspeak, the institutional computer acts as a *proxy server*. The user's browser delegates to it the task of accessing external web servers on its behalf. The proxy server's job is to serve pages to all clients in the institution. It manages the cache. Whenever it receives a request, it looks to see whether there is a local copy, checks the remote copy's date over the web in case it has changed, and if not, serves it up. Otherwise, the system retrieves the content from the web, sends it to the browser, and stashes it in the cache in case it's requested again in the future. A well-designed caching service decreases traffic significantly, particularly if it makes smart decisions about which pages should be cached and when to ditch them to make room for new entries. Intelligent caching policies yield a dramatic reduction in network traffic.

CRAWLERS

Search engines spawn massive crawling operations that account for a fair proportion of overall web traffic. The load they impose on individual servers depends on the volume of other traffic that the site attracts. For large and popular commercial sites that already process a huge volume of requests, the additional load that crawlers impose is negligible. For small specialist sites, crawlers frequently account for more than 50 percent of the traffic, and for sites that get few requests, they could well consume an even greater proportion of resources. Fortunately, only a few companies download large numbers of pages, and the massive crawling performed by major search engines is an extreme example.

The web ecosystem is inherently protected because of two properties. First, the number of competing search engine companies is necessarily rather small.[37] Second, even if these companies decided to make substantial capital investments to increase their crawling rate, the bandwidth of individual servers inherently restricts the overall volume of traffic on the web. This is the same argument that was raised when introducing the uncertainty principle in Chapter 3. Individuals may increase the capacity of their own web connection, only to find that it doesn't help when trying to download information from a sluggish server. The same holds for search engines, whose crawling efficiency is limited by the bandwidth of web servers internationally.

---

[37] In the next chapter, we will describe a "rich get richer" tendency which suggests that economic reasons tend to stifle growth in competing search engine companies.

Things could change quickly. The web ecology could be significantly perturbed by crawling if different retrieval models were adopted. As an extreme example, suppose all users decided to create their own individual copy of the pages that are of interest to them by unleashing a personalized robot to inspect the web and return relevant information. Given the current Internet infrastructure, this would result in a state of global congestion, a deadly embrace. New retrieval models such as this could easily radically disturb the ecology.

Of course, the web may protect itself: the new scheme might soon become so slow that no one used it. Or it may not: the well-known "tragedy of the commons" is that public land can be rendered worthless when subjected to overgrazing, yet it is in each individual's self-interest to use it as much as possible. The interests of the individual conflict with those of the group as a whole. New web retrieval models may need to conform with ecology restrictions to limit the load imposed by robots to a reasonably small percentage of ordinary page requests.

As we observed in Chapter 3, crawlers incorporate the principle that each web server can take steps to avoid unwanted downloading of its site. Crawling is permitted by default: it's up to the system administrator to withdraw permission by placing an appropriate specification in a configuration file (called *robot.txt*). A particular site operator might exclude search engines because, although she wanted to put information on the web for the benefit of a restricted group of people who knew the location, she did not want it to be available to all and sundry. For instance, a spin-off company might choose not to be searchable on the web because of an agreement with investors. An alternative is to protect your data using a password. Note, incidentally, what a different place the world would be if the default were the other way around—if crawlers could only visit sites that had explicitly given permission rather than being denied access to sites that explicitly withdrew permission.

PARASITES

Crawling isn't the only process that must observe restrictions. The idea of using huge numbers of computers on the Internet to perform intensive computational tasks is exploited by the *SETI@home* project, a Berkeley-based venture that is analyzing radio signals in a search for extraterrestrial intelligence. Anyone can join the project and donate computer time to help in the search by downloading special software that runs when their computer is otherwise idle. As we playfully observed in Chapter 3, most computers spend most of their time running the screen saver: SETI puts their idle moments to more productive use. However, this is an opt-in system: the resources that are harnessed are ones that have been willingly volunteered. By 2006, 5.5 million computers had been enlisted, and 2.5 million years of processing time had been donated.

A robot that recruited your computer's resources without explicit permission would be a sinister proposition. Zombies are supernatural powers that, according to voodoo belief, can enter and reanimate a dead body. A "zombie attack" is a nefarious scheme for seeking out an unused, unprotected computer—and there are many forgotten machines on the Internet—and entering it with an alien program. For example, purveyors of junk e-mail manage to commandeer machines in other countries, particularly developing ones where lower levels of technical savvy results in generally weaker security, and use them as servants. If the computer happens to be one that is derelict, it could serve its new master for months without being detected. Eventually the breach is discovered, and the computer's innocent owner harassed, perhaps disconnected, by the Internet community. Of course, the solution is to take proper security precautions to avoid being hijacked in this way.

Astonishingly, it turns out that computers on the Internet whose operation has not been compromised at all can be unknowingly recruited to undertake computation on behalf of another. This is done by cunningly exploiting the protocols that support Internet communication. Remote computers already perform computation, stimulated by ordinary requests to download pages. At a lower level of operation, such requests are broken into packets of information and delivered to the remote site. Every packet is checked at its destination to ensure that it was delivered without transmission errors. This requires a small computation by the computer that receives the packet. The trick is to formulate a problem in such a way that it is solved when massive numbers of remote computers perform these routine checks.

Such a technique was described in a letter to *Nature* in 2001. There is a classic set of problems in computer science, the infamous "NP-complete" problems, for which no efficient solution methods are known. However, these problems yield easily to a tedious and inefficient brute-force approach, where candidate solutions are generated and tested one by one. An example is the "traveling salesman" problem, which seeks the shortest route between a given set of cities. You can try out all possible routes—there is an exponentially large number of them—but no more efficient solution methods are known. One computer was used to generate possible solutions, possible routes in this example, each of which was encoded as an Internet packet. The clever part was to formulate the packets in such a way that the check calculation revealed whether or not it was the true solution. Because of the way the Internet protocol works, only valid solutions to the problem were acknowledged by a return message. On all other packets the check failed, so they were discarded.

This ingenious construction illustrates the idea of what was aptly called *parasitic computing*. Fortunately, it is not effective for practical purposes in its current form. The small amount of computation that the remote server performs for free is far outweighed by the effort required by the host to transmit the packet in the first place. The researchers who developed the scheme remarked that their technique needed refinement but noted that although it was "ethically challenging," it overcame one of the limitations of the *SETI@home* approach, which is that only a tiny fraction of computer owners choose to participate in the computation. Whether it could in fact form the basis of a viable scheme for commandeering other people's resources to do your work is a moot point.

A distributed infrastructure, like the Internet, relies on cooperation among all parties, and trust is essential for successful communication. Parasitic computing exploits trust by getting servers to solve a particular problem without authorization. Only a tiny fraction of each machine on the Internet would amount to colossal overall computational power, the largest computer on earth. Whereas *SETI@home* exploits the resources of computers that explicitly subscribe to its mission, parasitic computing uses remote resources without asking permission.

In a sense, parasitic computing demonstrates the Internet's vulnerability. But it isn't really very different from crawling. Crawling happens behind the scenes, and most people don't know about it, but when they find out they tolerate it because the result is used for their own good—it allows them to search the web. Crawling exclusively for private or commercial purposes would be a different matter. Similarly, if parasitic computing became practical, it might be tolerated if it were used to attack complex problems of general scientific or public interest that required huge computational resources. But the idea of enslaving the Internet and forcing it to perform private computations is repugnant.

RESTRICTING OVERUSE

In any case, the ecosystem must be protected to limit pollution and avoid abuse, and in the future this may require active steps. It is clear that the privileges of crawling and parasitic computing cannot be extended to everyone. It seems reasonable to ask schemes that use global Internet resources to at least make their results publicly available. Whether further policing will be required to protect the ecology, and what form that should take, are important open questions.

WebCrow is a good example of the issues that are already arising. During the crossword competition, it downloaded as many as 200 pages per minute. Search engines offer a great public service, which in this case is being used to solve crosswords—not for private profit but in a curiosity-driven public research program. Whereas there are natural limits to the load that can be imposed by individual human queries, machines that are programmed to make queries can soak up limitless resources. If the idea of creating automatic systems that make intensive use of the web were scaled up to significant proportions, this would impact human access. In fact, it is already happening.

Individual search engines already place restrictions on the number and rate of queries that are processed from any one site, an example of local administration of the web ecology. However, these limits are imposed individually and arbitrarily by organizations which themselves consume public resources through crawling in an unregulated way. The web community needs to face up to such conundrums with sensitivity and wisdom. Regulating ecologies is not easy!

RESILIENCE TO DAMAGE

Broken links, hardware failure in the Internet communication infrastructure, and software bugs, are examples of natural damage that affect the web ecosystem. Although technologists can take steps to reduce the damage and localize its impact, it will never be possible to rid the web of defects entirely. Overall, the web's reliability and the extent to which it resists local damage is generally superior to the reliability and dependability of individual computers, considering the hardware and software problems they typically suffer. A fault in a single memory chip prevents you from running your favorite program—indeed, your computer will likely not even be able to bootstrap the operating system.

Bugs have plagued us ever since people began their adventures in the sphere of technology. Almost all artifacts exhibit brittle behavior when reacting to the fault of a single component. On the other hand, natural systems have strong resilience to damage. They don't crash just because a component fails. The human brain is the most striking example of such admirable behavior. In contrast to faults in the transistors of a microchip, the brain's response to the death of neurons is a graceful degradation in the ability to perform cognitive tasks.

Similar behavior is found in artificial neural networks, one of the few artifacts that exhibit robust fault-tolerance. Neural networks trained to recognize handwritten characters continue to work even if you break a few connections or remove some neurons. As with the human brain, behavior becomes compromised after much damage, but even then, the system can often relearn the task and recover its original performance, or something like it. Neural networks and the World Wide Web share with natural systems, such as the brain, an inherent resilience to damage. What do they have in common? A network-based structure!

What happens to the overall connectivity of the web when links are broken? And what happens on the Internet when a fault arises in one of the routers that directs the traffic? Such questions are of great practical importance and have been widely studied. If the network were a random graph, created by randomly selecting pairs of nodes and attaching links between them, theoretical analysis shows that removing nodes beyond a certain critical threshold could fragment the network into small clusters. In the web, this would cause serious problems, for if enough links became broken, search engine crawlers wouldn't be able to explore it properly.

In fact, despite the continual incidence of natural damage, the web does not break into fragments, but retains its overall connectivity. What it shares with many natural systems is the power-law distribution of the number of links that connect the nodes, introduced in Chapter 3 (page 89). And this makes scale-free networks more robust to faults than the classical Gaussian distribution. Intuitively, the reason is that robustness stems from the presence of a number of massively connected hubs. Since there are far more nodes with just a few links than there are hubs, most faults don't affect hubs. But it is the hubs that are primarily responsible for the network's overall connectivity.

The innate resistance to damage that scale-free networks exhibit is very strong indeed. You can gradually remove nodes without the network fragmenting into clusters, provided that the exponent of the power law lies below a certain critical threshold.[38] This property holds for both the Internet and the web, and their steadfast resilience under adversity has been observed experimentally.

VULNERABILITY TO ATTACK

The fault-tolerance of scale-free networks is predicated on the fact that damage affects links randomly. If critical nodes are purposely targeted, that's a different matter altogether. Random damage is what tends to occur in nature. But with artificial systems, it would be unwise to neglect the possibility of deliberate attack.

Unfortunately, healthy resistance to damage has a flip side: scale-free networks are particularly vulnerable to deliberate aggression. The reason is quite obvious: they inherit their connectivity principally from the hubs. These are unlikely to suffer much from random damage since, though large, hubs contain a small minority of the overall links. But they are prime targets for deliberate attack. Resilience to random damage comes hand in hand with fragility under assaults that are perpetrated intentionally. If we want to preserve the web's ecosystem, we have to study the risk of attack.

Targeted network attacks can have consequences that are far more serious than the fragmentation that occurs when hubs are destroyed. If an important Internet node is brought down, the problem is not just the broken connections that ensue. The traffic that it handled previously will be directed to other nodes, creating an overload. The resulting cascade effect resembles the massive power outages that our highly networked world has begun to experience—but worse. On the Internet, difficulties in information delivery are indicated by the lack of a receipt. This eventually causes nodes to resend the information, which increases traffic and escalates the problem. Destroying a single important hub causes serious network congestion—perhaps even a global catastrophe.

---

[38] In fact, it has been shown theoretically that the critical value is 3. For the web, the power-law exponents have been empirically determined to be 2.1 for inbound links and 2.7 for outbound links (Broder et al., 2000).

Despite their great technical sophistication, computer attacks are reminiscent of medieval sieges, and there are similarities in the strategies for attack and defense. The effective defense of a fort requires weapons and, if the battle lasts for days, adequate stores of food and medical supplies. If any of these resources are destroyed, the consequences are serious. The same is true for computer networks: in addition to the main targets, there are many critical supporting elements. Attacks are directed not only at major hubs, but also at sites that contain anti-virus software and security upgrades. When discussing ecological vulnerability, we need to consider the whole question of security, with emphasis on the overall integrity of the web rather than the local effect of attacks on a single computer or large organization.

VIRUSES

As everyone knows, computers can be attacked by contaminating them with a virus. This idea originated in the 1972 novel *When Harlie was One*, which described a computer program that telephoned numbers at random until it found another computer into which it could spread.[39] A virus is a piece of program code that attaches copies of itself to other programs, incorporating itself into them, so that as well as performing their intended function, they surreptitiously do other things. Programs so corrupted seek others to which to attach the virus, and so the infection spreads. To do so the programs must be executed; viruses cannot spread from one computer to another on their own.

Successful viruses lie low until they have thoroughly infiltrated the system, only then revealing their presence by causing damage. Their effect can be mischievous, ranging from simulated biological decay of your screen to sounds that suggest your computer is being flooded by water. They can equally well inflict serious damage, destroying files or—perhaps even worse—silently corrupting them in subtle and potentially embarrassing ways.

Viruses cannot spread without communication. In the early days, they thrived in personal computer environments where users shared floppy disks or other removable media, by infiltrating the system's hard disk. Nowadays networks provide a far more effective vehicle for virus infection. Infection can occur when you download any kind of program—computer games are common carriers—or open an e-mail attachment. Even word processor and spreadsheet documents are not immune. Clicking your mouse to open an attachment is just so easy it's irresistible. Users who are unaware, or only vaguely aware, of the threat often experience the potentially disastrous effects of viral attacks.

---

[39] The first actual virus program seems to have been created in 1983, at the dawn of the personal computer era.

It is always necessary to guard against viruses when sharing any kind of computer program. They work by subtly altering files stored on your computer and can be detected by inspecting recent changes to files—particularly unexpected changes. Anti-virus software regularly examines recently changed files and analyzes them for traces of known viral code, moving them to a quarantine area to prevent you from inadvertently executing them.

Viruses may bother individual users, but they do not represent a serious threat to the overall integrity of the web. Today the main source of infection is e-mail, but although such attacks can be devastating for naïve users, they are ineffective on critical targets. Important hubs are run by trained professionals who are wise to the ways of viruses and take care to follow sanitary operating practices. As a result, viral attacks are unlikely to compromise the integrity of the entire network.

WORMS

There are more serious threats than virus infection. On November 3, 1988, a small "worm" program was inserted into the Internet. It exploited security flaws in the Unix operating system to spread itself from computer to computer. Although discovered within hours, it required a concerted effort (estimated at 50,000 hours), over a period of weeks, by programmers at affected sites, to neutralize it and eliminate its effects. It was unmasked by a bug: under some circumstances it replicated itself so quickly that it noticeably slowed down the infected host.

That flaw was quickly fixed. But others continually appear. In January 2003, Sapphire, a program of just 376 bytes, began to flood the Internet. It let itself in through an open communication port in a popular database system, the Microsoft SQL server, masquerading as an ordinary database request. Instead, it gave rise to a cascading failure in the database servers. First, it threw an error whose consequences had not been anticipated by the server designers. The error was not just a local server fault, but affected the entire installation. Having gained entry, the program repeated its malevolent effect, doubling the number of infected servers every few seconds. As a result, about 70,000 servers crashed in just ten minutes, causing widespread devastation. Fortunately, this malicious program neither destroyed files nor did any permanent damage, but it did result in a billion-dollar productivity loss—a so-called denial-of-service attack. This is just one of the worms that has inflicted damage on the Internet. Like most others, it exploited a portal that was insufficiently fortified.

Computer worms, like biological organisms, continually evolve. A crucial step in their evolution is the development of self-defense mechanisms. For instance, one worm (Blaster) caused infected machines to continually reboot themselves sufficiently quickly to make it difficult for the user to remove it and install an immunization patch. It simultaneously launched a denial-of-service attack on Microsoft's update service, the web's store of food and medicine.

The Internet is such an attractive target for evil-doers that attack strategies will certainly evolve. There will always be some onslaughts for which defenses have not been properly prepared. But considering the integrity of the web as a whole, the fact that its vulnerability is restricted to a limited number of crucial hubs suggests that effective protective defense mechanisms will be established. There are only a limited number of experts of sufficient technical caliber to pose serious security threats. Ethical, if not economic, arguments suggest that if the web is generally considered to be a worthwhile endeavor for society as a whole, more of these people might be persuaded to wield their intellectual weaponry to defend the fort than to mount attacks on it.

INCREASING VISIBILITY: TRICKS OF THE TRADE

There are countless different reasons that lead one to visit a web page. Regardless of your motivation and interests, the web is a place where speed is highly valued, so for a page to become widely visible, it must reside on a site with a sufficiently fast network connection. Once you reach the page, the quality of its content, and allure of its presentation, are good reasons to bookmark it for future visits. But, for the most part, the extent to which pages and sites are visible is determined by the ranking they receive from major search engines. These are the gateways through which we reach the treasure.

A typical search engine query returns tens or hundreds of thousands of pages. For pragmatic reasons, users can only view those near the beginning of the list. In practice, the visibility of pages is determined by search engines: most users view the web through the lens that the dragons provide. Pages that are not highly ranked are simply buried under a mountain of documents: for most of the world, they might as well not exist. Now that the web is indispensable to almost every aspect of our lives, some of the people who create or own pages are desperate to make them more visible.

Although the precise way in which search engines work is a closely guarded secret, the criteria they use to rank pages can be surmised by combining information from public documents, experimental evidence, and reverse engineering. A large and growing array of methods have been discovered that aspire to increase the visibility of web pages and web sites. *Boosting techniques* are directly concerned with elevating the rank of particular target pages. You can boost for specific query terms, or you can boost a site's overall visibility. In either case, the process involves including artificial text or creating artificial pages whose sole purpose is to fool—persuade, their proponents might say—search engines into increasing the target's rank. *Hiding techniques* have been developed to conceal these artifacts from human eyes—that is, to ensure that different

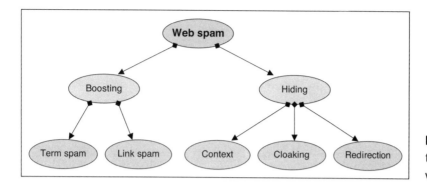

Figure 5.1 The taxonomy of web spam.

information is delivered to search engines and human readers. Figure 5.1 shows the techniques discussed in this section.

TERM BOOSTING

Chapter 4 explained how search engines assess the relevance of documents to a given query. They assign higher weight to documents that contain more of the query terms, particularly terms that appear often in the document but seldom in the collection as a whole. You should bear this in mind if you are working on a web page that you would like to be more visible with respect to a particular query. Deliberately repeat the query term: that will increase its influence. Avoid referring to it by pronouns: that wastes the opportunity for another mention. Increase the term's density by avoiding articles, function words, and other linguistic distractions. None of these are recipes for compelling prose. The resulting pages will be stilted and, if these hints are taken to extremes, completely unacceptable to human readers.

The contribution of each term to the rank depends on just where in the page it is located. For example, it's conjectured—but only the dragons really know the truth—that terms occurring early in the document, and particularly in the title, are deemed to be more relevant than others. Metatags also play an important role (perhaps). For instance, the *VIP* keyword that we attached to Felix in Chapter 3 is simply intended to fool the dragons. Logically, search engines ought to attach great import to metatags which, after all, are supposed to be a way of specifically indicating what the page is about. Inserting misleading terms here has the added advantage that readers will never see them. Terms can also be boosted by putting them into the URL, on the assumption that search engines break this down into components and use them in the ranking—probably with more weight than the ordinary words that occur in the body of the document.

As explained in Chapter 4 (page 113), the text that accompanies links into a web page—the anchor text—gives a clue to its content, ostensibly a more reliable clue than the words in the page itself, because it is apparently written by another person and represents an independent view. Another deceitful way of boosting rank is to create links to the page and insert critical terms into their anchor text. For example, the presence of this link

```
<a href="felix.html"> A true example of a VIP! </a>
```

in some *other* web page enriches Felix's own page—see Figure 3.11(b) on page 68—with the term *VIP* and is likely to be more effective than simply including *VIP* in a metatag or the text body, as in Figure 3.1(c). Replicating inbound links on a large scale boosts the term's weight significantly, more significantly than replicating the term in the body of the text. Unlike the previous techniques, the fake terms are added to a page other than the one being boosted. Note, incidentally, that it could be more effective to include *A true example of a VIP* than the single term *VIP* because the whole phrase might match a query in its entirety. It's a good idea to attach popular phrases that stand a chance of matching queries perfectly.

LINK BOOSTING

So far, we have discussed how to boost a page by adjusting the text it contains, or the text associated with links that point to it. As we learned in Chapter 4, inbound links play a crucial role in determining rank. Creating more links to a target page is likely to increase its standing. Like anchor-text boosting but unlike the other term-based methods, this one needs control over the pages from which the links originate. But the rewards are great. Whereas term boosting only increases the rank of a page with respect to a particular query, creating new links increases its rank *for all queries*. Moreover, if we can somehow create highly ranked pages, the links that emanate from them will be particularly valuable because of how the page-rank calculation works.

The easiest way to implement this boosting strategy is to create your own website. Of course, if you can somehow gain control of someone else's site—preferably a high-ranking one—so much the better. But you can sometimes accomplish the desired effect by legitimate usage of an existing site. For example, you might visit a high-ranking site like *www.whitehouse.gov* and sign the guest book there with a message that contains a link to your page. While you're at it, why not sign it several times? Or program a robot to crawl for sites containing guest books. Better still, simply use a search engine to find high-ranking guest books for you—and sign them in your stead. Why stop at guest books? Wikis are open collaborative environments, and most allow anyone to contribute to them. You might have to set up a user name and password, and then you can write what you like—including links to your own page. Again, you can program a robot to find blogs and wikis and add your graffiti automatically. It's not hard to hijack the cooperative social mechanisms of the web for your own nefarious purposes.

Now that you know how to create artificial links to your page, let's see how they can be used to greatest effect with the two link-analysis algorithms described in Chapter 4. Consider, first, PageRank and begin by focusing attention on a particular website that you want to boost. Surprisingly, its overall rank grows with the number of pages it contains. This is a straightforward consequence of the probabilistic interpretation of PageRank: a random walker is likely to stay longer and return more often to sites that are bigger. Given a certain amount of content, it's advantageous to distribute it among as many pages as possible. This is illustrated in Figure 5.2. The rule is simply that the same content is ranked higher if split into more pages.

The overall rank of a site can be increased by limiting the number of links to the outside world. Again, the explanation is a simple application of the random walk: the more links there are out of a site, the greater the chance of exit. If you must have external links, it is best to direct them from pages that have many outbound links within the site, because this reduces the probability of choosing the external links. In Figure 5.2(b), the outbound link from page 1 is preferable to that from page 2 because there is only a 25 percent chance of it being taken versus the 33 percent chance of exiting from page 2. Finally, it's best to avoid trapping states or "sinks" within your site, because then the random surfer will necessarily be forced to teleport away. Thus, you should add a link out of page 4 in Figure 5.2(b), as shown in Figure 5.2(c).

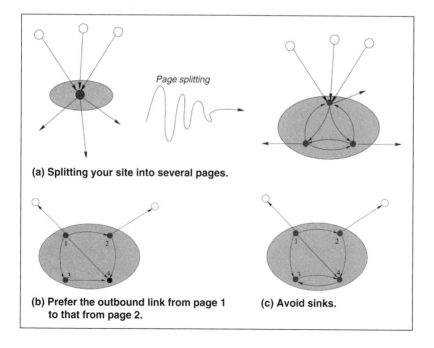

(a) Splitting your site into several pages.

(b) Prefer the outbound link from page 1 to that from page 2.

(c) Avoid sinks.

Figure 5.2 Insights from link analysis.

These strategies only affect the structure of your own website, the one you are trying to boost. You can implement them without having control of any external site. Another way of increasing ranking is to attract as many incoming links as possible. Each external link increases the overall rank of your site. This, of course, is the fundamental insight of PageRank: links are a sign that your site is well established, contains relevant information, and is sufficiently valued by others to be worth referring to. Suppose you control a site elsewhere from which you can send links to your own pages, the target community. The best way to manage this, from the point of view of maximizing visibility, is to create a site designed specifically to promote PageRank, often called a "link farm." This is illustrated in Figure 5.3, where each page in the promoting community sends a link to the target community. Of course, you should design the promotion community with the preceding rules in mind.

Other tricks can be used to boost pages in the eyes of the HITS scheme for hub/authority ranking. You can easily construct a highly ranked hub simply by sending many outbound links to sites that are known to have high authority—for instance, *cnn.com* or *www.sony.com*. To create a highly ranked authority, you need to engineer links to it from several good hubs. So, create many artificial good hubs using the previous method, and link these to the target, which in turn becomes a good authority. In principle, the process is only limited by your wallet and the cost of the pages you create.

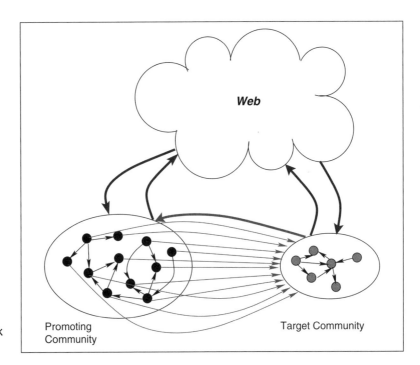

Figure 5.3 A link farm.

CONTENT HIDING

Term boosting tends to clutter up the page with unnatural and unwanted text, such as fake terms and hundreds of replications of the same word. Everyone can see that there's something wrong with the page. Here's a simple way of hiding all the extraneous text: color it the same as the background. Although the default text color is black, other colors can easily be specified in HTML. Human readers will not see words written in the background color, but the text is plainly visible in the HTML code and so search engines will—or may—be deceived.

The same applies to link boosting. Pages can include hordes of outbound links to improve their HITS hub ranking and the rank of other pages, but if these are visible, readers might smell a rat. It's the anchor text that makes links visible, and it can easily be concealed. When users mouse over a link anchor, the cursor changes shape to indicate that it can be clicked; so to avoid detection, you should not only have invisible anchors but make them as small as possible. The best choice is a one-pixel image of the background color. For instance, the anchor text *Click here* in Felix's page (Figure 3.1a) could be replaced by:

```
<a href="http://www.everwonder.com/david/felixthecat/">
      <img src="onepixel"></a>
```

A page can contain many hidden and virtually undetectable links expressed in this way, whose sole purpose is to deceive search ranking mechanisms.

Instead of hiding terms and anchors, here's a more radical technique known as "cloaking." Simply present different pages to search engines than those you show to ordinary users. When a web server receives a page request, it can identify where it comes from. If the source is a known crawler, serve up something different—something that contains various boosting tricks as well as the real content for the crawler to index. There is nothing to stop a web server from presenting robots with an entirely fictitious view of the site. Search engine operators today do not seem to disguise their robots as ordinary users, though they could. However, they probably do perform anonymous checks to determine whether what their crawlers are seeing is the same as what ordinary users see.

Another way to deceive search engines—and people—is to exploit HTML's ability to redirect users automatically from one page to another. You have probably experienced this when surfing the web, typically when a site has moved from one host to another. What you see is a page that invites you to update your bookmark with the new address, to which you are automatically redirected after a few seconds. If the delay time is set to zero, the original page—called the "doorway"—is not displayed at all and can be used to boost visibility through the techniques described earlier. Redirection is just another way of creating pages that are indexed by search engines but unseen by human users.

DISCUSSION

These are some ideas for boosting visibility. They are well known to search engine operators, who take pains to detect tricks and neutralize their effects. Other techniques will arise in the future, and it's hard to foretell their guise. The boosters and the dragons will continue to wage war. New tricks will emerge from the underworld; dragons will adapt; spammers will reverse-engineer their changes and exploit loopholes. In the middle, of course, are the users, innocently relying on the web for their daily information, ignorant of the battleground heaving beneath their feet. Boosting will continue to develop hand in hand with information hiding. The most effective techniques involve gaining control of a large number of websites, and people in the boosting business will team up with hackers who are expert in network attack and intrusion.

BUSINESS, ETHICS, AND SPAM

Everyone wants to increase their visibility on the web. One way is to pay the dragons for advertising services. A second is to recruit companies that boast expertise in "search engine optimization" and seek their advice about how to reorganize your site to increase its visibility; they will help you use some of the techniques described here. A third is to buy links from highly ranked pages. In the murky world of search engine optimization, some people run link farms and—for a fee—place links to your pages from pages they have artificially boosted. Building an extensive link farm or a set of highly ranked hubs is costly, and selling links is a way of amortizing the investment. A fourth is to buy highly ranked pages on auction sites such as eBay. The web has huge inertia, and pages retain their ranking even if their content changes completely, because sites that link to them take a long time to notice the changes and alter their links. Squatters look for pages whose naming license is about to expire and snap them up within seconds if the owner forgets to renew. The license database is online, and all this can be done by an agent program that operates automatically.

You might find it hard to persuade a search engine to sell you a higher rank. As mentioned in Chapter 4, most take great care to keep paid advertising distinct from their search results. They make it clear to the public that while advertising can be bought, placement in the search results cannot. Otherwise, the answer to any query might be biased by economic issues—and you, the user, would never know. Web search is good business because of its popularity and advertising potential; in reality, it is more concerned with making money than providing library-quality information retrieval services. But to maintain their standing, the dragons must keep a watchful eye on their user base by continually striving to offer an excellent and trustworthy information service. Although users might be hard put to find out whether search results are biased by commercialism, the betrayal of trust if the word got out probably makes it too dangerous for the dragons to contemplate.

Search engine optimization is also good business, and there are many companies that do it. While it is perfectly reasonable to strive to attract links from other sites by making your pages as alluring as possible, web spam is a consequence of extreme interpretations of popularity-seeking. Junk pages used to promote documents and advertisements pollute the ecosystem. While viruses and worms have dramatic effects that can easily be spotted, spam is more insidious. It's difficult to find neat ways of filtering it out. The free and easy publication style that characterizes the web provides fertile ground for spam. Unlike viruses and worms, its growth and diffusion don't violate any law. The killer lobster—the spam—has already entered the ecosystem, and it spreads by apparently respecting the spirit of its environment.

What's really wrong with making strenuous efforts to boost visibility? It opens the door to business, and one might well argue that ethics and business are unnatural bedfellows. Perhaps people cry about ethics only when they are on the defensive, when they are losers in the great world of commerce. Or are ethical considerations of crucial importance in order to preserve the web, encourage a healthy ecosystem, and facilitate its evolution? Surely search engine companies are aware that crawling is a parasitic operation that must be regarded as a privilege rather than a right? By the same token, search engine optimization enthusiasts should bear in mind the damaging effects of spam on the ecosystem as a whole.

Web visibility is becoming the target of stock-market-style speculation. As the fever takes hold, people pay to promote their sites, gaining top-ranked positions for crucial keywords—regardless of the quality of the information—and competing for people's attention. But there's only a finite amount of attention in the world. Will the bubble burst?

THE ETHICS OF SPAM

SPAM is ground pork and ham combined with spices, packed in cans. Originally called Hormel Spiced Ham, the name was invented to market this miracle meat, a savior of the allies in the Second World War. Its negative connotations originated when a zany British comedy troupe created a café full of Vikings singing "spam, spam, spam, ..." and rendering normal conversation impossible.[40] All e-mail users are depressingly familiar with the annoyance of

---

[40] In fact, they were echoing a 1937 advertising jingle—possibly the first ever singing commercial—to the chorus of "My Bonny Lies Over the Ocean." Instead of "Bring back, bring back / Oh, bring back my bonnie to me," the lyrics were "SPAM SPAM SPAM SPAM / Hormel's new miracle meat in a can / Tastes fine, saves time / If you want something grand / Ask for SPAM!"

finding meaningless jingles in their mailbox. Just as Monty Python's Vikings prevent you from communicating with friends at your table, the spam in your e-mail inbox threatens to drown out the real conversations.

The web is the café where the new Vikings sing. Now that you have learned the tricks of the visibility-boosting trade, it's not hard to imagine the lyrics. You encounter doorways that redirect you to a target page without announcing themselves on the screen; synthetic pages created automatically by software, comprised solely of links to other pages, particularly high-authority ones; pages containing long lists of terms that will match almost any query. What they all have in common is that they are junk. They are the killer lobsters that threaten to drown out real life in the ecosystem and make the lives of fishermen a misery.

Spam on the web denotes pages created for the sole purpose of attracting search engine referrals—either to the page itself or to some other target page. In 2004, 10 to 15 percent of web pages were estimated to be spam. It's not yet clear whether the growth trend will be reversed. These songs, these killer lobsters, are parasites that waste communication resources all over the planet. Once indexed by search engines, they pollute their results. Although they may increase visibility initially, sooner or later search engine operators react by changing their ranking algorithms to discriminate against spam—spam as they see it, that is. In their efforts to save the web by purifying search results, they might have a hard time distinguishing the real thing—and your innocent website may suffer. For sometimes one person's spam is another person's ham.

Web spam goes hand in hand with deceit. Visual tricks hide terms and links. Cloaks disguise pages with unseen surrogates. Doorways conceal surreptitious wormholes. Guest books contain mysterious messages. Wiki pages take forever to load because they are stuffed with invisible hyperlinked one-pixel images. In the extreme, entire sites are infiltrated and perverted to serve their new masters. Apart from intrusion, these deceptions are unlikely to run afoul of the law. But they raise ethical concerns—particularly if we aspire to cultivate the web into the ultimate interactive library, a universal and dynamic repository of our society's knowledge.

Concerns arise regardless of one's philosophical stance or school of thought. Whether we strive to obey Kant's categorical imperative to respect other rational beings or Bentham's utilitarianism principle to attain the greatest happiness and benefit for the greatest number of people, the deceit that web spam represents is harmful. It's harmful because, like e-mail spam, it wastes time and resources while producing nothing of value to society as a whole. PageRank—and, ultimately, human attention—is a zero-sum game: one site's enhanced visibility inevitably detracts from another. More seriously, not only is spam wasteful but, like any other kind of pollution, it compromises beauty and healthy growth—in this case, the beauty and healthy growth of our society's knowledge as represented in the universal library. Deceit neither respects other rational beings nor brings happiness and benefit to the greatest number of people.

There is nothing wrong with boosting one's own site by making it sufficiently informative and alluring to attract the genuine attention of others. We should not decry the boosting of visibility in general: the issue is the means that are used to reach the end. And whereas our discussion has singled out just a couple of popular schools of Western philosophy, the web is an international endeavor and other mores will prevail in different parts of the world. (And other problems: we already mentioned the prevalence of zombie attacks in developing countries.) We need a broader discussion of the web as a public good that is to be respected by all. It's unwise to neglect ethical issues when considering the future of an ecosystem.

ECONOMIC ISSUES

Visibility of knowledge is crucial if the web is to evolve into a universal library that serves society effectively. But in addition to being a repository of knowledge, the web is a shopping center too, and visibility plays a central role in driving commercial transactions. Promotion of websites is big business. Companies that undertake search engine optimization also help you submit your site to search engines and place it in appropriate directories. They advise on the design of your site, its visual impact and logical structure. They provide guidelines for selecting keywords in the title, inserting metatags, creating a site map, avoiding image buttons in links, and structuring internal links. Some also use unethical techniques for boosting visibility, like those just described.

Customers should be skeptical about promises from any company to position their pages "in the top ten" irrespective of content. These companies have no influence over the ranking schemes that search engines use. They cannot fulfill such promises without adopting unethical boosting techniques. Although they may succeed in boosting visibility, the victory will be short-lived. Search engine operators constantly watch for spam and adjust their algorithms to defeat new techniques. They are likely to discriminate heavily against what they see as artificially boosted pages. Your pages may appear briefly in the top ten and then drop out of sight altogether, far below where they were originally. It's no good complaining. This is war: there are no referees.

SEARCH ENGINE ADVERTISING

Web visibility in general, and search engine optimization in particular, is big business. But the dragons of the business are the search engines themselves.

They offer an invaluable service that we use every day for free. Their business model is to make money through advertising, inspired by the phenomenal commercial success of traditional broadcast advertising. Some sell placement within the search results, a straightforward way to offer an advertising service based on keywords in user queries. Others keep their search results pure and ensure that any advertisements are completely separate.

We use Google as an example; similar services are offered by other major search engines. It displays advertisements separately from search results. It gives advertisers access to a program that helps them create their own ads and choose keywords that are likely to attract the targeted audience. Whereas a few years ago advertisers paid Google whenever their ad appeared on a user's screen, today they pay only when a user actually clicks on the ad. Advertisers bid for keywords and phrases, and Google's software chooses the winner in an online auction that happens every time a user makes a query whose terms attract advertising.

For each ad, Google's software calculates the "clickthrough rate"—the proportion of times the ad is actually clicked. Up to a certain maximum number of ads are shown on the query results page. Originally they were sorted by the product of clickthrough rate and bid amount. This was justified not on the basis of maximizing revenue to Google (though that is exactly what it did), but rather by the idea of providing a valuable service to users by showing them ads they are likely to click. These ads are targeted to people with a particular information need. Google promotes ads not as distracters, but as rewarding opportunities in their own right.

At the end of 2005, Google began to take into account the content of the page that an ad pointed to (so-called "landing pages"). It began rewarding advertisers who provided a "good user experience" and penalizing those whose ads were seductive (or misleading) enough to generate many clickthroughs but led to a "disappointing user experience"—polite language for "spammy" pages. Advertisers in the latter category have been forced to bid higher if they wish to be seen. This caused controversy because the evaluation criteria were secret—indeed, it was not even known whether landing pages were assessed by humans or by a computer algorithm.

Advertisers adopt complex strategies to maximize their return on investment. Some change their bid dynamically throughout the day. For example, to gain maximum benefit from a scheduled TV program on a topic related to their product, they may increase their bid while it is airing. A clickthrough for insomnia pills in the middle of the night might be more valuable than one during the day; a clickthrough for raingear might be more valuable during a storm. Advertisers are interested in the *cost per action*, where an action is purchasing an item or signing up for a new account. The likelihood of a click turning into an action is called the "conversion rate." Canny advertisers monitor variations in the conversion rate and try to correlate them with the time of day, or external events, in an effort to find good ways of determining how much to bid in the auction.

The pay-per-click advertising model, coupled with sophisticated strategies for tweaking the bid price to make the best use of an advertising budget, has been a resounding success. However, it is susceptible to "click fraud," where users with no intention of buying a product or service click simply to deplete the advertiser's budget. This might be done systematically—manually or automatically—by someone in a rival company. You click repeatedly on a competitor's ad to use up their daily budget and force them out of the auction—and then reduce your bid. No one knows how much of this goes on: media estimates vary from 5 percent of clicks to 50 percent. Click fraud represents yet another threat for search engines. Some make concerted efforts to detect it and refrain from billing for clicks that they judge to be fraudulent.

CONTENT-TARGETED ADVERTISING

Google also places ads on other people's sites. When you join the service, it performs an automatic analysis of your site to determine what it is about and delivers ads that match the contents of each page, automatically integrating them visually into the page. When others visit your site, they also see the ads—which are matched to the page content. If they click on one, you get some money from the advertiser (so, of course, does Google). The service adapts to changes in your site's content by periodically reanalyzing it.

This is a bonanza for some websites. You collect revenue with no effort whatsoever! Indeed, you can generate it for yourself by clicking on the ads that Google has put on your page, another form of click fraud. But it's not the ultimate free lunch that it appears, because overtly commercial activity may put off those who visit your pages. The scheme rewards entrepreneurs who create sites designed for advertising rather than real content and boost their visibility in artificial ways. Another activity of search engine optimization companies is to advise on setting up pay-per-click accounts and to design websites that attract lucrative ads. Like click fraud, this may represent a further threat to search engines.

Does content-targeted advertising pollute the web, or does it provide a useful service, one valued by potential customers? It's a matter of opinion. But regardless of perspective, any sound and lasting business model must follow ethical principles. Is it ethical for a search engine to sell placement in its search results—that is, web visibility? Obviously not, if users are deceived. But suppose the search engine company declares that its business policy is to sell visibility, just as search optimization companies do. Our view is that the web is a public good, and those who exploit its resources by crawling (or parasitic computing) have an obligation to offer a useful public service, one that benefits a significant proportion of the web population. This is Bentham's utilitarianism principle of ethics, often expressed as the catchphrase "the greatest good for the greatest number." Whether selling placement in search results is compatible with that obligation is arguable at best.

THE BUBBLE

In Holland in the late sixteenth century, tulip bulbs exceeded gold in value. Strange as it may seem, ordinary people sold everything they possessed to buy tulips, anticipating that the price, already high, would continue to rise further. Their dream was to become rich. However, prices crashed and a prolonged financial crisis ensued. This is a classic early example of the havoc that irrational expectations can play with valuations. Ever since, speculative crazes have appeared with depressing regularity. Indeed, since the famous—or infamous—1929 financial crash, nine such events have been identified. They are called "bubbles"; they swell up with air under the pressure of a speculative market, and the ultimate burst is as sudden as it is inevitable.

Economic bubbles share a common cause: local, self-reinforcing, imitative behavior among traders. The growing economic importance of the web has given rise to a sort of fever of web visibility, where people artificially promote products and ideas in order to reap economic benefits and wield cultural influence. The currency is not tulips but eyeballs: we crave attention, readers, click-throughs, inbound links. But the risk of speculation lurks just beneath the surface. There is only a limited amount of attention in the world. If all website owners compete to push their pages higher in the search results, the process may become unstable. The pressure to buy additional visibility is local self-reinforcing imitation—precisely the conditions that accompany economic bubbles. As page promotion becomes more popular, the cost of visibility continues to increase, leading, perhaps, to a bubble of web visibility.

The bubble's growth is related to the quality of the information present. The lower the quality, the more artificial the promotion and the higher the probability of a burst. A true speculative bubble and its inevitable collapse into depression would have serious consequences for everyone connected with the web business. Search engines, as the information gateways, are in a position to control inflation by guaranteeing high-quality search results. This meets Bentham's utilitarianism principle of ethics. It also raises new concerns—practical, not ethical—about the strategy of selling placement in search results. Clean separation between commercial and noncommercial information, between ads and search results, seems an effective way to gently deflate the bubble. Even then, however, spam and artificial site promotion methods are powerful inflationary forces. The war against spam is also a war against inflation.

When ethics and economics point in the same direction, we should take heed! In this case, they both converge on the importance of paying particular attention to the quality of the information delivered by web search.

QUALITY

Jean-Paul Sartre, the renowned existential philosopher who won the Nobel Prize for literature in 1964, painted an evocative picture of the relationship between reader and reading material that is both sensuous and eerie:

> ... but it is always possible for him to enter his library, take down a book from the shelf, and open it. It gives off a slight odor of the cellar, and a strange operation begins which he has decided to call reading. From one point of view it is a possession; he lends his body to the dead in order that they may come back to life. And from another point of view it is a contact with the beyond. Indeed the book is by no means an object; neither is it an act, nor even a thought. Written by a dead man about dead things, it no longer has any place on this earth; it speaks of nothing which interests us directly. Left to itself, it falls back and collapses; there remain only ink spots on musty paper.
>
> *– Jean-Paul Sartre (1947)*

Transport this into the relationship between the surfer and the web, the prototype universal library. Information, left to itself, is dead—written by dead people about dead things. It's just ink spots on musty paper; limp pixels on a fictitious screen; neither an act nor even a thought. By downloading a page, we lend it our body and liberate it from the land of the dead. When we honor its link anchor with a click, we bring it temporarily to life: it possesses us. Through it we make fleeting contact with the beyond.

In the gigantic ecosystem of the web, how can we possibly discover information that is worth lending our mind to? Traditional publication is expensive. Books undergo a stringent review process before being published that greatly simplifies the reader's task of selecting relevant material—though it's still far from easy. But web publication is cheap, and the human review process can hardly be transposed to this domain. Instead, we rely on computers to rank the stuff for us. As we saw in the previous chapter, the schemes that search engines use are superficial. They count words and links, but they do not weigh meaning.

What are the frontiers of automatic quality assessment? We have been focusing on spam. This is part of the problem—an important part, and one that involves a fascinating duel between dragon and spammer, good and evil—but it's by no means the whole story. Can intelligent agents replace human reviewers? Is quality assessment a formal technical process, that is, an activity that is susceptible to automation, even though a complex one that has not yet been cracked by artificial intelligence research? Or is it a creative process, on the same level as the production of quality content that is worth taking down from the shelf and breathing life into? More immediately, can we expect to benefit in the near future from filters that are capable of offering high-quality individualized views of the web, thus excluding spam? We return to these questions in the final chapter.

THE ANTI-SPAM WAR

Visibility fever has spawned a global market of customers who vie with one another for the top-ranked listing for queries relevant to their business. Just as the dragons compete among themselves to offer a better service, so do search engine optimization companies. Both are concerned with web visibility, but from opposite directions. In some cases their interests converge: for example, both seek to protect customers who buy advertisements against click fraud.

When search engine optimization borders on spamming, the competition becomes war, and both sides use sophisticated weaponry. Search engines jealously guard the secrecy of their code—especially their ranking policy, the crown jewels of their operation. While lack of transparency is undesirable from the point of view of serving society's information needs, it seems the only way to protect the web from spam. We are trapped in an irresolvable dilemma—unless we are prepared to consider major changes to the basic model of the web.

Perhaps documents, like the inhabitants of a sophisticated ecosystem, should have to undergo rigorous testing before they are permitted to evolve and reproduce. Individuals who are too simple often have a hard time finding an evolutionary niche. In the web, no document is actually threatened, no matter how atrocious its content. This is a mixed blessing. Universal freedom to publish is a great thing, the force that has driven the web's explosion. Yet a completely unrestricted environment is precisely what has sown the seeds of war.

Sun-Tzu, a Chinese general from the sixth century B.C., wrote a landmark treatise on military strategy in his seminal book *The Art of War*, and many of his lessons apply outside the military. For example, long-term strategic planning is often greatly superior to short-term tactical reaction. Instead of the present series of skirmishes, the time may have come to ponder more broadly an overall plan for the web. Perhaps spammers should be thinking of individualizing and improving search services rather than initiating parasitic attacks on the treasure the dragons guard—and society should find ways of rewarding this. The strategy for dragons might be to transcend their fixation on a single ranking policy, which makes them especially vulnerable to attack.

THE WEAPONS

Spammers use software tricks, some dramatically referred to as "bombs," that arise from the boosting and hiding techniques described earlier. While some can easily be detected, others are lethal. The boosting of PageRank is an insidious example. The promoting community can include any content whatsoever and embed its links within an arbitrary network of connections. However, although it can be concealed, a characteristic interconnection pattern underlies the network, and this gives search engines a chance to discover the bomb lurking within.

Search engines devise shields against the spammers' weapons. For example, in 2004 Google proposed a simple way to defeat guest-book spam. The idea was to introduce a new kind of link called "nofollow" that anyone can use. These links work in the normal way, except that search engines do not interpret them as endorsing the page they lead to. In an unprecedented cooperative move,

MSN and Yahoo, as well as major blogging vendors, agreed to support Google's proposal. Technically it involves adding a nofollow tag to existing links, rather than defining a completely new link, so existing applications—web servers and browsers—are unaffected. It's not hard for guest-book software, and wiki and blog systems, to scan user-entered text and place the nofollow tag on all links therein.

Like spammers, search engines employ secrecy and occasionally deceit. As mentioned earlier, they probably crawl the web in disguise to check for cloaking. Spammers fill honey pots with attractive information (for example, copies of useful public documents, or copied hubs) to deceive legitimate websites into linking to them. Search engines, if they spot this happening, simply artificially downgrade the honey pot's PageRank or HITS score. The code is kept secret and no one will ever know, except that the spammer's efforts will mysteriously prove ineffectual.

One way in which search engines can purify their results is based on the simple observation that reputable sites don't link to disreputable ones—unless they have actually been infiltrated, which is rare. Suppose a person manually inspects sample pages and labels them as good or bad, ham or spam, trusted or untrustworthy. Links from trusted pages almost always lead to other trusted ones, and this allows a trust map of the web to be drawn up. However, good sites can occasionally be deceived into linking to bad ones—honey pots are an explicit attempt to engineer this—so it is advantageous to keep inference chains short. Of course, if an error is discovered, it can immediately be corrected by hand-labeling that page.

When propagating trust from a given number of hand-labeled sample pages, the result can be improved by selecting ones that lead directly to a large set of other pages, so that their trust status can be inferred directly. Indeed, we should select pages that point to many pages that in turn point to many other pages, and so on. This leads to a kind of inverse PageRank, where the number of outlinks replaces the number of inlinks, measuring influence rather than prestige.

As time goes by, spammers' bombs become ever more sophisticated. Effective defenses like the trust mechanism are likely to benefit significantly from human labeling. Machine learning technology should prove a powerful ally. Given a set of examples that have been judged by humans, automated learning methods generalize that judgment to the remaining examples. They make decisions on the basis of a model that is determined during a learning phase and is designed to minimize error on the human-labeled examples. This defense mechanism exhibits a feature that is highly prized by search engines: even if spammers know what learning algorithm is used, the model cannot be predicted because it depends on the training examples. Moreover, if spammers invent new tactics, the dragons can relabel a few critical pages and learn a new defensive model from scratch.

THE DILEMMA OF SECRECY

In 1250 B.C., the city of Troy was finally destroyed after ten years of unsuccessful siege. In one of the first notable examples of the importance of secrecy in military action, the Greeks built a hollow wooden horse, filled it with soldiers, and left it in front of the city gates. The rest, as they say, is history. Well over three millennia later, during World War II, secrecy remained a crucial ingredient in a totally different technological context. German scientists refined an earlier Polish invention into Enigma, an encryption machine whose purpose was to keep radio communications—such as planned U-boat attacks—secret. The code was cracked by British scientists led by Alan Turing, the father of computer science, who invented a computer specifically for that purpose and made a significant contribution to the Allied victory.

Secrecy also plays a central role in the dragons' war against spammers. Spammers hide their work, of course; otherwise it would be easy for the dragons to discriminate against improperly boosted pages. The software code that implements the dragons' ranking policies is kept secret, for knowing it would give spammers an easy target on which to drop their bombs. Moreover, the policies can be surreptitiously changed at will—and they are.

Search engines use secrecy to help combat spam, which is necessary to keep our view of the web in good order. But secrecy is a crude weapon. In the realm of computer security, experts speak disparagingly of "security by obscurity." In the past, computers kept lists of users and their passwords in obscure files. This information had to be heavily guarded because it was an obvious point of weakness: if it got out, the entire system would instantly be compromised. The modern approach is to employ cryptographic devices such as one-way functions—ones that scramble information in a way that cannot be reversed—to store the password file. Then it does not need to be kept secret, for it is no use to an interloper. The passwords that users present are scrambled and checked against the file to determine whether to grant access, but the file cannot be unscrambled to reveal them. Today's dragons rely on security by obscurity, creating a serious weakness: a huge incentive to bribe a disgruntled or corrupt employee, or otherwise crack the secret.

There is an even more compelling objection to the dragon's secrecy. Users have a legitimate reason to know the recipe that governs the emergence of certain web pages from underneath a mountain of documents. What are you missing if you inspect the first three, or the first twenty, pages from the ranking? What if the ranking policy changes? The view of the web that the dragons present is arbitrary and changes mysteriously at unpredictable times. We are trapped in a dilemma: users want to know how their information is selected—indeed, they have a right to—but if this information were made public, spam would increase without bound, with disastrous consequences. And, of course, publishing the details of the ranking policy would create far more interest among spammers than among most ordinary users.

TACTICS AND STRATEGY

Spammers and dragons are waging a tactical war by engaging in a succession of minor conflicts. They perform optimizations aimed at preserving and expanding their own businesses, which are both based on web visibility. Spammers seek to control as many pages as possible. They typically create their own websites, though if they can manage to attract links from other sites—preferably ones of high repute—so much the better. But this is not the whole story. As in real war, alliances can be very effective. Spammers interconnect their link farms for mutual benefit or through economic agreements. Such alliances tend to improve the ranking of every member, boosting the visibility of each spammer's link farm, which in turn is used to boost the visibility of paying customers who suffer from visibility fever. Figure 5.4 shows a simple alliance in which two link farms jointly boost two targets.

Dragons do their best to render spammers ineffective, and particularly to break up alliances. The fact that their code is secret allows them to quietly shift the target. When spammers focus on a particular feature of the ranking algorithm that they believe crucially affects visibility, dragons can simply change that feature. Given the growing public distaste for spam, and the fact that the dragons provide the only means for large-scale web search, they can mount broad public anti-spam campaigns, perhaps even supported by legislation. While this has its merits, it could be a double-edged sword, for ethical concerns can also be raised about the business model adopted by some search engines (e.g., selling placement in search results).

While fighting this tactical war, the dragons should also be hatching an overall strategic plot that reaches much further than individual battles. And for all we know, they are. New ideas might go far beyond the simple keyword-based query model. The web is suffering to an extent that is already beginning to create a dilemma for us users. Parents who ignore cries for help from teenagers often end up learning the hard way.

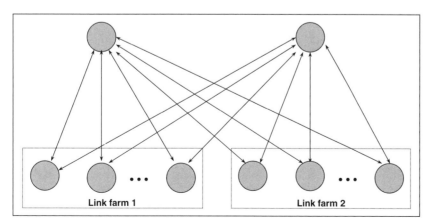

Figure 5.4 A spam alliance in which two link farms jointly boost two target pages.

SO WHAT?

The World Wide Web was created by scientists and quickly became the playground of academic computer researchers. Then commerce took over, introducing a competitive element into what until then had been a fundamentally cooperative environment. The playground became a battleground. As gateways to the web, search engines are the arbiters of visibility. Web visibility is free advertising to the most attractive possible audience—people who are actively seeking information related to your product. Promoting visibility has become an industry. There are perfectly legitimate ways to do this: make your pages attractive and informative and ensure that they are listed in the right places. But some people attempt to discover and exploit loopholes in how the dragons sift information. This has the effect of polluting our information universe, and search engine companies work hard on our behalf to eliminate the deleterious effects of web spam on their search results.

Next we turn to broader questions of the control of information, both on the web and in our society.

WHAT CAN *YOU* DO ABOUT ALL THIS?

- Donate some computer time to a good cause (*SETI@home*?).
- List the websites you rely on—ones whose failure you are most vulnerable to—and spend a day without them to see how vulnerable you are.
- Install a spyware prevention program on your PC.
- Hide a message in e-mail spam (try *spammimic*).
- Find a link farm.
- Learn the market price of PageRank (try *eBay*).
- Find a web page that contains some hidden content.
- Find web pages of search engine optimization companies and learn what they do.
- Learn about Google's AdSense.
- Discuss different boosting methods from an ethical point of view.

NOTES AND SOURCES

The WebCrow program was designed by one of the present authors, Marco Gori, along with Marco Ernandes, a Ph.D. student at the University of Siena. It soon attracted the attention of another student, Giovanni Angelini, who began to improve it using techniques from computational linguistics. It was announced in *Nature* (Castellani, 2004) and is sponsored by Google under their Research Program Awards.

The idea of parasitic computing was developed by Barabási and his colleagues at Notre Dame University, who also announced their results in a seminal paper in *Nature* (Barabási et al., 2001). The consequences of gradual breakdown in the network of links in the web are analogous to the consequences of faults in the routing computers of the Internet, a topic that has been widely investigated and is addressed in Barabási's (1999) book, *Linked*. Shlomo Havlin and colleagues at Bar-Ilan University in Israel discovered the intriguing result that you can remove nodes from power-law networks without fragmenting them into clusters, provided the exponent of the power law is not greater than 3 (Cohen et al., 2000). Intrusion detection was introduced by Dorothy Denning (1987), who initiated the academic study of viruses, worms, and their detection. A systematic treatment with historical references can be found in Bace (2000).

Many studies of how to combat web spam are undertaken by search engine companies but are not made available to the public. Gyongyi and Garcia-Molina (2005a) published a comprehensive survey that includes a taxonomy of boosting and hiding techniques currently used to enhance the visibility of websites. They estimated that in March 2004, spam represented 10 to 15 percent of web pages. The same authors observed that links from trusted pages generally lead to other trusted ones (Gyongyi et al., 2004) and discussed the insidious problem of spam alliances (Gyongyi and Garcia-Molina, 2005b). Google has indicated interest in technologies for the propagation of trust by registering a U.S. trademark for the word *TrustRank*. Fetterly et al. (2004) give interesting statistical analyses of how to locate websites containing spam. The topic of web visibility and the growth of a speculative bubble has been studied by Gori and Witten (2005). Johansen et al. (1999) discuss significant financial crashes between 1929 and 1998 and point out that almost all of them share common preconditions. Figures 5.2 and 5.3 are from Bianchini et al. (2005).

Finally, some brief notes about the literature cited in this chapter: Umberto Eco's masterpiece *The Name of the Rose* (Eco, 1980) was originally published in Italian as *Il Nome della Rosa* and has been likened to transplanting Sherlock Holmes to a medieval monastery, incorporating elements of the gothic thriller. Harlie in *When Harlie was One* (Gerrold, 1972) is a more endearing version of HAL 9000 in Stanley Kubrick's film *2001: A Space Odyssey* (1968). The story revolves around his relationship with the psychologist whose job it is to guide him from childhood to adulthood. Sartre's famous essay "What is Literature?" (Sartre, 1947) presents an Existentialist account of literature, which he argues is an important part of our difficult but essential task of facing up to human freedom. *The Art of War* (Sun-Tzu, 515–512 B.C.) is a definitive work on military strategy and tactics that has had a vast influence on Western military planning ever since it was first translated into a European language (French) two centuries ago.

WHO CONTROLS INFORMATION?

The underlying mantra of the web is that it's free for all, accessible by everyone. Even before the beginning, in the pre-dawn darkness, Tim Berners-Lee (1989) foresaw that "for an international hypertext to be worthwhile … many people would have to post information." The idea was always that anyone should be able to publish, and everyone should be able to read: there would be no central control. It was understood that the information itself would be the right stuff: good, useful, and reliable, even if not always completely correct. And the hyperlinks would be apt and relevant; they would take you on instructive and informative voyages of exploration. But if we look dispassionately at the web as it is today, we have to acknowledge that some of the characteristics it has acquired do not really comply with this wholesome vision.

The web is a victim of its own success. So many people are eager to publish that no one could possibly check that all the information is presented in good faith—let alone that it is correct and reliable. Indeed, it serves so many different communities and the content is so diverse that the very idea of information being "correct and reliable" and presented "in good faith" is hopelessly naïve, almost

---

A human in the node, and the insidious braids of control.

laughable—although in the early days, the user community, far smaller and more focused back then, would have shared a broad consensus on such matters.

This chapter is about the mechanisms that control the flow of information. A cardinal advantage of the web is that it eliminates many intermediaries that the traditional publishing industry places between the demand for information and its supply. But search engines are a new kind of intermediary—an extraordinarily powerful one—that stand between users and their right to be informed. In practice, they play a central role in controlling access to information. What does this mean for democracy on the web?

Despite their youthful immaturity and the crudeness of their retrieval mechanisms, search engines have become absolutely indispensable when working with online information today. The presence of these intermediaries between users and the information they seek is double-edged. On the one hand, we must thank the dragons for the invaluable service they offer to the community (and for free). On the other, we have to accept them as arbiters of our searches.

Search engines are the world's most popular information services. Almost all web users (85 percent) employ them. More than half (55 percent) use them every day. Without them, most sites would be practically inaccessible. They represent the only hope of visibility for millions of authors. They play a pivotal role in the distribution of information and consequently in the organization of knowledge. But there is no transparency in their operation. Their architecture is shrouded in mystery. The algorithms they follow are secret. They are accountable to no one. Nevertheless, they furnish our most widely used public service for online information retrieval. As we learned in the last chapter, they have not necessarily chosen secrecy: it is forced upon them by the dynamics of spam.

The search business is hotly competitive, and the dragons must offer excellent service in order to convince people to use them. However, as public companies, their primary responsibility must be to their shareholders, not their users. The object is to make a profit. Profit is a legitimate, honest, fair, and necessary aim of any commercial enterprise. But in this case, there is a delicate balance between performing the public service of ensuring information access and making money out of it on the way. Since they are the visibility arbiters of online information, the raw material from which new knowledge is wrought passes through the dragons' gates. This raises technical, economic, ethical, and political issues.

In traditional publishing, it is copyright law that controls the use and reuse of information. Copyright is society's answer to the question of how to reward authors for their creative work. On the web, most authors are not rewarded—at least, not directly. But when asking who controls information, we should take a close look at copyright law because, as we learned in Chapter 2, immense efforts are underway to digitize traditional libraries and place them online.

Does copyright apply to material that was born digital? The situation with regard to computer files, and particularly documents published on the web, is murky. Lawyers have questioned whether it is legal even to view a document on the web, since one's browser inevitably makes a local copy that has not explicitly been authorized. Of course, it is widely accepted that you can look at web documents—after all, that's what they're there for. If we allow that you can view them, next comes the question of whether you can save them for personal use—or print them, link to them, copy them, share them, or distribute them to others. Note that computers copy and save documents behind the scenes all over the place. For example, web browsers accelerate delivery by interacting with web proxy servers that selectively cache pages (see Chapter 5, pages 147–148).

Search tools are at the confluence of two powerful sources of data. They enable access to all the information on the web, and they log user queries over time. Like telephone calls, query records are sensitive information: they allow customer profiling, and they reflect citizens' thought processes. The privacy policy that they adopt is of crucial importance for all of us.

In 1986, before the web era began, Richard Mason, a pioneer in the field of information ethics, wrote an influential and provocative article that identified four critical challenges we face in the information age: privacy, accuracy, property, and accessibility. Privacy concerns the question of what information people can keep to themselves and what they are forced to reveal. Accuracy deals with the authenticity and fidelity of information—and who is accountable for error. Property is about who owns information and what right they have to determine a fair price for its exchange. Accessibility relates to the criteria and conditions of access by people or organizations to particular pieces of information. Search engines, at the heart of information distribution on the web, are critically involved in all four areas.

THE VIOLENCE OF THE ARCHIVE

The web is a kind of collective memory that is fully open and public. Its contents can be examined, commented on, cataloged, referred to, retrieved, and read by everyone. You could think of it as a world archive whose contents—for the first time in the history of mankind—are not controlled by authorities and institutions, but rest directly in the hands of those individuals who can access and nurture it.

You might be surprised to learn that archives, which you probably think of as dusty caverns of forgotten nostalgia, are historical dynamite. They can be used to rewrite history by making parts of it simply vanish. Archives are not neutral records because history is written by the *winners*. In the case of conflict, the records that survive are those that support the interpretation of the conquerors. Archives do violence to the truth.

Controlling the means of information preservation—the archives—bestows the ultimate power. You can decide what is public and what is private, what is secret, and what is up for discussion. Once these issues have been settled, the archive's conservation policy sets them in stone for time immemorial. Archives are both revolutionary and conservative: revolutionary in determining what can and cannot be talked about, and conservative in propagating the decisions indefinitely. But information on the web belongs to society as a whole. Social control of the archive implies collective possession of history.

Free access to all was a signature of the early web. So was self-organization—or lack of it. Material accumulated chaotically, anarchically. But to be useful, information needs to be organized: it must be retrieved, studied, and interpreted before it can form the basis for new knowledge. As a leading contemporary philosopher put it in a book on the role of archives in the organization of knowledge:

> The archive is what determines that all these things said do not accumulate endlessly in an amorphous mass, nor are they inscribed in an unbroken linearity, nor do they disappear at the mercy of chance external accidents; but they are grouped together in distinct figures, composed together in accordance with specific regularities.
>
> – *Foucault (1989)*

The web by itself is not an archive in this sense. Archives involve rules that govern how their contents are organized and accessed and how they are maintained and preserved.

Transferring the ability to publish from institutions to individuals promises a welcome innovation: the democratization of information. The catch is that the effectiveness of publication is governed by the tools available for organizing information and retrieving content. And these tools are not publicly controlled; they're supplied by private companies.

Although traditional archives preserve knowledge (and therefore the possible directions for creating new knowledge), their contents do not evolve naturally but are controlled by man-made laws that govern what is and is not included. The postmodern deconstructionist philosopher Derrida noted this in a lecture given in London in 1994—coincidentally, just as the web was taking off. An archive is the historical a priori, a record of facts, discovered not deduced, that support subsequent interpretations of history. Derrida spoke of the "violence of the archive," which does not merely involve remembering and forgetting, inclusion and exclusion, but also occlusion—the deliberate obstruction of the record of memory. By *violence*, Derrida suggests the conflicts that arise as the archive suffers regressions, repressions, suppressions, even the annihilation of memory, played out against the larger cultural and historical backdrop. He broods on revisionist histories that have been based on material in archives—*archives of evil*—that do violence to the truth.

Viewed as an archive, the web embodies deep contradictions. No one controls its content: everybody is free to contribute whatever he or she feels is needed to build and preserve a memory of our society. However, nothing is permanent: online content suffers from link rot, and the only accurate references are spatio-temporal ones: location *and* access date. Existence does not necessarily imply access: in order to find things, we must consult the gatekeepers. The dragons are the de facto arbiters of online memory.

Another conundrum is that the notion of "archive" implies both an interior and an exterior: there must be some things that it does *not* contain. As Derrida enigmatically puts it:

> There is no archive without a place of consignation, without a technique of repetition, and without a certain exteriority. No archive without outside.
>
> *– Derrida (1995, p. 11)*

You need somewhere to put the archive ("consignation"), some way of accessing it ("repetition"), and an exterior to make it meaningful to talk about the interior. But the web is everywhere; it holds everything that is produced (or is at least capable of doing so). It is in constant flux. Where does its outside commence?

Again, the answer lies in the distinction between the web as a repository and the web as a retrieval system. Information retrieval is by nature selective, and different tools embody different biases. The web's exterior is represented not by absent documents, but by inherent bias in the tools we use to access it. The spirit of the web—the spirit of those pioneers who conceived and developed it—is kept alive by a continual process of conception and invention of new means of gathering, accessing, and presenting information. Users and developers share responsibility for ensuring that the web does not degenerate into a closed machine that can be interrogated in just one way, an oracle that spouts the same answers to everybody. The web was founded on the freedom of all users to share information. The same freedom should be reflected today and tomorrow in the continued evolution of new tools to access it.

WEB DEMOCRACY

In the beginning, life was simple: when you inserted links into your page, the targets were the pages that were most appropriate, most relevant. Today the web is so immense that visibility has become the dominant factor. If you don't know about my page, you certainly won't link to it. Nodes with many links are de facto more visible and tend to attract yet more links. Popularity is winning out over fitness. This makes it difficult for newcomers to gain prominence—but not impossible, as the fairytale success of Google, a latecomer in the search engine arena, illustrates. As the web becomes commercial, another factor in link placement is the questionable desire to maximize visibility artificially, as we learned in the previous chapter. Even outside the business world of search engine optimization, webmasters continually receive e-mail suggesting that "if you link to me, I'll link to you: it'll be good for us both."

As we all know, it's really hard to find good, reliable information. The problem is not just one of determining whether what you are looking at represents the right stuff—correct, reliable, presented in good faith, the right kind of truth for you. It's also that given a particular information need, crudely translated into a search engine query, there can be no single definitive list of the "best" results. The relevance of information is overwhelmingly modulated by personal preference, the context of the request, the user's educational level, background knowledge, linguistic ability, and so on. There are as many good replies to an inquiry as there are people who pose the question.

THE RICH GET RICHER

Received wisdom, underscored by rhetoric from all quarters, is that the web is the universal key to information access. However, we now know that things are not as straightforward as they appear at first sight. Over the last decade or so, the network theory sketched in Chapter 3 has been developed to explain how structure emerges spontaneously in linked organisms, like the web, that evolve continuously over time; structure that is shared by all scale-free networks. The very fact of growth determines the network's topological form. This structure, clearly understandable from the logical point of view, implies that when people publish information online, there is scant chance that it will actually be read by others. Indeed, Barabási, one of the pioneers of the study of the web as an enormous scale-free network, went so far as to observe:

The most intriguing result of our web-mapping project was the complete absence of democracy, fairness, and egalitarian values on the web. We learned that the topology of the web prevents us from seeing anything but a mere handful of the billion documents out there.

– Barabási (2002, p. 56)

How can this be? To probe further, let's examine a 2003–2004 study that took a snapshot of part of the web and then another one seven months later.

A sample of 150 websites was chosen, and all their pages were downloaded, plus the pages they linked to—a total of 15 million of them. The two snapshots had 8 million pages in common. The goal was to examine how the number of inlinks to each page changed over the period.

There were about 12 million new links. But surprisingly, a full 70 percent of these went to the 20 percent of the pages that were originally most popular in terms of their number of inlinks. The next 20 percent of pages received virtually all the remaining new links. In other words, the 60 percent of pages that were least popular in the original sample received essentially no new incoming links whatsoever! Even when the new links were expressed as a proportion of the original number of links, there was a negligible increase for the 60 percent of less-popular pages. This extraordinary result illustrates that, on the web, the rich get richer.

Suppose the increase was measured by PageRank rather than the number of inlinks. It's still the case that the top 20 percent of the original sample receives the lion's share of the increase, and the next 20 percent receives all the rest. But the total amount is conserved, for, as we learned in Chapter 4, PageRank reflects the proportion of time that a random surfer will spend on the page. It follows that the remaining 60 percent of pages suffer substantial decreases. Not only do the rich get richer, but the poor get poorer as well. In this sense, the web reflects one of the tragedies of real life.

Of course, you'd expect the rich to get richer, for two reasons. First, pages with good content attract more links. The fact that a page already has many inlinks is one indication that it has good content. If new links are added to the system, it's natural that more of them will point to pages with good content than to ones with poor content. Second, random surfers will be more likely to encounter pages with many inlinks, and therefore more likely to create new links to them. You cannot create a link to something you have not seen.

But these effects do not explain why the bottom 60 percent of pages in the popularity ranking get virtually *no* new links. This is extreme. What could account for it? The dragons.

THE EFFECT OF SEARCH ENGINES

In practice, the way we all find things is through web dragons, the search engines. Their role is to bestow visibility on as much information as possible by connecting all relevant content to well-posed queries. They are the web's gatekeepers: they let people in and help them find what they're looking for; they let information out so it can reach the right audience. What's their impact on the evolution of the web? The links to your page determine where it appears in the search results. But people can only link to your page if they find it in the first place. And most things are found using search engines.

At first glance, things look good. A democratic way for the web to evolve would be for random surfers to continually explore it and place links to pages they find interesting. In practice, rather than surfing, search engines are used for exploration. Consider a searcher who issues a random query and clicks on the results randomly, giving preference to ones higher up the list. Typical search engines take PageRank into account when ordering their results, placing higher-ranking pages earlier in the list. As we learned in Chapter 4 (page 116–117), PageRank reflects the experience of a random surfer, and so it seems that the experience of a random *searcher* will approximately mirror that of a random *surfer*. If that were the case, it would not matter whether links evolved through the actions of searchers or surfers, and the evolution of the web would be unaffected by the use of search engines.

Not so fast. Although this argument is plausible qualitatively, the devil is in the details. It implicitly assumes that random searchers distribute their clicks in the list of search results in the same quantitative way that random surfers visit pages. And it turns out that for typical click distributions, this is not the case. Buried deep in the list from, say, the 100th item onward, lie a huge number of pages that the searcher will hardly ever glance at. Although random surfers certainly do not frequent these pages, they do stumble upon them occasionally. And since there are so many such pages, surfers spends a fair amount of time in regions that searchers never visit.

To quantify this argument would lead us into realms of theory that are inappropriate for this book. But you can see the point by imagining that searchers *never* click results beyond, say, the 100th item (when was the last time you clicked your way through more than ten pages of search results?). The millions of pages that, for typical searches, appear farther down the list are completely invisible. They might as well not be there. The rich get richer and the poor do not stand a chance. More detailed analysis with a plausible model of click behavior has shown that a new page takes 60 times longer to become popular under the search-dominant model than it does under the random surfer model.

Google shot from obscurity (less than 5 percent of web users visited once a week) to popularity (more than 30 percent) in two years, from 2001 through early 2003. According to the preceding model, today, in a world where people only access the web through search, this feat would take 60 times as long—more than a century!

Surely, this must be an exaggeration. Well, it is—in a way. It assumes that people only find new pages using search engines, and that they all use the same one so they all see the same ranking. Fortunately, word of mouth still plays a role in information discovery. (How did you find your favorite web dragon?—probably not by searching for it!) And fortunately, we do not all favor the same dragon. Nevertheless, this is a striking illustration of what might happen if we all used the same mechanism to discover our information.

POPULARITY VERSUS AUTHORITY

Do web dragons simply manage goods—namely, information—in a high-tech marketplace? We don't think so. Information is not like meat or toothpaste: it enjoys special status because it is absolutely central to democracy and freedom. Special attention must be paid to how information circulates because of the extraordinarily wide impact it has on the choices of citizens. When people make decisions that affect social conditions or influence their activities, they must have the opportunity to be fully informed. To exacerbate matters, in the case of web search users are generally blithely unaware not only of just how results are selected (we're all unaware of that!), but of the very fact that the issue might be controversial.

As explained in Chapter 4, despite the internal complexity of search engines, a basic principle is to interpret a link from one page to another as a vote for it. Links are endorsements by the linker of the information provided by the target. Each page is given one vote that it shares equally among all pages it links to: votes are fractional. But pages do not have equal votes: more weight is given to votes from prestigious pages. The definition of prestige is recursive: the more votes a page receives, the more prestigious it is deemed to be. A page shares its prestige equally among all pages it chooses to vote for.

Search engines base prestige solely on popularity, not on any intrinsic merit. In real life, raw popularity is a questionable metric. The most popular politician is not always the most trustworthy person in the country. And though everyone knows their names, the most popular singers and actors are not considered to dispense authoritative advice on social behavior—despite the fact that the young adulate and emulate them. Why, then, do people accept popularity-based criteria in search engines? Do they do this unconsciously? Or is it simply because, despite its faults, it is the most efficacious method we know?

The way web pages relate to one another leads to the idea of an economy of links. Choosing to create a link has a positive value: it is a meaningful, conscious, and socially engaged act. Links not only imply endorsement within the abstract world of the web, they have a strong impact on commercialization of products and services in the real world. Their metaphysical status is ambiguous, falling somewhere between intellectual endorsement and commercial advertising. As we learned in the last chapter, the economy of links has real monetary value: there is a black market, and you can buy apparently prestigious endorsements from link farms. This offends common sense. It's a clear abuse of the web, a form of both pollution and prostitution that stems from a failure to respect the web as a common good. Nowadays such practices cannot be prosecuted by law, but they are firmly—and, some would say, arbitrarily—punished by today's search engines.

Search engines make sense of the universe that they are called upon to interpret. Their operators are strenuously engaged in a struggle against abuse. But despite their goodwill, despite all their efforts on our behalf, one cannot fail to observe that they enjoy a very unusual position of power. Although they play the role of neutral arbiter, in reality they choose a particular criterion which, whatever it is, has the power to define what is relevant and what is insignificant. They did not ask for this awesome responsibility, and they may not relish it. The consequences of their actions are immeasurably complex. No one can possibly be fully aware of them. Of course, we are not compelled to use their service—and we do not pay for it.

Defining the prestige of a web page in terms of its popularity has broad ramifications. Consider minority pages that lie outside the mainstream. They might be couched in a language that few people speak. They might not originate in prominent institutions: government departments, prestigious universities, international agencies, and leading businesses. They might not treat topics of contemporary interest. No matter how relevant they are to our query, we have to acknowledge the possibility that such pages will not be easily located in the list of results that a search engine returns, even though they do not belong to the deep web mentioned in Chapter 3. Without any conscious intent or plan—and certainly without any conspiracy theory—such pages are simply and effectively obliterated, as a by-product of the ranking. This will happen regardless of the particular strategy the dragons adopt. Obviously, no single ranking can protect all minorities. Selective discrimination is an inescapable consequence of the "one size fits all" search model.

There are so many different factors to take into account that it is impossible to evaluate the performance of a search engine fairly. Chapter 4 introduced the twin measures of precision and recall (pages 110–111). Recall concerns the completeness of the search results list in terms of the number of relevant documents it contains, while precision concerns the purity of the list in terms of the number of irrelevant documents it contains. But these metrics apply to a single query, and there is no such thing as a representative query. Anyway, on the web, recall is effectively incomputable because one would need to identify the total number of relevant documents, which is completely impractical. And, of course, the whole notion of "relevance" is contextual—the dilemma of inquiry is that no one can determine what is an effective response for questions from users who do not know exactly what they are seeking. A distinction can be made between relevance—whether a document is "about" the right thing in terms of the question being asked—and pertinence—whether it is useful to the user in that it satisfies their information need. It is very hard to measure pertinence. Add to this the fact that search engines change their coverage, and their ranking methods, in arbitrary ways and at unpredictable times.

This makes it clear that users should interact in a critical way with search engines and employ a broad range of devices and strategies for information retrieval tasks in order to uncover the treasure hidden in the web.

PRIVACY AND CENSORSHIP

Although everyone has a good idea of what *privacy* means, a clear and precise definition is elusive and controversial—and contextual. In many circumstances, we voluntarily renounce privacy, either in circumscribed situations or because the end justifies the means. Life partners arrive at various different understandings as to what they will share, some jealous of individual privacy and others divulging every little secret to their partner. In families, parents give their children privacy up to a certain level and then exercise their right to interfere, educating them and protecting them from external menaces—drugs, undesirable companions, violent situations. For certain purposes, we are all prepared to divulge private information. Whenever you take a blood test, you give the medical technician—a complete stranger—full access to extremely personal information. Privacy is not so much about keeping everything secret; it's more about the ability to selectively decline our right to protection when we want to. It's a matter of control.

Actual privacy legislation differs from one country to another. In this section, we examine privacy protection from a general, commonsense perspective and illustrate the issues raised by widespread use of pervasive information technology to manage and manipulate personal data. Protection is not just a matter of legal rules. We want to understand the underlying issues, issues that apply in many different contexts.

There are two major approaches to privacy: *restricted access* and *control*. The former identifies privacy as a limitation of other people's access to an individual. It is clear that a crucial factor is just who the "other people" are. Prisoners are watched by guards day and night, but no one else has access, and guards are prohibited from revealing anything outside the prison. There is no access from outside—complete privacy—but full access from inside—zero privacy. As another example, disseminating information about oneself must be considered a loss of privacy from the restricted-access point of view. However, revealing a secret to a close friend is quite different from unwittingly having your telephone tapped. The question is whether you have consented to the transfer of personal information.

According to the second view, privacy is not so much about hiding information about oneself from the minds of others, but the control that we can exercise over information dissemination. There is a clear distinction between involuntary violation of privacy and a decision to reveal information to certain people. One question is whether we are talking about *actual* or *potential* revelation of information. We might live in an apartment that is visible from outside with the aid of a telescope, but in a community where nobody ever uses such a device to spy. In strict terms of control, we sacrifice privacy because our neighbors' behavior is beyond our control, but the question is academic because no one actually exploits our lack of control.

This issue is particularly germane to cyberspace. Ubiquitous electronics record our decisions, our choices in the supermarket, our financial habits, our comings and goings. We swipe our way through the world, every swipe a record in a database. The web overwhelms us with information; meanwhile every choice we make is recorded. Internet providers know everything we do online and in some countries are legally required to keep a record of all our behavior for years. Mobile telephone operators can trace our movements and all our conversations. Are we in control of the endless trail of data that we leave behind us as we walk though life? Can we dictate the uses that will be made of it? Of course not. This state of affairs forces us to reflect anew on what privacy is and how to protect it in the age of universal online access.

PRIVACY ON THE WEB

When defining privacy, various modalities of protection of personal data can be distinguished, depending on the communication situation. In private situations, of which the extreme is one-on-one face-to-face interaction, we are less protective of the data we distribute but in full control of our audience. In public situations the reverse is true; the audience is outside our control, but we carefully choose what information to reveal. A third communication situation concerns channels for the processing of electronically recorded information.

In this third situation, there are two different principles that govern online privacy. The first, *user predictability*, delimits the reasonable expectations of a person about how his or her personal data will be processed and the objectives to which the processing will be applied. It is widely accepted that before people make a decision to provide personal information, they have a right to know how it will be used and what it will be used for, what steps will be taken to protect its confidentiality and integrity, what the consequences of supplying or withholding the information are, and any rights of redress they may have. The second principle, *social justifiability*, holds that some data processing is justifiable as a social activity even when subjects have not expressly consented to it. This does not include the processing of sensitive data, which always needs the owner's explicit consent. It is clear that these two principles may not always coincide, and for this reason there will never be a single universally applicable privacy protection policy. It is necessary to determine on a case by case basis whether a particular use of personal data is predictable and whether and to what extent it is socially justifiable.

User predictability resembles the medical ethics notion of "informed consent," which is the legal requirement for patients to be fully informed participants in choices about their health care. This originates from two sources: the physician's ethical duty to involve patients in their health care, and the patients' legal right to direct what happens to their body. Informed consent is also the cornerstone of research ethics. While not necessarily a legal requirement, most institutions insist on informed consent prior to any kind of research that involves human subjects. Social justifiability extends informed consent and weakens it in a way that would not be permitted in the ultra-sensitive medical context.

Every user's network behavior is monitored by many operators: access providers, websites, e-mail services, chat, voice over IP (VoIP) telephone services, and so on. Users who are aware of what is going on (and many aren't) implicitly consent to the fact that private information about their online habits will be registered and retained for some period of time. We can assess the privacy implications by considering every piece of data in terms of its predictability and justifiability, and verify the system's legitimacy—both moral and legal—according to these principles.

Our information society involves continual negotiation between the new possibilities for communication that technology presents and the new opportunities it opens up for monitoring user behavior. There is both a freedom and a threat; privacy protection lies on the boundary. As users, we choose to trust service providers because we believe the benefits outweigh the drawbacks. The risk is loss of control of all the personal information we are obliged to divulge when using new tools.

We are never anonymous when surfing the net: the system automatically registers every click. Service providers retain data in accordance with national laws such as the U.S.A. Patriot Act.[41] Although they are not compelled to do so, many individual websites keep track of our activities using the cookie mechanism. As explained in Chapter 3 (pages 73–74), cookies reside on the user's computer and can be erased at will, either manually or by installing software that periodically removes them, paying special attention to suspected spyware. Technically speaking, users retain control of this privacy leak. But practically speaking, they do not, for most are blithely unaware of what is

---

[41] The name is an acronym for *Uniting and Strengthening America by Providing Appropriate Tools Required to Intercept and Obstruct Terrorism*. This Act began in 2001 and was so controversial that it had to be renewed by the U.S. Senate every year; most of its provisions were finally made permanent in 2006. The Electronic Privacy Information Center (EPIC) has more information.

going on, let alone how to delete cookies (and the risks of doing so). Moreover, the balance between freedom and threat arises again, for cookies allow websites to personalize their services to each individual user—recognizing your profile and preferences, offering recommendations, advice or opportunities, and so on.

PRIVACY AND WEB DRAGONS

It is impossible to draw a clear line between protection of privacy and access to useful services. Certainly users should be aware of what is going on—or at the very least have the opportunity to learn—and how to use whatever controls are available. Every website should disclose its policy on privacy. Many do, but if you do have the patience to find and read them, you may discover that popular websites have policies that allow them to do more than you realized with the personal data you give them.

Here is a lightly paraphrased version of the privacy policy of a major search engine (Google):

We only share personal information with other companies or individuals if we have a good faith belief that access, use, preservation or disclosure of such information is reasonably necessary to (a) satisfy any applicable law, regulation, legal process or enforceable governmental request, (b) enforce applicable Terms of Service, including investigation of potential violations thereof, (c) detect, prevent, or otherwise address fraud, security or technical issues, or (d) protect against imminent harm to the rights, property or safety of the company, its users or the public as required or permitted by law.[42]

This example is typical: the policies of other major search engines are not materially different. Yahoo pledges that it will not share personal information about you except with trusted partners who work on its behalf, and these partners must in turn pledge that they will not use the information for their own business purposes. For instance, an insurance company interested in purchasing personal queries on medical conditions cannot procure them from search engines, either directly or indirectly. However, as you can see from the policy quoted here, under some circumstances personal information can be shared. Governments can access it if it relates to criminal activity, and the company can use it to investigate security threats. A further clause states that if the company is acquired or taken over, users must be informed before the privacy policy is changed. In a sense, the philosophy behind search engine privacy reflects the norm for telephone companies: they must prevent the circulation of personal data.

Most companies routinely track their customers' behavior. There is enormous added value in being able to identify individual customers' transaction

---

[42] Extracted from Google's privacy policy at *www.google.com/intl/en/privacypolicy.html#infochoices*.

histories. This has led to a proliferation of discount or "loyalty" cards that allow retailers to identify customers whenever they make a purchase. If individuals' purchasing history can be analyzed for patterns, precisely targeted special offers can be mailed to prospective customers.

Your web queries relate to all aspects of your life (at least, ours do). People use their favorite search engine for professional activities, for leisure, to learn what their friends are doing, or to get a new date—and check up on his or her background. If you subscribe to their services, web dragons monitor your queries in order to establish your profile so that they can offer you personalized responses. In doing so, they keep track of what you are thinking about. When opting for personalized service, you face an inescapable dilemma: the more facilities the service offers, the more privacy you will have to renounce. However, unless you are working outside the law, your private data is not expected to circulate outside the dragon's lair.

As an example of unanticipated circulation of personal information, in April 2004, dissident Chinese journalist Shi Tao was convicted of disclosing secret information to foreign websites and condemned to ten years in jail. Vital incriminating evidence was supplied to the Chinese government by Yahoo's Hong Kong branch, which traced him and revealed his e-mail address, Internet site, and the content of some messages. Commenting on the case during an Internet conference in China, Yahoo's founder Jerry Yang declared:

> We don't know what they wanted that information for, we're only told what to look for. If they give us the proper documentation in a court order, we give them things that satisfy local laws. I don't like the outcome of what happens with these things. But we have to follow the law.[43]

CENSORSHIP ON THE WEB

During 2004, Google launched a Chinese-language edition of its news service, but in an emasculated version:

> For users inside the People's Republic of China, we have chosen not to include sources that are inaccessible from within that country.[44]

Self-censorship was judged necessary in order to launch the service. In 2002, the company had crossed swords with the Chinese government, and in some areas of the country it seems that Google cooperated by withdrawing selected pages and redirecting to a Chinese search engine from Google's home page.

---

[43] *www.washingtonpost.com/wp-dyn/content/article/2005/09/10/AR2005091001222.html*

[44] *googleblog.blogspot.com/2004/09/china-google-news-and-source-inclusion.html*

In summer 2004, Google invested heavily in Baidu, a government-approved Chinese search engine. Early in 2006, after a long period of uncertainty, Google finally announced that it was actively assisting the Chinese government in censoring results from its main search service.

Human rights groups responded in a blaze of outrage whose flames were fanned by the company's self-proclaimed motto, "Do no evil." Of course, web dragons cannot impose their service in defiance of a hostile government that is prepared to censor access from any Internet address. They have just two choices: to go along with censorship or to refrain from offering their service. Meanwhile, when Microsoft was criticized in mid-2005 for censoring the content of Chinese blogs that it hosted, it retorted:

Microsoft works to bring our technology to people around the world to help them realize their full potential. Like other global organizations we must abide by the laws, regulations and norms of each country in which we operate.[45]

China today presents a golden opportunity for profit in the business of web search and related technologies. Major search engines and leading Internet companies are jockeying for a favorable market position. The problem is that local regulations sometimes dictate controversial decisions concerning personal freedom. In parts of the world where free speech is in jeopardy, the enormous power wielded by information filters placed between users and Internet services becomes all too evident, as does the danger of monitoring user behavior. The flip side is that withdrawing search services could cause damage by restricting cultural and business opportunities.

Privacy and censorship are critical problems on the web. Both involve a balance between transparency and protection of individuals from information disclosure. People need to be protected both by keeping private information secret and by censoring certain kinds of information. The problem is to define the boundary between permissible and illicit diffusion of information, balancing the rights of the individual against community norms. For example, criminals sacrifice their right to privacy: when the police demand information about a cyber thief, the community's right to be protected against illegal appropriation may outweigh the suspect's right to privacy. Censorship is justified when transparency is deemed to damage a segment of society. Almost everyone would agree that young children should be protected from certain kinds of content: social software helps parents censor their children's viewing.

These issues cannot be dealt with mechanically because it is impossible to draw a line based on formal principles between the community's right to know

---

[45] *news.bbc.co.uk/1/hi/world/asia-pacific/4221538.stm*

and the individual's right to privacy. Moreover, any solutions should respect cultural diversity. Decisions can only be made on a case by case basis, taking into account the context and the type of information. These difficult judgments depend on social norms and pertain to society as a whole. They should not be left to automatic filters or to private companies with legitimate business interests to defend. Society must find a way to participate in the decision process, open it up, allow debate and appeal. Online privacy and censorship will remain open questions. There is an inescapable tradeoff between the opportunities offered by new information technologies and the threats that they (and their administrators) pose to our core freedoms.

COPYRIGHT AND THE PUBLIC DOMAIN

Digital collections are far more widely accessible than physical ones. This creates a problem: access to the information is far less controlled than in physical libraries. Digitizing information has the potential to make it immediately available to a virtually unlimited audience. This is great news. For the user, information around the world becomes available wherever you are. For the author, a wider potential audience can be reached than ever before. And for publishers, new markets open up that transcend geographical limitations. But there is a flip side. Authors and publishers ask, how many copies of a work will be sold if networked digital libraries enable worldwide access to an electronic copy of it? Their nightmare is that the answer is *one*. How many books will be published if the entire market can be extinguished by the sale of one electronic copy to a public library?

COPYRIGHT LAW

Possessing a copy of a document certainly does not constitute ownership in terms of copyright law. Though there may be many copies, every work has only one copyright owner. This applies not just to physical copies of books, but to computer files too, whether they have been digitized from a physical work or created electronically in the first place—born digital, you might say. When you buy a copy of a work, you can resell it but you certainly do not buy the right to redistribute it. That right rests with the copyright owner.

Copyright subsists in a work rather than in any particular embodiment of it. A work is an intangible intellectual object, of which a document is a physical manifestation. Lawyers use the word *subsists*, which in English means "to remain or continue in existence," because copyright has no separate existence without the work. Copyright protects the way ideas are expressed, not the ideas themselves. Two works that express the same idea in different ways are independent in copyright law.

Who owns a particular work? The creator is the initial copyright owner, unless the work is made for hire. If the work is created by an employee within the scope of her employment, or under a specific contract that explicitly designates it as being made for hire, it is the employer or contracting organization that owns the copyright. Any copyright owner can transfer or "assign" copyright to another party through a specific contract, made in writing and signed. Typically an author sells copyright to a publisher (or grants an exclusive license), who reproduces, markets, and sells the work.

The copyright owner has the exclusive right to do certain things with the work: thus copyright is sometimes referred to as a "bundle" of rights. In general, there are four rights, though details vary from country to country. The *reproduction right* allows the owner to reproduce the work freely. The *distribution right* allows him to distribute it. This is a one-time right: once a copy has been distributed, the copyright owner has no right to control its subsequent distribution. For example, if you buy a book, you can do whatever you want with your copy—such as resell it. The *public lending right* compensates authors for public lending of their work—though an exception is granted for not-for-profit and educational uses, which do not require the copyright holder's consent. The remaining rights, called *other rights*, include permitting or refusing public performance of the work, and making derivative works such as plays or movies.

Copyright law is complex, arcane, and varies from one country to another. The British Parliament adopted the first copyright act in 1710; the U.S. Congress followed suit in 1790. Although copyright is national law, most countries today have signed the Berne Convention of 1886, which lays down a basic international framework. According to this Convention, copyright subsists *without formality*, which means that (unlike patents), it's not dependent on registering a work with the authorities or depositing a copy in a national library. It applies regardless of whether the document bears the international copyright symbol ©. You automatically have copyright over works you create (unless they are made for hire). Some countries—including the United States—maintain a copyright registry even though they have signed the Berne Convention, which makes it easier for a copyright holder to take legal action against infringers. Nevertheless, copyright still subsists even if the work has not been registered.

The Berne Convention decrees that it is always acceptable to make limited quotations from protected works, with acknowledgement and provided it is done fairly. The United States has a particular copyright principle called "fair use" which allows material to be copied by individuals for research purposes. The U.K. equivalent, which has been adopted by many countries whose laws were inherited from Britain in colonial times, is called "fair dealing" and is slightly more restrictive than fair use.

Making copies of works under copyright for distribution or resale is prohibited. That is the main economic point of the copyright system. The Berne Convention also recognizes certain moral rights. Unlike economic rights, these cannot be assigned or transferred to others; they remain with the author forever. They give authors the right to the acknowledgment of their authorship and to the integrity of their work—which means that they can object to a derogatory treatment of it.

THE PUBLIC DOMAIN

Works not subject to copyright are said to be in the "public domain," which comprises the cultural and intellectual heritage of humanity that anyone may use or exploit. Often, works produced by the government are automatically placed in the public domain, or else it sets out generous rules for their use by not-for-profit organizations. This applies only in the country of origin: thus, works produced by the U.S. government are in the public domain in the United States but are subject to U.S. copyright rules in other countries.

Copyright does not last forever, but eventually expires. When that happens, the work passes into the public domain, free of all copyright restrictions. No permission is needed to use it in any way, incorporate any of its material into other works, or make any derivative works. You can copy it, sell it, excerpt it—or digitize it and put it on the web. The author's moral rights still hold, however, so you must provide due attribution.

Today the internationally agreed Berne Convention sets out a minimum copyright term of life plus 50 years, that is, until 50 years after the author dies. This presents a practical difficulty, for it is often hard to find out when the author died. One way is to consult the authors' association in the appropriate country, which maintains links to databases maintained by authors' associations around the world.

The duration of copyright has an interesting and controversial history. Many countries specify a longer term than the minimum, and this changes over the years. The original British 1710 act provided a term of 14 years, renewable once if the author was alive; it also decreed that all works already published by 1710 would get a single term of 21 further years. The 1790 U.S. law followed suit, with a 14-year once-renewable term. Again, if an author did not renew copyright, the work automatically passed into the public domain.

In 1831, the U.S. Congress extended the initial period of copyright from 14 to 28 years, and in 1909 it extended the renewal term from 14 to 28 years, giving a maximum term of 56 years. From 1962 onward, it enacted a continual series of copyright extensions, some one or two years, others 19 or 20 years.

In 1998, Congress passed the Sonny Bono Copyright Term Extension Act, which extended the term of existing and future copyrights by 20 years.[46]

The motivation behind these moves comes from large, powerful corporations who seek protection for a miniscule number of cultural icons; opponents call them the "Mickey Mouse" copyright extensions. Many parts of the world (notably the United Kingdom) have followed suit by extending their copyright term to life plus 70 years—and in some countries (e.g., Italy), the extension was retroactive so that books belonging to the public domain were suddenly removed from it.

The upshot is that copyright protection ends at different times depending on when the work was created. It also begins at different times. In the United States, older works are protected for 95 years from the date of first publication. Through the 1998 Copyright Extension Act, newer ones are protected from the "moment of their fixation in a tangible medium of expression" until 70 years after the author's death. Works made for hire—that is, ones belonging to corporations—are protected for 95 years after publication or 120 years after creation, whichever comes first.

The original copyright term was one-time renewable, if the copyright holder wished to do so. In fact, few did. Focusing again on the United States, in 1973 more than 85 percent of copyright holders failed to renew their copyright, which meant that, at the time, the average term of copyright was just 32 years. Today there is no renewal requirement for works created before 1978: copyright is automatically given for a period of 95 years—tripling the average duration of protection.

No copyrights will expire in the twenty-year period between 1998 and 2018. To put this into perspective, one million patents will pass into the public domain during the same period. The effect of this extension is dramatic. Of the 10,000 books published in 1930, only a handful (less than 2 percent) are still in print. If the recent copyright extensions had not occurred, all 10,000 of these books would by now be in the public domain, their copyright having expired in 1958 (after 28 years) if it was not renewed, or 1986 (after a further 28 years) if it was renewed. Unfortunately, that is not the case. If you want to digitize one of these books and make it available on the Internet, you will have to seek the permission of the copyright holder. No doubt 98 percent of them would be perfectly happy to give you permission. Indeed, many of these books are already in the public domain, having expired in 1958. You could find out which, for there is a registry of copyright renewal (though it is not available online) that lists the books that were renewed in 1959. However, for the remaining works, you would have to contact the copyright holders, for which there is no such registry. There will be a record from 1930, and again from 1959, of who registered and extended the copyright. But you'd have to track these people down.

---

[46] The Act is named in memory of former musician Sonny Bono, who, according to his widow, believed that "copyrights should be forever."

The problem is a large one. It has been estimated that of the 32 million unique titles that are to be found in America's collective libraries, only 6 percent are still in print, 20 percent have now passed into the public domain, and the remainder—almost 75 percent—are orphan works: out of print but still under copyright. As Lawrence Lessig put it in his book *Free Culture* (from which much of the preceding information was taken),

> Now that technology enables us to rebuild the library of Alexandria, the law gets in the way. And it doesn't get in the way for any useful copyright purpose, for the purpose of copyright is to enable the commercial market that spreads culture. No, we are talking about culture after it has lived its commercial life. In this context, copyright is serving no purpose at all related to the spread of knowledge. In this context, copyright is not an engine of free expression. Copyright is a brake.
>
> *— Lessig (2004, p. 227)*

RELINQUISHING COPYRIGHT

As we have explained, the Berne Convention makes copyright apply without formality, without registration. Anything you write, every creative act that's "fixated in a tangible means of expression"—be it a book, an e-mail, or a grocery list—is automatically protected by copyright until 50 years after you die (according to the Berne Convention's minimum restrictions) or, today in the United States, 70 years after you die (assuming you did not write your grocery list as a work made for hire). People can quote from it under the principle of fair use, but they cannot otherwise use your work until such time as copyright expires, unless you reassign the copyright.

If you wish to relinquish this protection, you must take active steps to do so. In fact, it's quite difficult. To facilitate this, a nonprofit organization called the Creative Commons has developed licenses that people can attach to the content they create. Each license is expressed in three ways: a legal version, a human-readable description, and a machine-readable tag. Content is marked with the CC mark, which does not mean that copyright is waived but that freedoms are given to others to use the material in ways that would not be permissible under copyright.

These freedoms all go beyond traditional fair use, but their precise nature depends on your choice of license. One license permits any use so long as attribution is given. Another permits only noncommercial use. A third permits any use within developing nations. Or any educational use. Or any use except for the creation of derivative works. Or any use so long as the same freedom is given to other users. Most important, according to the Creative Commons, is that these licenses express what people can do with your work in a way they can understand and rely upon without having to hire a lawyer. The idea is to help reconstruct a viable public domain.

The term "copyleft" is sometimes used to describe a license on a derivative work that imposes the same terms as imposed by the license on the original work. The GNU Free Documentation License is a copyleft license that is a counterpart to the GNU General Public License for software. It was originally designed for manuals and documentation that often accompany GNU-licensed software. The largest project that uses it is Wikipedia, the online encyclopedia mentioned in Chapter 2 (page 65). Its main stipulation is that all copies and derivative works must be made available under the very same license.

COPYRIGHT ON THE WEB

The way that computers work has led people to question whether the notion of a copy is the appropriate foundation for copyright law in the digital age. Legitimate copies of digital information are made so routinely that the act of copying has lost its applicability in regulating and controlling use on behalf of copyright owners. Computers make many internal copies whenever they are used to access information: the fact that a copy has been made says little about the intention behind the behavior. In the digital world, copying is so bound up with the way computers work that controlling it provides unexpectedly broad powers, far beyond those intended by copyright law.

As a practical example, what steps would you need to take if you wanted to digitize some documents and make them available publicly or within your institution? First, you determine whether the work to be digitized is in the public domain or attempts to faithfully reproduce a work in the public domain. If the answer to either question is yes, you may digitize it without securing anyone's permission. Of course, the result of your own digitization labor will not be protected by copyright either, unless you produce something more than a faithful reproduction of the original. If material has been donated to your institution and the donor is the copyright owner, you can certainly go ahead, provided the donor gave your institution the right to digitize. Even without a written agreement, it may reasonably be assumed that the donor implicitly granted the right to take advantage of new media, provided the work continues to be used for the purpose for which it was donated. You do need to ensure, of course, that the donor is the original copyright owner and has not transferred copyright. You cannot, for example, assume permission to digitize letters written by others.

If you want to digitize documents and the considerations just noted do not apply, you should consider whether you can go ahead under the concept of fair use. This is a difficult judgment to make. You need to reflect on how things look from the copyright owner's point of view, and address their concerns.

Institutional policies about who can access the material, backed up by practices that restrict access appropriately, can help. Finally, if you conclude that fair use does not apply, you will have to obtain permission to digitize the work or acquire access by licensing it.

People who build and distribute digital collections must pay serious attention to the question of copyright. Such projects must be undertaken with a full understanding of ownership rights, and full recognition that permissions are essential to convert materials that are not in the public domain. Because of the potential for legal liability, prudent collection-builders will consider seeking professional advice. A full account of the legal situation is far beyond the scope of this book, but the *Notes and Sources* section at the end contains some pointers to sources of further practical information about copyright, including information on how to interpret fair use and the issues involved when negotiating copyright permission or licensing.

Looking at the situation from an ethical rather than a legal point of view helps crystallize the underlying issues. It is unethical to steal: deriving profit by distributing a book on which someone else has rightful claim to copyright is wrong. It is unethical to deprive someone of the fruit of their labor: giving away electronic copies of a book on which someone else has rightful claim to copyright is wrong. It is unethical to pass someone else's work off as your own: making any collection without due acknowledgement is wrong. It is unethical to willfully misrepresent someone else's point of view: modifying documents before including them in the collection is wrong even if authorship is acknowledged.

WEB SEARCHING AND ARCHIVING

What are the implications of copyright for web searching and archiving? These activities are in a state of rapid transition. It is impractical, and also inappropriate, for legal regulation to try to keep up with a technology in transition. If any legislation is needed, it should be designed to minimize harm to interests affected by technological change while enabling and encouraging effective lines of development. Legislators are adopting a wait-and-see policy, while leading innovators bend over backward to ensure that what they do is reasonable and accords with the spirit—if not necessarily the letter—of copyright law.

As you know, search engines are among the most widely used Internet services. We learned in Chapter 3 (page 71) that websites can safeguard against indiscriminate crawling by using the robot exclusion protocol to prevent their sites from being downloaded and indexed. This protocol is entirely voluntary, though popular search engines certainly comply. But the onus of responsibility has shifted. Previously, to use someone else's information legitimately, one had to seek permission from the copyright holder. Now—reflecting the spirit of the web from the very beginning—the convention is to assume permission unless the provider has set up a blocking mechanism. This is a key development with wide ramifications. And some websites threaten dire consequences for computers that violate the robot exclusion protocol, such as denial of service attacks that will effectively disable the violating computer. This is law enforcement on the wild web frontier.

Other copyright issues are raised by projects such as the Internet Archive (mentioned in Chapter 2, page 51) that are storing the entire World Wide Web in order to supply documents that are no longer available and maintain a "copy of record" that will form the raw material for historical studies. Creating such an archive raises many interesting issues involving privacy and copyright, issues that are not easily resolved.

> What if a college student created a Web page that had pictures of her then current boyfriend? What if she later wanted to "tear them up," so to speak, yet they lived on in the archive? Should she have the right to remove them? In contrast, should a public figure—a U.S. senator, for instance—be able to erase data posted from his or her college years? Does collecting information made available to the public violate the "fair use" provisions of copyright law?
>
> *— Kahle (1997)*

Copyright is a complex and slippery business. Providing a pointer to someone else's document is one thing, whereas in law, serving up a copy of a document is quite a different matter. There have even been lawsuits about whether it is legal to *link* to a web document, on the basis that you could misappropriate advertising revenue that rightfully belongs to someone else by attaching a link to their work with your own advertising. The web is pushing at the frontiers of society's norms for dealing with the protection and distribution of intellectual property.

The legal system is gradually coming to grips with the issues raised by web search. In 2004, a writer filed a lawsuit claiming that Google infringed copyright by archiving a posting of his and by providing excerpts from his website in their search results. In a 2006 decision, a U.S. district court judge likened search engines to Internet service providers in that they store and transmit data to users without human intervention, and ruled that these activities do not constitute infringement because "the necessary element of volition is missing." Earlier that year, a federal judge in Nevada concluded that Google's cached versions of web pages do not infringe copyright. However, at the same time, a Los Angeles federal judge opined that its image search feature, in displaying thumbnail versions of images found on an adult photo site, does violate U.S. copyright law.

Those who run public Internet information services tell fascinating tales of people's differing expectations of what it is reasonable for their services to do. Search companies receive calls from irate users who have discovered that some of their documents are indexed which they think shouldn't be.

Sometimes users believe their pages couldn't possibly have been captured legitimately because there are no links to them—whereas, in fact, at one time a link existed that they have overlooked. You might put confidential documents into a folder that is open to the web, perhaps only momentarily while you change its access permissions, only to have them grabbed by a search engine and published for the entire world to find. Fortunately, major search engines make provision for removing cached pages following a request by the page author.

Search technology makes information readily available that, though public in principle, was previously impossible to find in practice. Usenet is a huge corpus of Internet discussion groups on a wide range of topics dating from the 1980s—well before anyone would have thought Internet searching possible. When a major search engine took over the archives, it received pleas from contributors to retract indiscreet postings they had made in their youth, because, being easily available for anyone to find, they were now causing their middle-aged authors embarrassment.

THE WIPO TREATY

A treaty adopted by the World Intellectual Property Organization (WIPO) in 1996 addresses the copyright issues raised by digital technology and networks in the modern information era. It decrees that computer programs should be protected as literary works and that the arrangement and selection of material in databases is protected. It provides authors of works with more control over their rental and distribution than the Berne Convention does. It introduces an important but controversial requirement that countries must provide effective legal measures against the circumvention of technical protection measures (digital rights management schemes, mentioned in Chapter 2, page 56) and against the removal of electronic rights management information, that is, data identifying the author and other details of the work.

Many countries have not yet implemented the WIPO Treaty into their laws. One of the first pieces of national legislation to do so was the U.S. Digital Millennium Copyright Act (DMCA), one of whose consequences is that it may be unlawful to publish information that exposes the weaknesses of technical protection measures. The European Council has approved the treaty on behalf of the European Community and has issued directives that largely cover its subject matter.

THE BUSINESS OF SEARCH

The major search engines were born not by design, but almost by chance, through the ingenuity of talented young graduate students who worked on challenging problems for the sheer joy of seeing what they could do. They realized how rewarding it would be to help others dig useful information out of the chaotic organization of the web. The spirit of entrepreneurship helped turn the rewards into immensely profitable businesses. Some were more successful than others: luck, timing, skill, and inspiration all played a role. Early market shakedowns saw many acquisitions and mergers.

By the end of 2005, three major search engines (Google, Yahoo, and MSN) accounted for more than 80 percent of online searches in the United States. Measurements are made in the same way as for TV ratings: around 1 million people have agreed to have a meter installed on their computer to monitor their search behavior. And these three were serviced by only two paid advertising providers (Google uses its own AdWords/AdSense; MSN and Yahoo both use Overture, owned by Yahoo).

Google leads the growing market of paid search advertisements. Its $6 billion revenue in 2005 almost doubled the previous year's figure and was predicted to increase by 40 percent in 2006 and maintain a compound annual growth of 35 to 40 percent over the following five years. By 2005, Google was already larger than many newspaper chains and TV channels; during 2006, it became the fourth largest media company in the United States (after Viacom, News Corporation, and Disney, but before giants such as NBC Universal and Time Warner).

Paid search accounts for nearly half of all Internet advertising revenue (in 2005). Spending on online advertising is projected to double by 2010, when it will constitute more than 10 percent of the general advertising market in the United States. One-fifth of Internet users already consider online advertising more effective than radio, newspapers, and magazines. Not only will paid search take the lion's share of online advertising, it will also drain revenue from conventional broadcast media.

THE CONSEQUENCES OF COMMERCIALIZATION

This lively commercial interest pushes in two directions. On the one hand, websites strive to gain good positions in search engine rankings in order to further their commercial visibility. On the other, search engines strive to outdo one another in the quality of service they offer in order to attract and retain customers. The resulting tension explains the web wars of Chapter 5. There is huge commercial value in being listed early in the results of search engines. After all, there's no need to waste money on advertising if you are already at the top of the class! It means life or death to many small online businesses.

Countless poignant real-life stories describe casualties of the war between search engines and spammers. You start a small specialist Internet business.

Quickly realizing the importance of having high rankings on major search engines, you subscribe to a commercial service that promises to boost them. Little do you know that it utilizes dubious techniques for website promotion of the kind described in Chapter 5. In fact, such considerations are quite outside your experience, knowledge, and interests—your expertise is in your business, not in how the web works. The crash comes suddenly, with no warning whatsoever. Overnight, your ranking drops from top of the search results for relevant queries to the millionth position. Only later do you figure out the problem: the search engine has decided that your promotional efforts amount to spam.

The web is a capricious and erratic place. Meanwhile, users (as we saw earlier) place blind trust in their search results, as though they represented objective reality. They hardly notice the occasional seismic shifts in the world beneath their feet. They feel solidly in touch with their information, blissfully unaware of the instability of the mechanisms that underlie search. For them, the dragons are omniscient.

THE VALUE OF DIVERSITY

You might recall from Chapter 2 that France's national librarian warned of the risk of "crushing American domination in the definition of how future generations conceive the world" and threatened to build a European version (page 54). Shortly afterward, Jacques Chirac, President of the French Republic, initiated a mega-project: a Franco-German joint venture to create European search engine technology, funded from both public coffers and private enterprise. *Quaero*, Latin for *I search*, is a massive effort explicitly aimed at challenging U.S. supremacy in web search. The project involves many research institutes in France and Germany, as well as major businesses. Project leaders understand that they must be creative to succeed in the ultra-competitive market of online search. Quaero will target its services to various market areas. One is general web search; another will be designed for businesses that work with digital content; and a third version is aimed at the mobile phone market.

European leaders believe it is politically unwise to leave the fabulously profitable and influential business of online search to foreign entrepreneurs. In addition to economic concerns, they worry about the cultural value of services that organize and access the information on the web, services that are used to preserve and transmit cultural heritage. The Franco-German project aims to augment perceived American cultural hegemony with a European perspective. But wait, there's more. Japan has decided to create its own national search engine, through a partnership of major Japanese technical and media companies: NEC, Fujitsu, NTT, Matsushita, and Nippon public television (NHJ).

Large cooperative enterprises, organized on a national or regional scale with a component of public leadership and funding, are a far cry from the lone young geniuses working for love rather than money, who created the search engines we have today and grew into talented entrepreneurs whose dragons are breathing fire at the advertising legends of Madison Avenue. Will the new approach lead to better search? If the object is really to forestall cultural hegemony, will search engines be nationalized and funded from taxes? Does jingoism have a role to play in the international web world? These are interesting questions, and it will be fascinating to watch the results play out—from the safety of the sidelines.

However, we believe these efforts are addressing the wrong problem. The real issue is not one of cultural dominance in a nationalistic sense, but rather cultural dominance through a universal, centralized service, or a small set of services that all operate in essentially the same way. The activity of searching should recognize the multifarious nature of the web, whose unique characteristic is the collective production of an immense panoply of visions, the coexistence of countless communities. What users need is not a competition between a few grand national perspectives, but inbuilt support for the very idea of different perspectives. While it is understandable for them to want a piece of the action, the Europeans and Japanese have declared war on the wrong thing.

In order to truly represent the immense richness of the treasure, preserve it, and provide a basis for its continued development and renewal, we need an equally rich variety of methods to access it, methods that are based on different technologies and administered by different regimes—some distributed and localized, others centralized. Not only is content socially determined; so is the research process itself. Although we talk of research as though it were a single concept, it covers a grand scope of activities that share only a broad family resemblance. We research different kinds of objects, from apples to archangels, from biology to biography, from cattle prods to cathodes. And different objects imply different kinds of search. When we seek an evening's entertainment, we are not doing the same thing as when we seek precedents for a homicide case. Different activities imply different criteria and involve different elements for success.

Search is a voyage of understanding. In the real world, early European explorers set the scene for what was to become a huge decrease in our planet's ecological diversity. Today, in the web world, we are concerned for the survival of diversity in our global knowledge base.

PERSONALIZATION AND PROFILING

Sometimes we search for a particular object, such as an article we read long ago or the name of the heroine of *Gone with the Wind*. More often, what we seek is imprecise; the question is not well formulated, and our goal is unclear even to ourselves. We are looking more for inspiration than for an answer. Wittgenstein, the twentieth-century philosopher we met in Chapter 1, thought that search is more about formulating the right question than finding the answer to it. Once you know the question, you also have the response. When we embark on a quest online, we are looking more for education than for a fact. Too often, what we get is a factoid—a brief item that is factual but trivial. The trouble is, this affects the way we think and what we tend to value.

History and legend are replete with quests that are ostensibly a search for a physical treasure (the Golden Fleece, the Holy Grail, a missing wife) but end up transforming the hero and his friends from callow youths to demigods (Jason and the Argonauts, the medieval knights Parsifal, Galahad, and Bors, D'Artagnan and his trusty musketeers). Are today's search tools up to supporting epic quests? If only he'd had a search engine, Jason might have ended up as he began, an unknown political refugee from Thessaly.

Everyone who works in the search business knows that to respond properly to a question, it is necessary to take the user, and his or her context, into account. Keyword input is not enough. Even a full statement of the question would not be enough (even if computers could understand it). In order to resolve the inevitable ambiguities of a query, it is essential to know the user's perspective, where she is coming from, why she is asking the question. We need the ability to represent and refine the user's profile.

From a search engine's point of view, personalization has two distinct aspects. First, it is necessary to know the user in order to answer his questions in a way that is both pertinent and helpful. Second, knowing the user allows more precisely targeted advertising that maximizes clickthrough rate and hence profit. Google's AdWords system, for example, is an advanced artificial intelligence application that applies contextual analysis to connect user keywords with sponsored links in the most effective possible way. MSN demonstrated a demographic targeting tool for its contextual advertising service at the 2005 Search Engine Strategies Conference in Chicago. Perhaps search could be even more effective if the same degree of attention were paid to exploiting context in generating the search results themselves, in order to satisfy the user's real information need.

User profiles are based on two kinds of information: the user's "clickstream" and his geographical location. Search engines can analyze each user's actions in order to get behind individual queries and understand more of the user's thoughts and interests. It is difficult to encapsulate a request into a few keywords for a query, but by taking history into account, search engines might be able to fulfill your desires more accurately than you can express them. Localization provides a powerful contextual clue: you can be given a response that is personalized to your particular whereabouts—even, with GPS, when you are browsing from a mobile phone. This maximizes advertising revenue by sharply focusing commercial information to geographically relevant customers. It increases clickthrough by not overloading users with irrelevant advertisements. It saves sponsors from wasting their money on pointless advertising that may even aggravate potential customers. It provides an attractive alternative to broadcast media like TV advertising.

Personalization is a major opportunity for search companies. Personal service that disappeared when we abandoned village shops for centralized supermarkets is making a comeback on the web. Leading online marketers like Amazon already provide impressive personal service. A user's location and clickstream gives deep insight into what she is doing and thinking. The privacy dilemma emerges in a different guise. The tradeoff between personalization and privacy will be one of the most challenging questions to arise in years to come.

Web search is by no means the only field where new technology raises serious privacy concerns. Consider the vast store of call information collected by telecommunication companies, information that is even more sensitive. In principle, search technology could retrieve information from automatic transcriptions created by state-of-the-art speech recognition systems. Policies can change and evolve in different ways, and users should be keenly aware of the risks associated with the use of any information service—particularly ones that are funded from advertising revenue.

SO WHAT?

Information is not as neutral as you might have supposed. Ever since humans began keeping written records, control over the supply and archiving of information has been a powerful social, political, and historical force. But the web is no ordinary archive: it's created and maintained by everyone—an archive of the people, for the people, and by the people.

Access, however, is mediated by the dragons. They strive to determine the authority of each page as judged by the entire web community, and reflect this in their search results. Though it sounds ultra-democratic, this has some unexpected and undesirable outcomes: the rich get richer, popularity is substituted for genuine authority, and the sensitive balance between privacy and censorship is hard to maintain. In a global village that spans the entire world, the tyranny of the majority reigns.

How will these challenges be met? While we cannot predict the future, the next and final chapter gives some ideas. An important underlying theme is the reemergence of communities in our world of information.

WHAT CAN *YOU* DO ABOUT ALL THIS?

- Hunt down private information about some important personage.
- Next time you fill out a web form, analyze each field to determine why (and whether) they need this information.
- Find the "prejudice map" and learn how it works.
- Compare results for sensitive searches in different countries.
- Learn what your country's doing about the WIPO copyright treaty.
- Slap a Creative Commons license on the next thing you write.
- Read the story of someone who feels a dragon has threatened his livelihood.
- Find discussions on the web about blogs and democracy.
- Try separate searches for countries—for example, *united states, united kingdom, south africa, new zealand*—and compare the results.
- Investigate the privacy policy of major search engines.

NOTES AND SOURCES

Tim Berners-Lee wrote the prophetic words at the beginning of this chapter in 1989. Pew Internet & American Life Project[47] have surveyed search engine users (the results quoted on page 178 are from a January 2005 survey). A pioneering paper on information ethics is Mason (1986). Brennan and Johnson (2004), Moore (2005), and Spinello and Tavani (2006) are recent collections that discuss the ethical issues raised by information technology. In 2005, the *International Review of Information Ethics* devoted a special issue to ethical questions concerning search engines (Vol. 3).

Derrida's (1996) charming, though complex, monograph on Freud's inheritance gives a provocative and stimulating account of the role of archives in contemporary society; we have drawn upon the interesting commentary by Steedman (2001). Introna and Nissenbaum (2000), writing well before most people realized that there was any problem at all, discuss the links between web democracy and search engines. A well-informed book that raises this issue is Battelle's *The Search* (2005), which includes many fascinating facts about the commercialization of search engines. The study of web snapshots taken seven months apart (page 183) is described by Cho and Roy (2004); it was they who modeled the random *searcher* and contrasted him with the random *surfer* to obtain the extraordinary result that it takes 60 times longer for a new page to become popular under

---

[47] *www.pewinternet.org*

random searching. Belew (2000) gives a theoretical perspective on traps that people fall into when finding out new information.

The notion of privacy as a limitation of other people's access to an individual is defended by Gavison (1980). Various modalities of protection of personal data, and the two principles that relate to online privacy, are identified in European Directive 95/46/EC on the protection of individuals with regard to the processing of personal data and the free movement of such data. This directive is discussed by Elgesem (1999) and can be contrasted with the American perspective found in Nagenborg (2004). Lessig (1999, 2002) argues that privacy should be considered as property, though this view is by no means universal. Tavani and Moor (2000) argue for the restricted-control approach.

The information about the dissident Chinese journalist Shi Tao of the *Dangdai Shang Bao* (Contemporary Business News) is from a September 2004 press release from Reporters Without Borders[48] (see also the *Washington Post*, September 11, 2005).[49] The OpenNet Initiative (2005) has published a report on the filtering of the Internet in China. Hinman (2005) contains an interesting discussion of online censorship, with many pointers to further information. There are websites that display Google results from selected countries (e.g., the United States and China) side by side, to allow you to explore the differences for yourself.[50] Document queries for *falun gong* and image queries for *tiananmen* yield interesting comparisons.

Turning now to copyright, Samuelson and Davis (2000) provide an excellent and thought-provoking overview of copyright and related issues in the Information Age, which is a synopsis of a larger report published by the National Academy of Sciences Press (Committee on Intellectual Property Rights, 2000). An earlier paper by Samuelson (1998) discusses specific digital library issues raised by copyright and intellectual property law, from a U.S. perspective. The Association for Computing Machinery has published a collection of papers on the effect of emerging technologies on intellectual property issues (White, 1999). We learned a lot from Lessig's great book *Free Culture* (Lessig, 2004), which has strongly influenced our perspective. Lessig is also the originator of the Creative Commons, whose licenses can be found on the web[51]—as can the GNU GFDL license.[52] The lawsuit we cited on

---

[48] *www.rsf.org*

[49] *www.washingtonpost.com/wp-dyn/content/article/2005/09/10/AR2005091001222_pf.html*

[50] For example, CenSEARCHip at *homer.informatics.indiana.edu/censearchip* and ComputerBytesMan at *www.computerbytesman.com/google*

[51] *creativecommons.org*

[52] *http://www.gnu.org/copyleft/fdl.html*

page 200 which claims that Google infringed copyright is Parker *v.* Google; the one about the legality of cached copies is Field *v.* Google, and the one concerning image search is Perfect 10, a purveyor of nude photographs, *v.* Google.

There's plenty of information on copyright on the web. Staff at Virginia Tech have developed a useful site to share what they learned about policies and common practices relating to copyright.[53] It includes interpretations of U.S. copyright law, links to the text of the law, sample letters to request permission to use someone else's work, links to publishers, advice for authors about negotiating to retain some rights, as well as current library policies. Georgia Harper at the University of Texas at Austin has created an excellent "Crash Course in Copyright" that is delightfully presented and well worth reading.[54] Some information we have presented about the duration of copyright protection is from the website of Lolly Gasaway, director of the Law Library and professor of law at the University of North Carolina.[55]

Two major measurement services of search engine performance are comScore qSearch system and Nielsen/Netratings Mega View Search reporting service. The revenue and growth predictions for Google (page 202) are from Goldman Sachs and Piper Jaffray, a securities firm. Figures regarding advertising revenues come from the Interactive Advertising Bureau (IAB); projections are by Wang (2005). Two examples of the casualties of the war between search engines and spammers are the sad tales of *exoticleatherwear.com* and *2bigfeet.com* from the *Wall Street Journal* (February 26, 2003) and Chapter 7 of Battelle (2005), respectively.

---

[53] *scholar.lib.vt.edu/copyright*

[54] *www.utsystem.edu/ogc/intellectualproperty/cprtindx.htm3*

[55] *www.unc.edu/~unclng/public-d.htm*

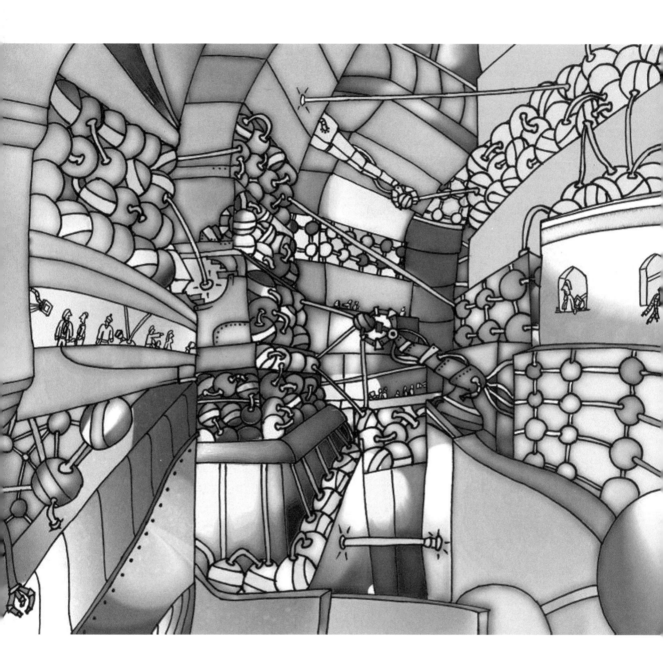

CHAPTER

7

THE DRAGONS EVOLVE

A ll is not well with *the universe (which others call the Web)*. It's a democratic storehouse of information in which everyone who wants can have a say. It's beginning to subsume traditional books and journals—not to mention audio, video, and other electronic entertainment media. The web dragons—search engines—are wonderful tools to help you find what you want. We all use them every day and (when we remember to think about it) are grateful for their existence. We could not even begin to estimate how many searches we did when writing this book; it would be an astronomical figure on a par with the number of times we clicked *save* in the word processor. Web dragons are marvels of technology, miraculous in how much they search, how quickly they respond, how many users they serve simultaneously, and how they work continually, cheerfully, and faithfully despite the notorious fallibility of hardware, software, and networks. And they're free.

Yet something is awry. We chose to call search engines "dragons" because of their fantastic power. Dragons are mysterious: no one *really* knows what drives them (and no one ever will). They're mythical: the subject of speculation, hype, legend, old wives' tales, and fairy stories. They guard immense riches—in this

The new theater: the audience watches the web evolve.

211

case, society's repository of knowledge (what could be more valuable than that?). Most of all, dragons enjoy a veiled positive/negative ambiguity. Are they evil? Magic? They are certainly independent, and unpredictable. In oriental folklore, they possess awesome beauty and wisdom; they are loved, even worshipped. The metaphor suits search engines well.

Think back to Chapter 1's philosophers and techno-visionaries: Socrates and Plato, Peirce and Wittgenstein, Wiener and Bush, Licklider and Engelbart, Nelson and Berners-Lee. The thread common to all is the social nature of knowledge. The value of knowledge—"content," as web pundits would put it—is not intrinsic, but lies in its communication, its use in the learning process, the way it feeds upon itself and provides the basis for its own growth. This is also true of the search service the dragons provide: it's about communication too. But it's not about *societies*—or rather, the web *is* about societies, but the dragons *do not recognize that*. When you search, they mediate between you and the treasure—they find it for you. But they do not involve you in any kind of social process. They connect you with the web. Not you, your friends, and the web; or you and your neighborhood web; or you and your professional colleagues' web. Just you, alone in the universe.

We all want to belong to communities. How many different ones are *you* in? How important are they to your life (and you to theirs)? How many acquaintances are in your address book, your mobile phone, your e-mail aliases? How many web pages are bookmarked in your browser? Technology is changing—improving—our ability to create communities for work and play. How many friends are on your kid's SMS buddy list? How many buddies did you have at their age? We want our communities to be open and transparent: we want to understand and participate in the processes of membership and governance. We recognize that one size does certainly *not* fit all.

One of the great things about the web is that it's full of communities. The group affairs are the fastest-growing parts: from blogs to wikis, from chatrooms to podcasts, from large, well-run, socially moderated newsgroups to salacious late-night hot tubs. There's a plethora of different ways of organizing web communities. Some are anonymous, some pseudonymous. Some are moderated, others immoderate. Some require special qualifications to join, others are open. Some recognize tribal elders, others favor equality. Some have multiple tiers of members: serfs, commoners, lords and ladies, royalty—or in contemporary terminology, lurkers, contributors, moderators, gurus.

Web communities come and go. Some explode in a blaze of flames and acrimony; others silently fade away. It's a dynamic, community-based world out there. The dragons will evolve to respond to these needs by offering personalized services that do not treat everyone in exactly the same way.

It would be crazy to make any serious pretense to forecast the development of the web and its dragons over the next decade as it matures from a young teenager into a young adult. But we can sketch out some directions that would help expand the scope of today's search engines and address some of their deficiencies. We see them as a first step, an amazing first step, but nevertheless just the beginning. There will be a shift in direction in information retrieval to recognize the social nature of knowledge, and the importance of communities that are controlled and run by people. Information is contextual; so is the web; so will web searching be. The visionaries of Chapter 1 foresaw all this (if not the web itself).

To prepare you for the discussion ahead, here is the thread that weaves through this chapter. We begin by stressing the value of diversity and decentralization. The world would be fatally impoverished if everyone accessed their information through a single mechanism (or a single dragon), and we believe that healthy diversity must continue indefinitely—and it will. We then examine personalization, a prime area of research and development for today's dragons (among many others). Immense power can be harnessed by analyzing each individual user's behavior as reflected in his or her clickstream. The dragons will get to know you, perhaps even better (in some respects) than you know yourself—through your actions.

From individuals we move to communities. More than a technological artifact, the web is a global community—or rather, an assemblage of millions of interlinked communities. The dragons recognize this by allowing you to search within a particular terrain; some try to automatically classify search results by community. But a community is more than a subset of the universe; it's a certain *perspective* on it. We foresee new developments in ranking techniques that will sort information according to different *perspectives*, ones that you can choose.

The web is a distributed global community, but dragons are centralized (though their programs run on computational grids). We go on to describe "peer-to-peer" architectures that distribute not only information but also control. This means that reliability must be built in from the ground up. It also introduces the issue of trust: how can independently operated computers (which are necessarily untrusted) store information in a trustworthy manner? Modern peer-to-peer protocols are capable of protecting privacy, resisting censorship, and limiting access. What allows us to trust people is their reputation: can this extend to a decentralized worldwide environment where identity is virtual and not physical?

Next, we turn to larger-scale institutional communities—the kind that build libraries. Libraries add value to information through the act of selection and organization. Organization implies metadata, which is a community affair because, on a worthwhile scale, it transcends what any person can do alone. Digital libraries will proliferate and coexist with the web at large: dragons will find ways to acknowledge the existence of high-quality, organized material, and integrate it into their search results alongside regular web pages.

Finally, we are all about to experience how radically centralized services can change the way we perceive our computational environment. The chasm between your personal filespace and the web will narrow, perhaps disappear. Just as they now provide your gateway to the web and perhaps even organize your email and calendar, dragons will in the future help you with your own files. They will provide storage and backup. They will assist with organization. Soon they will offer computational services: word processors, spreadsheets, databases. This will change the nature of collaboration and also the nature of privacy. Today the dragons aspire to be your one-stop information service; tomorrow they will be your personal secretary and workplace.

THE ADVENTURE OF SEARCH

Our first prediction—more a plea, really—is diversity. Searching presents a perennial compromise between authoritarian and libertarian, between predefined classification structures and free collective association, between Leibniz's dream of reason and the princes of Serendip. Though these are extreme positions, there is a good case for each end of the spectrum. But in truth, there is no conclusive reason to prefer one over the other, because everything depends on the context of the search. The only practical way to cope is to have a selection of different browsing techniques and search environments. The preservation of diversity lies at the foundation of all healthy ecologies, and the web is no exception.

What does the word *information* really mean? The root term (Latin *informatio*) has several different nuances. Etymologically, it derives from *in* and *forma*, meaning literally "to give or create a form." This provides the basis of at least three different concepts. First, information is an idea, an image of a notion—which could be innate (given a priori) or the fruit of acquired knowledge (derived a posteriori). Second, it is a diagram or sketch such as architects use, like a document in outline. Third, it is the transmission of knowledge—in other words, education. All these interpretations encapsulate the idea of producing a new "form."

In order to manage information—and to seek it—we should first establish what kind of form we are dealing with. Is it the conception of a new idea; or the organization of something whose germ is already present in the guise of an initial sketch; or the communication of a well-organized discipline, ready to be learned? Each case calls for different techniques. When undertaking research in an environment where everything has been neatly classified, such as a standard library, we remain within the confines of an organized corpus of information and our queries must follow the logic of the classification. In contrast, when seeking something that is not yet established—grasping at an elusive new idea that hovers just beyond the brink of our mind's reach—we embark on a serendipitous trial-and-error adventure without being sure that what we find will be exactly what we are looking for.

Although it seems antithetical to the preconceived structures advocated by trained librarians, there is at least one library whose organization is willfully serendipitous. In Warburg's Library, now based in London, books are found almost by chance, using the ingenuity of the researcher:

> The manner of shelving the books is meant to impart certain suggestions to the reader who, looking on the Library Holdings for one book, is attracted by the kindred ones next to it, glances at the sections above and below, and finds himself involved in a new trend of thought which may lend additional interest to the one he was pursuing.
>
> – Bing (1935)

The Library's emblem is taken from a 1472 woodcut, shown in Figure 7.1(a), which depicts the four elements of which the world was thought to be made—earth, air, fire, and water—along with the two pairs of opposing qualities—hot and cold, moist and dry—from which these elements were constructed. The diagram throws in the four seasons of the year and the four humors of man to complete an image of cosmic harmony. The Library's classification scheme is based on an analogous four-category scheme, less archaic but equally mysterious, depicted in Figure 7.1(b).

Organization versus serendipity; classification versus spontaneity. Each has advantages and disadvantages: we cannot disregard one in favor of the other. Searching in a well-classified environment means that what you find is organized, relevant to the question, and quickly accessible. But it brings the risk of finding only what the librarian (be it man or machine, person or program, human cataloger or search engine) has introduced into the categories that represent the world of information. In contrast, serendipitous exploration provides no clues, no signposts indicating which way to go to find what you need.

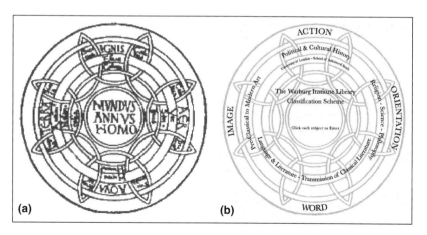

(a) (b)

Figure 7.1 The Warburg Library: (a) its emblem and (b) its classification scheme.

The voyage might be exhausting, frustrating, even ultimately fruitless. But striking discoveries and connections that would never occur in a pre-organized information space may await you. Translating into the web experience, random exploration through an unknown land of hyperlinks with no guide may be a waste of time (though perhaps enjoyable). On the other hand, a structured manager through which all users access information forces everyone to submit to the same discipline, the same preconceptions. We cannot appreciate the gorgeous panorama of information through a single porthole.

Not only are there different types of information that need different means of access, but users have diverse motivations when interrogating the web. They may seek a specific answer to a well-formulated question, or may just want to be entertained. They may set out in quest of a solution to an advanced scientific research problem, or may need help in completing a crossword puzzle. They may seek introductions to new people, or want to find an old friend's missing address. They may intend to purchase a particular new computer, or just want to establish a feeling for prices and characteristics of different brands of machines. They may seek a particular song, or just good music of a certain genre. A multiplicity of tools and strategies for research provides richness in itself and increases the probability of satisfying different information needs.

The web's foremost goal is to facilitate communication by decentralizing the publication of information. As Berners-Lee put it:

> I do not pin my hopes on an overpowering order emerging spontaneously from the chaos. I feel that to deliberately build a society, incrementally, using the best ideas we have, is our duty and will also be the most fun. We are slowly learning the value of decentralized diverse systems and of mutual respect and tolerance.
>
> – *Berners-Lee (2000, p. 223)*

To maintain the web as a healthy living organism, decentralized diversity should be the model for future search tools. We can best exercise mutual respect and tolerance by permitting the web to be interrogated in different ways, allowing a panoply of visibility metrics to coexist, fostering the creative anarchy that has made the web the adventure it is today.

PERSONALIZATION IN PRACTICE

As we write, about 250 million people access the web regularly. By and large, they all do so in the same way, regardless of where they live or what their lifestyle, culture, and needs and expectations are. It's unlikely that this is really what people want. *Personalization* is the web's new buzzword. We discussed the issue of personalized profiles at the end of Chapter 6 (pages 204–205) and mentioned privacy concerns raised by centralized storage and utilization of personal information.

Web queries are valuable pieces of information. Search engines already analyze them intensely in order to serve users better. Spelling correction is just one example. Sometimes you can donate information about how you surf the web. Simply by downloading the Alexa toolbar, introduced ten years ago, each member of the community contributes information about their usage, what's important and what's not.[56] At the end of 2005, the same company introduced a "web search platform" that lets subscribing developers create personalized information services by combining user profiles with the repository of web content gleaned by Alexa's crawlers, and other information such as traffic flow.

MY OWN WEB

Each user necessarily accesses only a tiny fraction of the web. However, the search technologies described in Chapter 4 don't exploit locality. Instead, they use global ranking techniques in an attempt to present the ostensibly most pertinent information first. A different approach would let users navigate in their *own* web, and even give them the opportunity to annotate the contents.

My Own Web is one of the directions in which web dragons are evolving. It's a first step toward the integration of personal, community, and generic search. The idea is to let users work on a subset of the web that they define by selecting web pages. This can be extended by sharing bookmarks, enabling people to organize communities and inherit the pages of other community members, on the basis that your friends and those with whom you share information are excellent sources of high-quality information. People and communities can create a sort of "persistent memory" of pages they find of interest. They could add value to the information space by tagging items with metadata and providing textual comments about the content. Of course, these notes should also be searchable. The end result is a high-quality view of a defined subset of the web.

You have to register to take advantage of personalization features, because the system must retain a detailed history of your activities and annotations. Privacy is protected to ensure that others cannot access your personal web archive, unless you explicitly share it within designated communities. Searches can be restricted to your own private information space, or the community's, or the web at large. Of course, tagging items with metadata can help improve search results. Yahoo mentions a new ranking algorithm called MyRank that is designed to rank the pages that you and your community have saved within its system.[57]

---

[56] *www.alexa.com*

[57] *myweb2.search.yahoo.com*

In contrast to global link analysis, personal web subsets are impervious to spam. So are those created by a community, provided its members are trustworthy. In principle, communities could be treated as social networks whose members are themselves subject to PageRank-style peer evaluation. (Reputation management systems are described further on pages 227–229.) Different weights could be applied to the recommendations of community members. Whereas on the web at large, page contents are often deliberately misrepresented by malicious tagging, tagging by trusted peers has the potential to improve search significantly.

One way to create a community is by bilateral agreement: you invite someone to share your web, and they accept the invitation. Another is unilateral: you decide to share your personal web and let anybody see it. The current state of affairs is unilateral in the other direction: you have no choice but to see everyone else's web insofar as the page ranking mechanism is concerned. Making use of these distinctions goes beyond universal ranking, which is spammable, to new models that emphasize the fit between the search method and the needs of individual users.

The evolution toward personalization that we have described adopts a centralized view of web search in which the dragons guard critical private information. Are the privacy policies of search engines strong enough to encourage widespread use of personalized services? The issue is so important that it could stimulate radical architectural innovations. For instance, your own web might be safer if it were stored locally on your computer, or on your organization's proxy server. Regardless of where it resides, the dragons will have to offer strong and realistic guarantees on the privacy of communities and their members.

ANALYZING YOUR CLICKSTREAM

We have seen how users might create their own personalized quality views of the web. Personalization can also be based on implicit actions rather than explicit decisions. Take online shopping as an example. In order to give users a unique and customized experience, a focus on personalization seems essential—just as in real shopping. It is the store, not the customer, who must take the initiative and do whatever is necessary to provide a personalized experience. Suppose you walk into a department store that you visit every couple of months. You examine a few items in a desultory fashion, and glance around inquiringly. A good manager organizes things in such a way that helpful sales staff are right there to interact with you. A good management philosophy emphasizes the importance of understanding your profile so as to provide better service. It's no accident that "customer" and "customize" share the same stem!

Online personalization works the same way. On the web, the staff who assist the user are software agents—programs that emulate the services shop assistants provide. Human staff can anticipate needs because they know something about the customer's profile. Such knowledge comes from previous interactions: perhaps over the last few moments as they observe the customer's age, sex, and dress (and whether they are accompanied by a spouse); perhaps over the last few years from personal experience of the customer; perhaps from a database of past purchases. Computer systems often treat personalization simplistically—like allowing you to view a website in your favorite colors. In reality, personalization is about reacting meaningfully on the basis of a user's profile, anticipating his or her needs. Profiles could be created by asking users to fill out a form or inferred less intrusively from background analysis of their clickstream.

Regardless of the function of a website, profiles permit personalized access by taking account of user needs when selecting the interface and the information to be presented. The "cookies" described in Chapter 3 (pages 73–74) provide the underlying mechanics. A type of program called a "recommender system" predicts items (books, news, music) that may interest a user on the basis of his profile. It must be intelligent enough to filter the information so as to discover relevant items for the user.

There are two different approaches to information filtering. The first is to rely on text analysis to discover whether or not a particular web page is relevant to a particular user's profile. The second is to exploit other users: if someone buys an item, this item is recommended to others with similar profiles. These approaches can be integrated to further improve the result. While it is hard to provide quantitative measures of recommendation quality, there are good automated ways to perform accurate text categorization that prove useful for filtering. Simple collaborative schemes such as those popularized by Amazon can be amazingly effective.

COMMUNITIES

Contemporary dragons have treated the web as though it were an objective reality. That's how computer scientists, who created the dragons, were trained. It's not that they believe that the web reflects "the truth"—of course it doesn't. But they do believe it stands as an identifiable artifact that can be distinguished from the rest of the world. It can be counted and measured like any other objective reality.

However, it's not an objective reality, it's a social artifact. And the bad guys—spammers—are trying to distort it for their own commercial purposes. How can we combat deliberate distortion? Today's dragons play referee. They patch things up by inventing ad hoc measures and (necessarily) keeping them under wraps. This is the natural reaction of the computer scientist. Spam is a bug, and we must find ways to eliminate it, or at least ameliorate the damage it causes.

SOCIAL SPACE OR OBJECTIVE REALITY?

This book's message is that the problem is far more fundamental. We cannot treat the web as an objective reality because it forms part of the fabric of our society. Spam is a social problem, not a technical one, and will not yield to solutions that are purely technical. And spam is just the first crack in the edifice. The web is developing and taking over more of our intellectual life (for example, by subsuming traditional literature). The dragons are developing and aspire to collaborate more closely with us in our quest for information (for example, by adding specialized search in domains such as health and geography, literature and science, and in commercial areas such as shopping and entertainment). It is inappropriate for them to treat the web as an objective reality: they must recognize social relationships between its users, for whom the web is a substrate. Spam is just the tip of the iceberg.

The dragons search the web and present what they find as the truth—not the absolute truth, but the truth as reflected by the web. They work by counting and weighing. But this is not sustainable. You cannot count and weigh an infinitude, for reasons that are not technical but social. Spam happens. It happens because the web is a community that anyone can join, with no controls and no responsibility. Spam does not happen in my family, my neighborhood, my workplace, my professional society, my sports club, my music group. We have social controls.

As the dragons seek to serve us better, their view of the web as objective reality will break down further. For example, they localize some searches ("pizzas in Tucson") and present the result on maps. But maps are social artifacts, not objective realities. What should they label that continent-sized island in the southern hemisphere?—should it be called the "West Island of New Zealand," or "Australia"? (That's a joke. But analogous questions about, say, Northern Ireland, Tibet, or Taiwan are not a joke.) Geographic labels are not objective reality but political choices.

The dragons must not be drawn into acting as the world's referee in order to preserve the myth of objective reality. That might work for things we can (almost) all agree on, such as pyramid scams or child pornography, but it will not continue to function as society and the web converge and the dragons move into new territory. The only solution is to recognize the existence of myriad communities with their own social controls.

Today's dragons treat the web as a single, measurable entity. The way they evaluate different points of view is to weigh them as though they were objective realities. Take the deep divisions of our time: pro-choice versus pro-life, evolution versus creationism, traditional family values versus gay rights, Palestine versus Israel, Christian versus Muslim. Even to name them stirs strong emotions! Or, slightly less inflammatory, consider a discussion that erupted some time ago as to whether the web is pro- or anti-vaccination. It doesn't make sense to talk about these issues—or retrieve information on them—by counting words and weighing links. Different communities have different perspectives.

What we need is an open structure that recognizes communities but does not dictate or control them. They should be allowed to form in any way, and grow, develop, fragment, reorganize, or die. People will find ways to organize them. The dragons should recognize them and allow you to search within them.

SEARCHING WITHIN A COMMUNITY PERSPECTIVE

Search engines let users restrict their search to a particular area of the web—a particular domain such as Italy (*.it*) or a particular site such as the Library of Congress (*www.loc.gov*). This is a popular and useful facility. It focuses the search results by filtering out those pages that do not belong to that domain or site. Of course, the order of search results—the visibility of the pages—is still determined by the global web community. The perspective is a holistic one, shaped by all the web—the universe.

Imagine a different model. Suppose the *point of view* was restricted to a particular domain. Instead of filtering the results to show only pages from the domain, let's compute visibility with respect to that domain alone, not the entire universe. In principle, this is not hard to do. Recall the calculations described in Chapter 4 that use the link structure to produce sensibly ordered results when searching in a web. Suppose only those links that emanate from pages in a particular part of the web—ones in pages from Italy (*.it*) or pages in the Library of Congress (*www.loc.gov*)—were used as the basis for the calculation. Then the ranking would reflect the structure of the Italian subgraph of the web, or the Library of Congress's subgraph. These minority viewpoints might differ from the overall ranking obtained from the whole web, representing the Italian perspective, or the Library of Congress's perspective, on the query. Of course, they might be the same.

In fact, the HITS algorithm described in Chapter 4 does restrict consideration to the links in a subset of the web. We called that set the "neighborhood graph" of the query. It is produced by finding all pages that contain the query terms, and adding the pages that they link to, the ones *they* link to, and so on, until the subgraph is large enough. This is a crude way of finding part of the web that is relevant to the query. The idea is that it will reflect different communities that use the query terms in different ways. We could characterize it as the query's "own" perspective on the web (or a rudimentary form of that perspective). Given query X, it is a rough and ready approximation to the part of the web that is particularly relevant to X.

What we are proposing here is different. Any coherent subgraph of the web represents a community of some kind (Italy, or the Library of Congress). By taking only the subgraph's links into account, we get the community's perspective on the query. The search results will list all pages that contain the query terms, just as before. But—crucially—they will be in a different order. Visibility will be determined by the community rather than the web as a whole. And in a world where responses to queries number in the millions or billions, visibility is everything. Of course, we might still want to restrict the results to pages in a particular domain. We might seek a community's view on pages within that community (Italy's view on Italian wine), or on pages in another community (Italy's view on French wine), or in the web at large (Italy's view on global warming). The point of view and the focus of the query are two different things.

DEFINING COMMUNITIES

So far we have talked as though a community is the same thing as a subdomain of the web (*.it*, or *www.loc.gov*). If we left it at that, it would be fairly simple for search engines to implement community search. Subdomains form a hierarchy. Any given page belongs to a single point in the hierarchy (e.g., *www.loc.gov/rr/askalib*), and this domain belongs to a higher-level one (*www.loc.gov/rr*), and still higher ones (*www.loc.gov*), right up to the top-level domain (*.gov*). The structure is hierarchical because each level is wholly included within the one above.

Real communities are more complex, less structured. Consider the community of biologists, or the community of skateboarding aficionados. They can be identified with subgraphs of the web, but not with single subdomains. One can imagine an existing society of biologists (the *American Society for Cell Biology*) wanting to be considered as a community for web search purposes. Then they—or you—could ask questions like, "What do American cell biologists think of global warming?" (or Italian wine). An ad hoc group of skateboarders, who may not be organized into an existing society, might want to form their own community for web search. They're probably far more interested in their own community's view of a radical new skateboard design than the view of the web at large, polluted by commerce and (from their perspective) ignoramuses. What if any group of people could create a list of pages and domains that represent their point of view and give it to search engines as a perspective that can be named in a search?

There are countless different ways in which people can organize themselves. A community could be created by a dictator, or run elections to admit new members, or rely on an inner circle of graybeards to make membership decisions, or be completely open—anyone can join. The web at large is completely open. Community search puts communities themselves in charge. It lets them define whose perspective will be taken when evaluating web visibility. As a side effect, they can control spam (if they wish to). By divorcing community rules from web search, search engines can get out of the awkward and unwelcome business of acting as web police.

In Chapter 3, we explained focused crawling (pages 70–71), where, with a particular topic in mind, a crawler starts from a seed page and selectively expands links that appear to be on-topic using some automated way of evaluating the target page's content. In Chapter 4 (pages 116–117), we met the random surfer, doomed to click his way around the web forever, landing on each page with a probability that is proportional to its ranking according to the PageRank scheme. Now imagine a random focused surfer, who only clicks links on pages belonging to a particular community. It might be topic-defined (as focused crawlers are) or socially defined (a list of pages and domains that belong). In either case, the probability that the surfer lands up on a page is governed by the page's community-determined visibility. Web visibility is modeled by the random surfer; community visibility corresponds to a random *focused* surfer.

Imagine being able to register communities with search engines and specify one or more communities along with any query. Then you could participate more actively in the enterprise of information access by defining your own perspective and by inventing new social mechanisms for organizing communities. Instead of being members of the audience, we would all be able to participate in the business of web search, through our communities.

From the dragon's point of view, this is a lot to ask. There is a vast number of potential communities. In fact, the number grows exponentially with the size of the universe, leading to truly unimaginable figures when applied to the web.

PRIVATE SUBNETWORKS

The interaction between web browser and web server that was discussed in Chapter 3 (page 64) is an example of what is called the "client-server" model of computing. Users access information through their web browser, the client, which makes requests behind the scenes to web servers to obtain the necessary information. This structure dates back to the 1960s, when computers were so scarce and expensive that they had to be shared by many users. As we learned in Chapter 1 (pages 15–16), the idea of time-sharing was a breakthrough that allowed people on "dumb terminals" to share the resources of a single central machine by sending it requests that were queued and processed in turn, according to their priority.

Time-sharing works well when there is a profound difference between the information processing capability of the client and that of the server. Because the server is much more powerful, the client accepts that it must wait to be processed. It respects the queue discipline because it has no choice: its place is determined by "the system" and programmed into the central server. This resembles the contractual arrangement between citizens and the State: we obey the system by paying taxes and waiting in hospitals because some services can only be delivered by a central authority.

Enter Moore's law. The number of transistors on a chip doubles every 18 months; in other words it grows tenfold every five years. Today's clients are every bit as powerful as massive servers were just a decade ago. This presents new opportunities that are more balanced than the dictatorial time-sharing regime. Today's new structure is peer-to-peer (often dubbed p2p). Peers are equals, like the knights who sat around King Arthur's table. Though they ceded authority to the king, that was a purely symbolic gesture which reflected their shared purpose rather than any real transfer of power.

Though the idea of peer-to-peer communication has been known since the early days, the Internet adopted the client-server model instead. Today, however, there is renewed interest in peer-to-peer networks, which become ever more practical as the capabilities of typical client computers increase. In a pure peer-to-peer arrangement, each peer acts as both client and server; there is no central authority that oversees the network. However, various semi-structured and semi-centralized networks are commonly viewed as part of the complex galaxy of peer-to-peer architectures. The underlying philosophy is that there is no difference between peers when performing the roles of client and server. This innovation gives rise to new ways of looking at networks and their operation, typically by setting up private subnetworks within the Internet's overall framework.

PEER-TO-PEER NETWORKS

Peer-to-peer protocols got off on the wrong foot. Not long ago, they became widely publicized as a populist tool for infringing copyright protection. Subnetworks arose for the express purpose of "sharing"—stealing—private copies of music and video content that was protected by copyright. As we noted in Chapter 6, possessing a copy of a document certainly does not constitute ownership in terms of copyright law; the same goes for CDs and DVDs. Decentralized networks are a way of decentralizing responsibility, making prosecution difficult. Consequently, the finger of blame was directed toward the technology itself rather than those who were using it for illegal purposes.

In 2005, the U.S. Supreme Court found the developers of two peer-to-peer systems (Grokster and StreamCast Networks) guilty of being responsible for copyright violations. The court did not address the question of whether the peer-to-peer technology itself is illegal, but focused on the actions of the companies and whether they encouraged illicit use of their system. Whether we lay the blame on the technology per se, or its users, is a highly controversial question. In 1984, the U.S. Supreme Court adjudicated a case between Sony Corporation and Universal Studios concerning the legality of video recorders, and established the so-called Betamax principle, which decrees that the inventor of a technology is not liable for its misuse by others. The reasoning was that although video recorders can be used to copy TV programs illegally, this is not their only use, and so Sony, the owner and distributor of the technology, should not be obliged to assume responsibility for the different uses that clients made of it.

Despite the negative reputation it has earned for promoting copyright infringement, the peer-to-peer architecture has striking potential for information distribution. It provokes fresh ways of thinking about how content can be distributed over a network. There are many examples of peer-to-peer subnetworks[58] that allow people to discover and download content stored on other people's machines, without knowing anything about that device—who owns it, its Internet address, or where in the world it is. All kinds of information can be distributed without any restriction, without any centralized control, without any need for organization or administration, and without any vulnerable points of failure.

In some respects, the centralized time-sharing structure is strengthening its hold over today's computing environment. Web dragons centralize Internet search. They and other commercial portals are eager to gain the attention of more eyeballs in order to increase their popularity and therefore boost advertising revenue. To do this, they are providing more facilities, which users access through their browser. What began with simple data conversion and display, like currency converters and zoomable maps, is escalating into applications like spreadsheets, word processors, calendar accessories, photo editing, and even complete office software suites. In some ways, network services are better than ones on our own computer because of the increasingly mobile computing environment: we want to access our personal information base using smart phones and personal digital assistants, as well as from our home and office desktops and laptop machines. We return to this shortly (pages 236–238).

Peer-to-peer subnetworks offer a refreshing alternative to this trend toward centralization. There are already schemes that pay particular attention to protecting the privacy, security, and anonymity of their members. Documents can be produced online and stored in anonymous repositories. Storage can be replicated in ways that guard data from mishap far better than any institutional computer backup policy, no matter how sophisticated. Documents can be split into pieces that are encrypted and stored redundantly in different places to make them highly resistant to any kind of attack, be it physical sabotage of backup tapes, security leaks of sensitive information, or attempts to trace ownership of documents. Your whole country could go down and your files would still be intact.

---

[58] Today they are called BitTorrent, Dagster, eDonkey2000, FastTrack, Freenet, Gnutella, FreeHaven, Kademilia, Oceanstore, Mnemosyne, Tarzan. By tomorrow everything will have changed.

Despite—or because of—its apparently haphazard and unregulated structure, the peer-to-peer architecture has encouraged the development of tools that are capable of protecting privacy, resisting censorship, and controlling access.[59] The underlying reason is that distributing the management of information, shunning any kind of central control, really does distribute responsibility—including the responsibility for ensuring integrity and anonymity. There is no single point of failure, no single weakness. Of course, no system is perfect, but the inventors and developers of peer-to-peer architectures are addressing these issues from the very outset, striving to build robust and scalable solutions into the fabric of the network rather than retrofitting them afterward.

Leading-edge systems[60] guarantee anonymity and also provide a kind of reputation control, which is necessary to restore personal responsibility in an anonymous world. It is hard to imagine how distributing your sensitive information among computers belonging to people you have never met and certainly do not trust can possibly guarantee privacy!—particularly from a coordinated attack. Surely the machines on the network must whisper secrets to each other, and no matter how quietly they whisper, corrupt system operators can monitor the conversation. The last part is true, but the first is not.

Strange as it may seem, new techniques of information security guarantee privacy using mathematical techniques. They provide assurances that have a sound theoretical foundation rather than resting on human devices such as keeping passwords secret. Even a coordinated attack by a corrupt government with infinite resources at its disposal that has infiltrated every computer on the network, tortured every programmer, and looked inside every single transistor, cannot force machines to reveal what is locked up in a mathematical secret. In the weird world of modern encryption, cracking security codes is tantamount to solving puzzles that have stumped the world's best minds for centuries.

Today's peer-to-peer architectures are moving fast and developing haphazardly. In the future, standards will be established that allow different structures to coexist. Various subnetworks will collect content from users and distribute it around in such a way that it remains invisible—mathematically invisible—to other users. In these collective repositories, we will, if we wish, be able to share resources with our chosen friends and neighbors, ones who we consider reliable and who have common interests.

Search will change. In a world where content is divorced from network structure, new strategies will be needed. In keeping with the distributed nature of the information, and in order to preserve scalability, computation will also

---

[59] Today's favorites are Groove, MojoNation, Oceanstore, Mnemosyne, and Dagster.

[60] Freenet, FreeHaven.

be distributed. Queries will propagate through the network: they will somehow flow from the place where the user makes a request to the place where the answer is stored. The routing strategy is the key to success. Flooding queries through the entire network is infeasible because it does not scale with the number of queries; random walk strategies are infeasible because they do not scale with the number of nodes. Instead, neighbors will be selected on the basis of their past behavior.

Popular content will be proactively but invisibly replicated to make it more readily accessible. In nature, a tsunami strikes; in the network, the obscure term *tsunami* suddenly begins to be uttered by queriers all over the world; within seconds, copies of the relevant information have migrated to all corners of the network. In weeks or months, interest has waned and so have the copies. A wave of tragedy in the real world; a surge of interest (compassionate? inquisitive? prurient?) in the populace; a wave of traffic on the network. Information mirrors the minds of people. The *web (which others call the universe)* moves one step closer to the real thing.

A REPUTATION SOCIETY

One of the challenges of peer-to-peer computing is managing the collective use of resources efficiently. This affects traditional architectures too, but their organization offers at least some assurances that individuals will not hog resources unduly, and steps can be taken to excommunicate them if they do. The fact that peer-to-peer networks are self-organized exposes them to greater risks, ranging from inherent technological problems such as scalability and traffic management to deliberate attacks: denial of service, consuming resources without contributing any, poisoning with files whose content belies their description, impersonation, spamming.

Anonymity lies at the root of many human problems. Untrammeled anonymity leads to a breakdown in personal responsibility. Regrettably, we are all apt to behave badly if we are not held accountable for our actions. However, anonymity coupled with reputation control is a different matter. A reputation system is a way of determining ratings for a collection of personae. Even though people may act pseudonymously, their assumed character can win or lose their reputation, a reputation that is independent of the actor.

The best-known reputation systems are those run by online auction sites. A rating—positive, negative, or neutral—is recorded after each pair of users conducts a transaction. Your reputation comprises the proportion of positive and negative transactions in your history. More sophisticated schemes weight the contribution to the second user's reputation by the first user's reputation, just as the PageRank algorithm described in Chapter 4 weights links— endorsements—by the endorser's rank. Like page rank, reputation is subject to spam attacks, whose prevalence depends on how cheaply new personae can be obtained and on the cost of transactions.

The reliability of a reputation system is based on its security. Centralized systems are necessarily operated by particular institutions, and people's trust in them is determined by the prestige and perceived integrity of the institution. It is far more difficult to preserve the integrity of a scheme that is distributed. Peer-to-peer networks generate reputation locally as the consequence of individual interactions and diffuse it through the network to yield a global evaluation of each node. The difficulty is keeping the information safe and secure. Reputation evaluation methods differ with respect to what is measured (history of uploads, satisfaction, level of user participation, popularity of the content) and the degree of centralization. Some schemes penalize malicious behavior; others adopt micropayment mechanisms. Credit might be earned by donating disk space and processing power, and spent on access to distributed file storage.

Another way of avoiding risks on the network is to model what we do in real life: keep within our circle of friends. Friend-to-friend protocols are private peer-to-peer systems in which people allow direct connections only to their "friends," others whom they trust enough to allow them direct access to their computer.[61] Like underground resistance networks, this diffuses responsibility, and systems can grow large without compromising anyone's anonymity. In a peer-to-peer network, anyone who accesses your computer knows its address and can thus reveal your real identity; friend-to-friend networks limit the spread of such knowledge. The richness of the friendship network governs the efficiency of its operation: it is difficult to transmit nonlocal messages through environments that harbor distrust. One solution is to assume that friendship is transitive: a friend of a friend is automatically a friend. This allows more efficient communication but gives weaker assurances of anonymity.[62] Another is to create some nodes that are connected to other, not necessarily friendly, nodes and take special precautions to protect these potential vulnerabilities.[63]

Restricting interactions to your circle of close friends is a conservative strategy that palls after a while, whereas taking the risk of interacting with strangers promises unlimited adventure. Online auctions would never catch on if you could only trade with people you already know. Can the comfortable security of friend-to-friend interaction be combined with the benefit of a public reputation system in a peer-to-peer environment that lacks central institutions?

---

[61] Today's friend-to-friend networks are Ants P2P and GNUnet; Mute and Napshare are peer-to-peer networks that can be configured into friend-to-friend ones.

[62] For example, DirectConnect.

[63] For example, Freenet.

We keep confronting the same dilemma: you have to give information away in order to obtain certain benefits—whether higher-quality documents or more reliable search results. Can strong encryption combine with reputation measurement to make it possible to trust people who are not known on a personal basis, but are guaranteed by the system itself? This is a challenge for the future.

THE USER AS LIBRARIAN

We explained earlier how communities of users might define their perspective by identifying a subgraph of the web that they care about. People want to participate by promulgating their own point of view. Another way they can do this is by publishing their own collections of information. When talking about archives in Chapter 6 (page 179–181), we remarked that the web is a conundrum because the notion of "archive" implies both interior and exterior: there must be some things an archive does *not* contain. Not everything is recorded in the web, of course, but being in constant flux, it is impossible to say where its outside commences. The very utterance in which you mention something that is on the outside may itself find its way onto the web, altering the status of the thing you were talking about by insinuating it into the fold. The web is the universe: boundless, all-embracing.

THE ACT OF SELECTION

People add value to information by the act of selection. Take a set of documents, bind them together (whether physically, like an anthology of stories or poetry, or virtually, like a website), and give the collection an identity—by publishing it in book form, or simply declaring *here it is*—the URL. The act of selection creates a new artifact, an archive—this time a proper one, with both interior and exterior. You are not just saying that these documents are in the collection, you are declaring (by implication) that all others are *not* in the collection. Making a selection is making a distinction, giving a certain set of items an identity that the others do not have. This is something the web at large does not do.

Ever since the Alexandrian principle—that libraries should strive to contain everything—was abandoned (as discussed in Chapter 2), selection has been central to the notion of a library. If "data" is characterized as recorded facts, and "information" is the creation of a form—a set of patterns, or expectations, that underlie the data (page 214)—then one possible way to define "knowledge" is the accumulation of your set of expectations, and "wisdom" as the value attached to knowledge. All information is not created equal, and it is wisdom that librarians contribute by making decisions about what to include in a collection—difficult decisions!—and following up with appropriate ways of organizing and maintaining the information. It is exactly these features that distinguish libraries from the web at large. In our world, where the web contains everything, digital libraries are focused subcollections, selected, organized, and maintained by people or institutions.

When people make collections, they begin—or should begin—by formulating a clear conception of what it is they intend to achieve. This might be called the "ideology" of the enterprise. It is formulated in terms of the collection's *purpose*, the objectives it is designed to achieve, and its *principles*, the directives that will guide decisions on what should be included and—equally important—excluded. This is where the wisdom comes in. Selection implies that you care about what the collection does and does not contain, and this in turn suggests that you will look after it: organize it, maintain it, take steps to ensure that it is preserved, perhaps publish it in another form. Collections have curators, people who care for them.

COMMUNITY METADATA

Communities already play a formative role in mediating access to information. Take the university, one of many professional communities to which we authors belong. Through its library, our institutions subscribe to several online publication databases. When our laptop is connected to the university network, we automatically gain access to the contents of these databases. Mechanisms that used to be awkward five or ten years ago are gradually becoming refined to the point where they operate invisibly. We locate a document on the web that does not have open access, and, if we are working through our institution, it is automatically available to us without any further layer of authentication.

The production of metadata is also a community affair. Although automatic document analysis and metadata assignment is a lively research area, high-quality metadata can only be created by human beings. But people are small: the amount that any one person can do is limited. It is communities that organize and collate the work of individuals into a comprehensive and worthwhile body of metadata, communities that impose standards and control metadata quality. Communities are of many kinds: academic, social, recreational, professional, family, artistic. Their members care enough about documents that fall within their purview to muster the resources needed to index and catalog them. Some communities employ professional librarians; others rely on amateurs.

As we learned in Chapter 2, librarians have training and experience in assigning metadata to documents in a consistent way—and it's a tough job.

In the more varied and informal world of the web, metadata is more often assigned by non-librarians, whether professionals in other disciplines or dedicated amateurs. The term *folksonomy* is sometimes used to refer to collaborative efforts by volunteers to organize things on the web. It combines the relaxed connotations of *folk* with the rigid structure implied by *taxonomy*. Instead of adopting a formal classification, predefined and approved in advance, users are encouraged to tag documents with freely chosen keywords. These might apply to photographs in an image collection, text in personal document collections, items in blogs, and so on. They are used to assist with information retrieval.

The trouble with freely assigned tags is that different people may describe particular documents in completely different ways. In Chapter 2, we learned that even apparently objective attributes such as title and author can be surprisingly hard to determine consistently. The use of free vocabulary—folksonomies—for keywords and subject headings may lead to information being harder, not easier, to locate, because idiosyncratic terms creep in. Most librarians would argue that an agreed set of tags, assigned by people trained in their use, enables more reliable retrieval of content. On the other hand, information on the web is so vast, and growing so quickly, that it is hardly likely that library-quality metadata will ever be assigned to most of it.

Quality control is always a difficulty with volunteer labor. But an even more troubling issue arises when volunteer tagging becomes popular. Whenever people have an opportunity to freely contribute information, the problem of misuse lurks, whether for fun (a twisted kind of fun) or profit. If metadata is used to help find information, it can equally well serve to misfile it. When we discussed enriching documents with metatags in Chapter 3 (page 77), we mentioned an intriguing way of exploiting anonymity on the web to provide accurate image metadata. The crux was to accept a descriptive term only when two people who could not possibly communicate with each other assigned it independently. Perhaps this kind of approach can be extended to more general metadata assignment to allow reliable tagging by people who do it for fun, or as a community service.

Actions, they say, speak louder than words. Collaborative filtering is a way of extracting trends from the behavior of users—typically website visitors—and using this information to present suggestions to searchers. For example, online bookstores or music stores recommend books or songs on the basis of purchases by other people with apparently similar interests. Spamming is unlikely because these actions cost real money. The information obtained is a kind of metadata that is automatically inferred, not from the item's contents but from the behavior of actual users. However, it is a rather complex form of metadata: it does not rate items individually, but tracks relations between them—"people who bought that generally bought this too." It clusters items into different groups, but does not name the classes.

A fascinating example of the power of volunteer effort in the web community is Wikipedia, a free encyclopedia to which anyone can contribute. We have acknowledged it several times under *Notes and Sources* and used it as an example in Chapter 3, noting there that it has become a respected, though controversial, source of information. Wikipedia began in 2001 with the slogan, "the free encyclopedia that anyone can edit," and within five years the English version had grown to a million items (there are versions in many other languages), by far the largest encyclopedia the world has ever known. Some praise it as an example of what open communities can do; others dismiss it as a faith-based encyclopedia. The journal *Nature* reported that its science articles compared in accuracy to those in *Encyclopedia Britannica*.[64] Once Wikipedia gained a certain degree of prominence, problems started to arise. It began to attract graffiti, hoaxes, people editing their own—or their enemy's—biography. Once it became prominent, it gained potential as a soapbox for idiosyncratic ideas and practical jokes. In the unregulated global information community, when something grows popular, it automatically becomes a natural target for misuse.

DIGITAL LIBRARIES

Future web users, and user communities, will participate in collecting, organizing, and cataloging information on a large scale. Although centralized search engines make everything accessible in some sense, they impose a single point of view on the universe. As we have argued, the act of selection has value in its own right. Creating anthologies is easy: now—for the first time in history— anyone can assemble a large information collection and make it public. People like to collect and arrange information. Anyone can participate in this creative act, and it's something that most of us are good at and enjoy doing.

Metadata is the glue that cements a library together. Of course, hyperlinks are the web's mechanism for linking documents, and, properly used, they provide a richly intertwined structure that serves readers well. But a salient characteristic of a library is that it is easy to take a new book and make it a first-class member of the library: all you need is metadata to add to the catalog. In contrast, when adding a new document to a website that achieves its unity by rich and intelligent hyperlinking, you must not only process the document by inserting links to pertinent places elsewhere in the collection, but also edit the rest of the website to add appropriate links to the newcomer. It is as if you had to revise the entire contents of all the library's books when adding

---

[64] Wikipedia had an average of four mistakes per article versus *Britannica's* three. Of eight serious errors found in a sample of 42 science entries—including misinterpretations of important concepts—four came from each source.

a new one. If you don't, the new entrant is a second-class member of the collection. This is one reason why websites degenerate with time unless substantial effort is put into maintaining them.

Software systems for building digital libraries make it easy to create collections and organize them using metadata—along with, of course, full-text search. You might want a list of titles, a list of authors, a browsing structure for hierarchically organized subject metadata, a dynamic collage display for images, and integrated access to a domain-specific thesaurus that includes links to pertinent documents. Add to this searchable full-text indexes of key phrases, summaries, titles, and the entire document text. If you have the necessary metadata (or can download it, say, from the Library of Congress), you can import it, along with the documents, into a digital library system and put the collection on the web—perhaps at the same time issuing it as a stand-alone collection on removable media such as DVD (or an iPod). Unlike an ordinary website that is bound together by manually inserted hyperlinks, new documents can be added, with their metadata, and be fully integrated into the collection immediately and automatically. A community might use such a system to create a repository of information it is interested in, allowing members to upload new documents and metadata.

Today's web dragons do not let us, the users, participate in what they do, except by creating web pages that eventually, when crawled, become integrated into the same old search structure. They treat the web as a whole, without any boundaries: a democratic swamp. Future dragons will recognize the value of drawing users in as full partners in the information-seeking enterprise. We will be allowed to create collections, draw boundaries, organize, maintain, and care for the information within—in a word, to become curators. Dragons will acknowledge the information we contribute and accord it special treatment, so that searchers who wish to, will be able to use our organization to help them find information. Digital libraries will coexist with the web at large, acknowledging its presence and being acknowledged by the dragons that users turn to when they need information.

YOUR COMPUTER AND THE WEB

As you can well imagine, we, the authors, are writing this book on our laptop and desktop computers. On each system, the file we are editing is one of a few hundred thousand others. These are just our personal files—the total number of files on the disk, including system files and those of other users, is far larger. Our computers are not particularly large or powerful. In fact, one of us periodically backs up his laptop on a personal music player (just like those our kids have). As well as hundreds of thousands of files, the player can accommodate thousands of tunes and thousands of photographs—and still have plenty of free space left. In the few short months that elapse before you read these words, new versions will be available that make today's personal media devices seem like 78 RPM records.

In terms of sheer quantity, the number of documents on most people's personal computer constitutes a fair-sized library, far larger than all but the most immense personal libraries of yore. They certainly dwarf Europe's largest collection of the seventeenth century, Duke August's (mentioned in Chapter 2, page 33) with 135,000 works. They rival the great library of Alexandria, with 700,000 volumes at its zenith. If digitized, these classic collections would easily fit on an iPod.

PERSONAL FILE SPACES

The organization of our files falls woefully short of the standard set by even the most primitive of libraries. Indeed, the word *organization* is a misnomer. Even tidy people who take pains to keep their workplace clean and presentable have filespaces that are haphazard at best. The only real structure is the folders. Along with our personal files are tens of thousands of folders in which they reside. Folders are hierarchical; most are buried deep within the file system. The top-level folders are like rooms of a great mansion. Superficially the house looks tidy, but every door opens to reveal a disgusting mess. Let's peek into a few rooms.

One room holds all the e-mail. The user has placed it into folders that correspond approximately to topics, most of which have subfolders. Compared with other rooms, it is relatively well structured, because every e-mail has natural properties (sender, receiver, date, subject), and our user keeps it tidy because he (the person responsible for this particular mess is a man) works with it every day. Nevertheless, this room contains several closets called *misc* containing messages he can't be bothered to classify, and others called *old* that are probably obsolete but he daren't risk deleting. Many e-mails contain vital attachments. Most relate to projects that have entrails in other parts of the file structure, but there are no explicit links—the user has to try to remember where everything is.

Another room (is it a folder or a single file?—this particular user doesn't know or care) contains web bookmarks. These are also organized hierarchically but with a completely different structure from the e-mail folders. Again, most relate to projects stored elsewhere, though there are no links except those in the user's head.

The computer desktop is like another room. Mostly it contains links into other parts of the file structure. However, on it are several items in the "too hard to file" category. Really, our harried user should clean up his desk by putting them away. But some have been there for months, and the fact is that he hasn't yet got around to dealing with them. Perhaps he never will.

The other rooms represent top-level folders of the file structure. Some are covered in cobwebs: their doors haven't been opened for years. Others are used only sporadically. On entering some of these rooms, it would take considerable effort for our user, their owner, to recall what they contain and what they are for. Many are lingering vestiges of his distant past. Any given project has information in several widely scattered rooms: some file folders, some related e-mails, and some related bookmarks.

This particular computer is three years old, and most of the files are younger than this. However, there is an embarrassing room called "legacy files." When he receives a new computer, the user will not sort through his files. He'll just copy them—lock, stock, and barrel—into a *legacy* folder on his new computer. That's what he did when he bought this computer, and the *legacy* folder here contains within it a *legacy* folder for his previous computer. He has no idea what most of these files contain or whether they might prove important in the future. It would take major effort to look into them and clean them up. Like most of us, this particular user has no intention of doing so.

FROM FILESPACE TO THE WEB

Our personal computers spend most of their lives connected to the Internet. In their minds, users could regard the web as a massive extension of their readable filespace. However, in practice, they are forced to use completely different tools to access it, and they have to worry about managing the boundary between the two. For example, they explicitly and painstakingly download some parts of the web that may be needed now or in the future.

The level of organization of the web is higher than that of an individual personal computer. It comprises separate sites, which resemble a top-level folder—except that there are hundreds of millions of them. Each site has a hierarchical structure of pages that is evident from the URLs it contains. This reflects the organization of that particular site. It could be well organized, for the site may be institutionally owned and professionally managed. Even on sites that are personal workstations, the files that are on display on the web are usually better organized than the personal filespace mess. And, of course, unlike files, web pages contain explicit hyperlinks that have been deliberately inserted to reflect a structure intended for browsing, although many links have gone stale.

The way we find things in our personal filespace is by navigating through our folders, trying to go in the right direction to descend to the information we want. This worked well for hundreds, or thousands of files, and tens of folders, but it doesn't scale up. It cannot even begin to cope with anything like the size of today's web. That's why search engines were invented, to deal with this problem on the web, and they do an excellent job. It is an astonishing fact of history that a full decade elapsed between the introduction of search engines for the web in the mid-1990s, and the widespread commercial adoption of the same kind of advanced software technology for searching one's personal filespace: the Google desktop, Microsoft's *Stuff I've seen*, Apple's *Spotlight*.

UNIFICATION

What's the difference between information within your computer and information that's out there on the web? Nothing! In both cases, some of it is yours; some is other people's. Some is private, available only on your machine or the corporate intranet, protected by firewalls from the outside world; some is public. Some is well organized; some has just been dumped there. There is no good reason for you to conceptualize the web as a separate information space from your personal computer's filespace.

Future systems will provide uniform ways of accessing personal files, community and corporate information, and public information on the web at large. Most of the time your computer will be connected to the Internet, as it probably is today. Even when you disconnect your laptop, most of the files you want will be available. In the background, the information you are browsing—and the pages in their web neighborhood too—will be silently cached onto your disk. All the files you are likely to access will be replicated locally. You'll still be able to see them when you are disconnected (whether by a temporary breakdown or when traveling)—indeed, you probably won't notice disconnection. The only exception is when you use web search to explore a totally new area.

Uniform mechanisms will let you work with all the hierarchies that are separate in your computer today—your file folders, e-mail folders, web bookmarks, your personal website, the web at large—as one unified data structure. No longer will pieces of information related to a single project be scattered all over the place. There will be tools that help you manage all this. You will no longer have to feel ashamed of the mess that is your filespace.

The whole notion of where a file resides will become an anachronism. You will never know—or care. Robust replication techniques will be used to ensure backup; secure encryption techniques will be used to ensure privacy. The desktop search that we are finally starting to see today is just the beginning of a major unification of filespaces and the web. Looking back from the future, you will find it almost inconceivable that people used to have to manage the boundary between the web and their filespace themselves. Your grandchildren will be incredulous when you tell them about the bad old days.

THE GLOBAL OFFICE

History comes in cycles. In the beginning, computers were personal affairs: one person and his or her machine. Then, the advent of time-sharing allowed several users to share the scarce and costly resource of computer time. Next, the microprocessor revolution gave birth to the office and home computer, and machines became personal again. We have talked of unifying your filespace and the web into a shared global storage resource. The wheel is turning again: the dragons are beginning to provide processing services, a kind of planetary time-sharing system—not, this time, for the sake of economy, but for convenience. At locations with reliable electricity and abundant network connectivity, they are establishing massive computational farms on a scale that is absolutely unprecedented—they will house many hundreds of thousands of computers, perhaps millions of them.

As we write, Google leads the trend. First, it offered its own e-mail service, GMail. Then a calendar application. Next, it acquired a company that had developed a web-based word processor, Writely, that resembles Microsoft Word, but operates remotely, through web pages. Then it released a spreadsheet application. All these initiatives make it easy to share your documents with other people, something that is awkward to manage by emailing them back and forth. By the time you read this, more moves will have been made. We can look forward to a full office suite, completely different from conventional offerings because Google will provide the computer as well as the software. All you need is a web browser. Your office will be right there in any Internet café, any airport lounge, on any mobile phone.

How can you run a word processor or spreadsheet application over a web browser? What makes this possible is the AJAX technology mentioned in Chapter 4 (page 129), which doesn't require the whole page to be reloaded when a piece of it changes. The interaction between browser and server is more fine-grained than before. Only incremental changes are transmitted, and this happens in the background while you continue typing or editing. All the new products mentioned before use AJAX.

It's not just Google. Think Free, a small California company, has created a platform-independent Microsoft-compatible office package that runs not just on PCs, but also on mobile devices such as iPods. You can download the package and run the word processor, spreadsheet, and slide presenter locally on your desktop computer, or you can register with the company to receive some file space and then work remotely. New business models are emerging based on providing services rather than selling software. Microsoft also offers an online service (*live.com*); they may evolve toward a server version for corporate networks.

The online office seems a natural evolution of the web dragons' core business of global search. First information services, then information *processing* services. Users enjoy many attractive advantages. You can work on your data anywhere. Collaborate freely with anyone you want. Share data without worrying about the coherence of copies on different computers. Collaborative environments could dramatically affect the production of content. Intelligent search agents might make suggestions as you write, telling you of new information or recommending key citations—either from the web at large or from your community's information space.

The result will be a radically new computer ecosystem. As we noted in Chapter 3 (page 64), computers waste most of their time running screen savers; their real computational power is largely untapped. In contrast, central hosting services can balance the computational load—existing search engines already do this well. The big saving is not so much the cost of processing, for computers are cheap, but of maintenance. And maintenance not so much of hardware, but of software. No more upgrades! (just your web browser). The office system runs remotely, and the dragons tend it for you. Since there's no need to bless a version, the software can evolve continually, dispensing with today's fuss over new releases.

Web dragons will fight to be the leading players of this revolution because their business model is based on advertising, and therefore usage. No doubt users will also be prepared to pay for these services, since they could replace our entire computing environment. Of course, communication channels will have to evolve to support widespread deployment of the global office. There will be challenges in providing advanced office software functionality, and in perceived stability of software, but these can be overcome.

The impact on privacy is a more serious issue. You may worry that strangers could tap into your data as you work on the Internet. Once every bit of your life's data is under global control, how will you feel about whether it is safely protected against malicious tampering? Although these issues are critical, current technology is mature enough to offer strong guarantees of security. But you will have to place complete trust in the service itself. It's hard to know whether people will accept this. Perhaps the new regime will coexist with familiar desktop-based software. Nonprofessionals, especially casual users, will find the global office ideal, while companies might be more skeptical, particularly in the beginning. In the long run, if people no longer work at their office desk, mobility will be a key driver for the global office—and mobility inevitably compromises security.

SO WHAT?

We have come to the end of our journey. Before parting company, let us walk together though the argument of the book, lightly paraphrasing the *So What?* sections at the end of each chapter.

The World Wide Web, our brash young teenager, exploded suddenly onto the scene in the space of a few years. Although totally unexpected, it didn't arise out of nowhere: the groundwork had been laid over centuries by philosophers and over decades by technological visionaries. Though they knew nothing of the web itself, looking back over their work, we can see that they had a lot to say about it. Nevertheless, the web is an absolutely unprecedented phenomenon that is exerting a profound influence on the way we think, work, and play.

Chapter 2 visited the world of libraries, another strand of our intellectual heritage, with a fascinating history in its own right. Libraries did not sow the seeds of the web but are now rushing headlong toward convergence with it—indeed, the web is threatening to subsume libraries by taking over our literature. This convergence has the potential to be a great unifying and liberating force in the way in which we find and use information. But there is a disturbing side too: the web dragons, which offer an excellent free service to society, centralize access to information on a global scale, which has its own dangers.

Next, we studied the technical background to the web and the way it works: all those acronyms; new meanings for cookies and crawling; mysterious-sounding avatars and chatbots, blogs and wikis. We learned that there is a mathematical side too. The web is a huge network that, viewed from afar, shares the properties of scale-free random networks. The pattern of links does not give a sense of scale: it doesn't make much sense to talk about the "average" number of links into or out of a node. The connectivity imparted by links breaks the web up into distinct regions or continents. Zooming in, the details start to come into focus: the connection pattern is not random at all, but reflects the myriad communities that have created the web.

How can you possibly find stuff in this gargantuan information space? In the beginning, scientists developed large-scale full-text search techniques that work by counting words, weighing them, and measuring how well each document matches the user's query. This was an appropriate way of finding information in a set of unrelated documents. However, pages on the web are not unrelated: they are densely hyperlinked. Today's search engines acknowledge this by counting links as well as words and weighing them too. This is an appropriate way of measuring the objective reality that is the web. However, the dragons do not divulge the recipe they use to weigh and combine links and words. It's not a science open to public scrutiny and debate. It's a commercial trade secret.

More fundamentally, secrecy is an unavoidable side effect of the need to maintain the illusion of an objective reality—an illusory reality that the bad guys, the spammers, are trying to distort. The World Wide Web was created by scientists and quickly became the playground of academic computer researchers.

Then commerce took over, introducing a competitive element into what, until then, had been a fundamentally cooperative environment. The playground became a battleground. As gateways to the web, search engines are the arbiters of visibility. Web visibility is free advertising to the most attractive possible audience—people who are actively seeking information related to your product. Promoting visibility has become an industry. There are perfectly legitimate ways to do this: make your pages attractive and informative, and ensure that they are listed in the right places. But some people attempt to discover and exploit loopholes in how the dragons sift information. This has the effect of polluting our information universe, and search engine companies work hard on our behalf to eliminate the deleterious effects of web spam on their search results.

Next, we turned to broader questions of the control of information, both on the web and in our society. Information is not as neutral as you might have supposed. Ever since humans began written records, control over the supply and archiving of information has been a powerful social, political, and historical force. But the web is no ordinary archive: it's created and maintained by everyone, an archive of the people, for the people, and by the people. Access, however, is mediated by the dragons. They strive to determine the authority of each page as judged by the entire web community and reflect this in their search results. Though it sounds ultra-democratic, this has some unexpected and undesirable outcomes: the rich get richer, popularity is substituted for genuine authority, and the sensitive balance between privacy and censorship is hard to maintain. In a global village that spans the entire world, the tyranny of the majority reigns.

How will these challenges be met? While we cannot predict the future, this final chapter has given some ideas. We wish the dragons well in the war against spam, but we also welcome longer-term solutions for resolving the dilemma of secrecy. As communities become central to web search, life will grow tougher for spammers. The dragons are starting to transcend the single-objective-reality view of the web by acknowledging the importance of personal interaction; they are beginning to recognize communities too. Will peer-to-peer technology offer new perspectives in web search? Will curated digital libraries be where we go to find truly authoritative information sources? Finally, while struggling for leadership in search, the dragons have realized the advantage of broadening their mandate by supplying office tools that help users manage their own information. Will our information environment evolve toward distributed desktop systems equipped with integrated search, or toward centralized data supported by global hosting services? Will desktop office applications be displaced? Only time will tell. But one thing is certain: the dragons are aiming higher than search—they will change the very way we work and play.

WHAT CAN *YOU* DO ABOUT ALL THIS?

- List communities you belong to.
- Seek web resources for each one (blogs, newsgroups, forums, hubs).
- Choose a dragon and try out its personalization features.
- Clear out your search history.
- Learn about a leading-edge peer-to-peer network.
- Play with a collaborative web search system (such as *stumbleupon*).
- Download open-source digital library software and build your own collection.
- Check out an online office package.
- What information on your hard drive would *you* be prepared to move to an online hosting service?
- What online services might web dragons offer?

NOTES AND SOURCES

The images in Figure 7.1 are from the Warburg Institute's website.[65] The Library's emblem is taken from a woodcut in the edition of the *De natura rerum* of Isidore of Seville (560–636), printed at Augsburg in 1472, along with a quotation from the Hexameron of St. Ambrose (III.iv.18) describing the relationship between the four elements of which the world is made (Bing, 1935).

Androutsellis-Theotokis and Spinellis (2004) provide a detailed description of peer-to-peer distribution technologies, which we used as a source for most of the technical information on this subject. As usual, Wikipedia is a mine of valuable information and contains helpful articles on client-server, peer-to-peer, and friend-to-friend communication. Kaye (2004) discusses the future of social file-sharing techniques, while Bawa et al. (2003) present an interesting and innovative peer-to-peer searching strategy.

The journal *Nature* conducted a study in 2005 that concluded that science articles in Wikipedia were comparable in accuracy to those in the *Encyclopedia Britannica* (Giles, 2005). Britannica Inc. attacked Giles' study as "fatally flawed"[66]

---

[65] *www2.sas.ac.uk/warburg*

[66] *http://www.corporate.britannica.com/britannica_nature_response.pdf*

and demanded a retraction; *Nature* defended itself and declined to retract.[67] Wikipedia provides objective coverage of the controversy in its article about the *Encyclopedia Britannica*. You can read about digital libraries in books by Witten and Bainbridge (2003) and Lesk (2005). Open-source systems for building digital libraries include Greenstone, DSpace, and Fedora.

---

[67] *http://www.nature.com/press_releases/Britannica_response.pdf*

REFERENCES

Albert, R., Jeong, H., and Barabási, A.-L. (1999). "Diameter of the World Wide Web." *Nature*, Vol. 401, pp. 130–131.

Androutsellis-Theotokis, S., and Spinellis, D. (2004). "A survey of peer-to-peer content distribution technologies." *ACM Computing Surveys*, Vol. 36, No. 4, pp. 335–371.

Bace, R. G. (2000). *Intrusion Detection*. Macmillan Technical Publishing, Indianapolis.

Barabási, A.-L. (2002). *Linked: The New Science of Networks*. Perseus, Cambridge, Massachusetts.

Barabási, A.-L., and Albert, R. (1999). "Emergence of scaling in random networks." *Science*, Vol. 286, pp. 509–511.

Barabási, A.-L., Freeh, V. W., Jeong, H., and Brockman, J. R. (2001). "Parasitic computing." *Nature*, Vol. 412 (August), pp. 894–897.

Bardini, T. (2000). *Bootstrapping*. Stanford University Press, Stanford.

Battelle, J. (2005). *The Search: How Google and Its Rivals Rewrote the Rules of Business and Transformed Our Culture*. Penguin, New York.

Bawa M., Manku, G., and Raghavan, P. (2003). "SETS: Search Enhanced by Topic Segmentation." In *Proc. ACM Conference on Research and Development in Information Retrieval (SIGIR)*, pp. 306–313. Association of Computing Machinery, New York.

Belew, R. (2000). *Finding Out About*. Cambridge University Press, Cambridge.

Bellamy, J., Laurence, A., and Perry, G. (Editors) (2001). *Women, Scholarship and Criticism*. Manchester University Press, Manchester, U.K.

Bender, T. K., and Higdon, D. L. (1988). *A Concordance to Henry James's "The Spoils of Poynton."* Garland Reference Library of the Humanities, Vol. 648. Garland, New York.

Berners-Lee, T. (1989). "Information management: A proposal." In-house technical document, CERN (revised 1990 with R. Cailliau), *www.w3.org/History/1989/proposal.htm*.

Berners-Lee, T. (2000). *Weaving the Web*. Texere, London and New York.

Berners-Lee, T., Hendler, J., and Lassila, O. (2001). "The semantic web." *Scientific American* (May), pp. 35–43.

Berry, M. W., and Browne, M. (2005). *Understanding Search Engines: Mathematical Modeling and Text Retrieval*, 2nd edition. Society for Industrial and Applied Mathematics, Philadelphia.

Bharat, K., and Broder, A. Z. (1999). "Mirror, mirror on the Web: A study of host pairs with replicated content." *Computer Networks*, Vol. 31, No. 11–16, pp. 1579–1590.

Bianconi, G., and Barabási, A.-L. (2001). "Competition and multiscaling in evolving networks." *Europhysics Letters*, Vol. 54, No. 4, pp. 436–442.

Bianchini, M., Gori, M., and Scarselli, F. (2005). "Inside PageRank." *ACM Transactions on Internet Technologies*, Vol. 5, No. 1 (February), pp. 92–128.

Bing, G. (1935). "The Warburg Institute." *Library Association Record*, Vol. 5, p. 88.

Borges, J. L. (2000). *The Library of Babel*. David R. Godine, Jaffrey, New Hampshire.

Borodin, A., Roberts, G. O., Rosenthal, J. S., and Tsaparas, P. (2002). "Finding authorities and hubs from link structures on the World Wide Web." In *Proc. 11th International World Wide Web Conference*, pp. 415–429. ACM Press, New York.

Bowker, R. R. (1883). "The work of the nineteenth-century librarian for the librarian of the twentieth." *Library Journal*, Vol. 8 (September–October), pp. 247–250.

Brennan, L., and Johnson, V. E. (Editors) (2004). *Social, Ethical and Policy Implications of Information Technology*. Information Science Publishing, Hershey, Pennsylvania.

Brin, S., and Page, L. (1998). "The anatomy of a large-scale hypertextual Web search engine." *Computer Networks and ISDN Systems*, Vol. 33, pp. 107–117.

Broder, A. Z., Kumar, R., Maghoul, F., Raghavan, P., Rajagopalan, V., Stata, S., Tomkins, A., and Wiener, J. L. (2000). "Graph structure in the Web." *Computer Networks*, Vol. 33, No. 1–6, pp. 309–320.

Burges, C., Shaked, T., Renshaw, E., Lazier, A., Deeds, M., Hamilton, N. and Hullender, G. (2005). "Learning to rank using gradient descent." In *Proc. International Conference on Machine Learning*, Bonn, Germany, pp. 89–96.

Bush, V. (1945). "As we may think." *Atlantic Monthly*, Vol. 176, pp. 641-649; reprinted in Nyce and Kahn (1991), pp. 88–109.

Bush, V. (1959). "Memex II." In *Bush Papers, MIT Archive*; reprinted in Nyce and Kahn (1991), pp. 165–184.

Castellani, F. (2004). "Program cracks crosswords: Multilingual algorithm uses web to find words." *Nature* (*www.nature.com/news/2004/041004/full/041004-2.html*).

Cho, J., and Roy, S. (2004). "Impact of search engines on page popularity." In *Proc. World-Wide Web Conference*, May 11–22, pp. 20–29. Association for Computing Machinery, New York.

Chu, Y.-C., Bainbridge, D., Jones, M., and Witten, I. H. (2004). "Realistic books: A bizarre homage to an obsolete medium?" In *Proc. Joint Conference on Digital Libraries*, Tucson, pp. 78–86. Association for Computing Machinery, New York.

Clarke, V. M. (1875). *The Complete Concordance to Shakespeare*. W. Kent and Co., London.

Cohen, R., Erez, K., ben-Avraham, D., and Havlin, S. (2000). "Resilience of the Internet to random breakdowns." *Physical Review Letters*, Vol. 85, No. 21, pp. 4626–4628.

Committee on Intellectual Property Rights, Computer Science and Telecommunications Board (2000). *The Digital Dilemma: Intellectual Property in the Information Age*. National Academy Press, Washington, DC.

Cooper, L. (1911). *Concordance to the Poems of William Wordsworth*. Russell and Russell, New York.

Crane, D., Pascarello, E., and James, D. (2005). *Ajax in Action*. Manning, Greenwich, Connecticut.

Crawford, W., and Gorman, M. (1995). *Future Libraries: Dreams, Madness, and Reality*. American Library Association, Chicago.

Davison, B. D., Gerasoulis, A., Kleisouris, K., Lu, Y., Seo, H., Wang, W., and Wu, B. (1999). "DiscoWeb: Applying link analysis to Web search" (Extended abstract). In *Proc. Eighth International World Wide Web Conference*, pp. 148–149. ACM Press, New York.

Denning, D. E. (1987). "An intrusion detection model." *IEEE Transactions on Software Engineering*, Vol. 13, No. 2, pp. 222–232.

Derrida, J. (1996). *Archive Fever: A Freudian Impression*. University of Chicago Press, Chicago and London.

Diligenti, M., Maggini, M., and Gori, M. (2003). "A learning algorithm for web page scoring systems." In *Proc. 18th International Joint Conference on Artificial Intelligence*, Acapulco, pp. 575–580.

Dorogovtsev, S. N., Mendes, J. F. F., and Samukhin, A. N. (2001). "Giant strongly connected component of directed networks." *Physical Review E*, Vol. 64 (July).

Eco, U. (1980). *The Name of the Rose*. Translated by William Weaver from Italian; republished in English in 1994 by Harvest Books.

Egghe, L., and Rousseau, R. (1990). *Introduction to Informetrics*. Elsevier, New York.

Elgesem, D. (1999). "The structure of rights in Directive 95/46/EC on the protection of individuals with regard to the processing of personal data and the free movement of such data." *Ethics and Information Technology*, Vol. 1, pp. 283–293.

Erdös, P., and Reny, A. (1960). "On the evolution of random graphs." *Publications of the Mathematical Institute of the Hungarian Academy of Sciences*, Budapest, Vol. 5, pp. 290–297.

Faloutsos, M., Faloutsos, P., and Faloutsos, C. (1999). "On power-law relationships of the internet topology." *Proc. ACM SIGCOMM Computer and Communications Review*, Vol. 29, pp. 251–263.

Fetterly, D., Manasse, M., and Najork, M. (2004). "Spam, damn, and statistics." In *Proc. Seventh International Workshop on the Web and Databases (WebDB2004)*, Paris, June 17–18, pp. 1–6. Association for Computing Machinery, New York.

Flake, G. W., Lawrence, S., Giles, C. L. and Coetzee, F. M. (2002). "Self-organization and identification of web communities." *IEEE Computer*, Vol. 35, No. 3, pp. 66–71.

Foucault, M. (1984). "What is Enlightenment?" In *The Foucault Reader*, edited by Paul Rabinow, pp. 32–50. Pantheon, New York.

Foucault, M. (1989). *The Archaeology of Knowledge*. Routledge, London (reprinted 2005).

Foucault, M. (1994). "The art of telling the truth." In *Critique and Power: Recasting the Foucault/Habermas Debate*, edited by M. Kelly, pp. 139–148. MIT Press, Cambridge.

Furness, M. H. H. (1875). *A Concordance to Shakespeare's Poems: An Index to Every Word Therein Contained*. J. B. Lippincott and Co., Philadelphia.

Garfield, E. (1972). "Citation analysis as a tool in journal evaluation." *Science*, Vol. 178, pp. 471–479.

Gavison, R. (1980). "Privacy and the limits of law." *Yale Law Journal*, Vol. 89, pp. 421–471.

Gerrold, D. (1972). *When Harlie Was One.* Spectra; updated edition published in 1988.

Gibson, D., Kleinberg, J., and Raghavan, P. (1998). "Inferring Web communities from link topology." *Hypertext 1998*, pp. 225–234.

Giles, J. (2005). "Internet encyclopaedias go head to head." *Nature*, Vol. 438, pp. 900–901.

Gore, D. (1976). "The theory of the no-growth, high-performance library." In *Farewell to Alexandria*, edited by D. Gore, pp. 164–180. Greenwood Press, Westport, Connecticut.

Gori, M., and Witten, I. H. (2005). "The bubble of Web visibility." *Communications of the ACM*, Vol. 48, No. 3 (March), pp. 115–117.

Graham, L., and Metaxas, P. T. (2003). "Of course it's true; I saw it on the Internet!" *Communications of the ACM*, Vol. 46, No. 5, pp. 71–75.

Gulli, A., and Signorini, A. (2005). "The indexable web is more than 11.5 billion pages." In *Proc. World-Wide Web Conference*, May, Chiba, Japan.

Gyongyi, Z., Garcia-Molina, H., and Pedersen, J. (2004). "Combating Web spam by TrustRank." In *Proc. 30th Conference on Very Large Databases*, Toronto, pp. 576–587.

Gyongyi, Z., and Garcia-Molina, H. (2005a). "Web Spam taxonomy." In *Proc. First International Workshop on Adversarial Information Retrieval on the Web (AIRWeb)*, Chiba, Japan.

Gyongyi, Z., and Garcia-Molina, H. (2005b). "Link Spam Alliances." *Proc. 31st Conference on Very Large Databases*, Trondheim, Norway, pp. 517–528.

Heims, S. (1980). *John von Neumann and Norbert Wiener: From Mathematics to the Technologies of Life and Death.* MIT Press, Cambridge.

Hinman, L. M. (2005). "Esse est indicato in Google: Ethical and political issues in search engines." *International Review of Information Ethics*, Vol. 3, No. 6, pp. 19–25.

Hyde, T. (1674). *Catalogus Impressorum Librorum Bibliothecae Bodleianae*, Oxford University, Oxford, U.K.

Introna, L. D., and Nissenbaum, H. (2000). "Shaping the Web: Why the politics of search engines matters." *The Information Society*, Vol. 16, No. 3, pp. 161–185.

Johansen, A., Sornette, D., and Ledoit, O. (1999). "Predicting financial crashes using discrete scale invariance." *Journal of Risk*, Vol. 1, No. 4, pp. 5–32.

Jowett, B. (1949). *Plato: Meno.* Prentice Hall, Boston.

Kahle, B. (1997). "Preserving the Internet." *Scientific American*, Vol. 276, No. 3 (March), pp. 82–83.

Kant I. (1784). "What Is Enlightenment?" In *Foundations of the Metaphysics of Morals and What Is Enlightenment.* Macmillan, New York, 1990.

Kant I. (1798). *The Conflict of the Faculties.* University of Nebraska Press, Lincoln, 1992.

Kaye R. (2004). "Next-generation file sharing with social networks." Presented at O'Reilly Emerging Technology Conference, San Diego. Available online at OpenP2P.com, *www.openp2p.com/lpt/a/4671.*

Kleinberg, J. (1998). "Authoritative sources in a hyperlinked environment." In *Proc. ACM-SIAM Symposium on Discrete Algorithms.* Extended version published in *Journal of the ACM*, Vol. 46 (1999), pp. 604–632.

Lagoze, C., and Payette, S. (2000). "Metadata: Principles, practices and challenges." In *Moving Theory into Practice: Digital Imaging for Libraries and Archives*, edited by A. R. Kenney and O. Y. Rieger, pp. 84–100. Research Libraries Group, Mountain View, California.

Lana, M. (2004). *Il testo nel computer*. Bollati Boringhieri, Torino.

Langville, A. N., and Meyer, C. D. (2005). "A survey of eigenvector methods for Web information retrieval." *SIAM Review*, Vol. 47, No. 1, pp. 135–161.

Langville, A. N., and Meyer, C. D. (2006). *Google's PageRank and Beyond: The Science of Search Engine Rankings*. Princeton University Press, Princeton, New Jersey.

Lawrence, S., and Giles, C. L. (1999). "Accessibility and distribution of information on the web." *Nature*, Vol. 400, No. 6740 (July), pp. 107–109.

Lesk, M. (2005). *Understanding Digital Libraries*, 2nd edition. Morgan Kaufmann, San Francisco. Originally published in 1997 with the title *Practical Digital Libraries: Books, Bytes, and Bucks*.

Lessig, L. (1999). *Code and Other Laws of Cyberspace*. Basic Books, New York.

Lessig, L. (2002). "Privacy as Property." *Social Research*, Vol. 69, No. 1 (Spring), pp. 247–269.

Lessig, L. (2004). *Free Culture: How Big Media Uses Technology and the Law to Lock Down Culture and Control Creativity*. Penguin, New York.

Library of Congress (1998). *Library of Congress Subject Headings*, 21st edition. Library of Congress Cataloging Policy and Support Office, Washington, DC.

Licklider, J. C. R. (1960). "Man-computer symbiosis." *IEEE Transactions on Human Factors in Electronics*, Vol. HFE-I, March 4–11.

Licklider, J. C. R., and Taylor, R. W. (1968). "The computer as a communication device." *Science and Technology* (April).

Mann, T. (1993). *Library Research Models*. Oxford University Press, New York.

Mason, R. O. (1986). "Four ethical issues of the information age." *Management Information Systems Quarterly*, Vol. 10, No. 1, pp. 5–12.

Moore, A. D. (Editor) (2005). *Information Ethics*. University of Washington Press, Seattle and London.

Moulton, W. F., and Geden, A. S. (1897). *A Concordance to the Greek Testament*, 1st edition. T. & T. Clark, Edinburgh.

Moulton, W. F., and Geden, A.S. (1977). *A Concordance to the Greek Testament*, 5th edition. T. & T. Clark, Edinburgh (revised by H. K. Moulton).

Nagenborg, M. (2004). "Privacy and terror: Some remarks from a historical perspective." *International Journal of Information Ethics*, Vol. 2 (November).

Nyce, J. M., and Kahn, P. (1991). *From Memex to Hypertext, Vannevar Bush and the Mind's Machine*. Academic Press, San Diego.

OpenNet Initiative (2005). "Internet filtering in China 2004–2005: A country study." Available at *opennetinitiative.net/studies/china/ONI_China_Country_Study.pdf*.

Parrish, S. M. (1959). *A Concordance to the Poems of Matthew Arnold*. Cornell University Press, Ithaca, New York.

Peirce, C. S. (1868a). "Questions concerning certain faculties claimed for man." *Journal of Speculative Philosophy*, Vol. 2, pp. 103–114.

Peirce, C. S. (1868b). "Some consequences of four incapacities." *Journal of Speculative Philosophy*, Vol. 2, pp. 140–157.

Pennock, D. M., Flake, G. W., Lawrence, S., Glover, E. J., and Giles, C. L. (2002). "Winners don't take all: Characterizing the competition for links on the web." *Proc. National Academy of Sciences*, Vol. 99, No. 8 (April), pp. 5207–5211.

Phelps, T. A., and Wilensky, R. (2000). "Robust hyperlinks and locations." *D-Lib Magazine*, Vol. 6, No. 7/8 (July/August).

Rheingold, H. (2000). *Tools for Thought*. MIT Press, Cambridge.

Samuelson, P. (1998). "Encoding the law into digital libraries." *Communications of the ACM*, Vol. 41, No. 4 (April), pp. 13–18.

Samuelson, P., and Davis, R. (2000). "The digital dilemma: A perspective on intellectual property in the information age." Presented at the Telecommunications Policy Research Conference, Alexandria, Virginia, September.

Sartre, J.-P. (1947). *"What Is Literature?" and Other Essays*. Republished in 1988, with introduction by S. Ungar, by Harvard University Press, Cambridge.

Smith, M. (2005). "Eternal bits." *IEEE Spectrum* (July), pp. 22–27.

Spinello, R., and Tavani, H. T. (Editors) (2006). *Readings in Cyberethics*, 3rd edition. Jones and Bartlett Publishers, Sudbury, Massachusetts.

Steedman, C. (2001). "Something she called a fever: Michelet, Derrida, and Dust." *American Historical Review*, Vol. 106, No. 4, pp. 1159–1180.

Sun-Tzu (515–512 B.C.). "The Art of War." In Sun-Tzu and von Clausewitz, K. (2000). *The Book of War: Sun-Tzu's "The Art of Warfare" and Karl von Clausewitz's "On War."* Modern Library, New York.

Svenonius, E. (2000). *The Intellectual Foundation of Information Organization*. MIT Press, Cambridge.

Tavani, H. T., and Moor, J. H. (2000). "Privacy protection, control of information, and privacy-enhancing technologies." In *Proc. Conference on Computer Ethics— Philosophical Enquiry*. Dartmouth College, Hanover, New Hampshire, pp. 293–304.

Thiele, H. (1998). "The Dublin Core and Warwick Framework: A review of the literature, March 1995–September 1997." *D-Lib Magazine*, Vol. 4, No. 1 (January).

Thompson, J. (1997). *A History of the Principles of Librarianship*. Clive Bingley, London.

Thomson, W. (1891). "Electrical units of measurement." In *Popular Lectures and Addresses, 1891–1894*, Vol. 1. Macmillan and Co., London. (Thomson was also known as Baron Kelvin.)

von Ahn, L., and Dabbish, L. (2004). "Labeling images with a computer game." In *Proc. ACM Conference on Human Factors in Computing Systems*, pp. 319–326. ACM Press, New York.

Waldrop, M. M. (2002). *The Dream Machine: J. C. R. Licklider and the Revolution That Made Computing Personal*. Penguin Books, New York.

Wang (2005). "The changing face of advertising in the digital age." Parks Associates Industry Report, Dallas (*www.parksassociates.com*).

Weibel, S. (1999). "The state of the Dublin Core metadata initiative." *D-Lib Magazine*, Vol. 5, No. 4 (April).

White, J. (Editor) (1999). *Intellectual Property in the Age of Universal Access*. ACM Press, New York.

Wiener, N. (1948). *Cybernetics: or Control and Communication in the Animal and the Machine*. MIT Press, Cambridge.

Wiener, N. (1950). *The Human Use of Human Beings*. Houghton Mifflin, Boston.

Witten, I. H., and Bainbridge, D. (2003). *How to Build a Digital Library*. Morgan Kaufmann, San Francisco.

Witten, I. H., and Frank, E. (2005). *Data Mining*. 2nd edition. Morgan Kaufmann, San Francisco.

Witten, I. H., Moffat, A., and Bell, T. C. (1999). *Managing Gigabytes: Compressing and Indexing Documents and Images*. Morgan Kaufmann, San Francisco.

Wittgenstein, L. (2003). *Philosophical Investigations*. Blackwell, London.

Wolf, G. (1996). "Steve Jobs: The next insanely great thing." *Wired Magazine* (February), pp. 50–55.

Wu, J. (Editor) (1999). *New Library Buildings of the World*. Shanghai Public Library, Shanghai, China.